Falling for Football

To / WINSTON,

YOU HAVE THE HONOUR OF
THIS BEING MY FIRST BOOK
SIGNING – FLOG IT IN 2024.

GREG

www.ockleybooks.co.uk

Published by Ockley Books Ltd

First published 2014

All text copyright of the authors.

The moral right of all the authors to be identified as the authors of this work has been
asserted. All chapters edited by Adam Bushby and Rob MacDonald.

ISBN 978-0957141049

Front Cover designed by Michael Atkinson

Layout & design by Michael Kinlan

Printed & bound by:

Riley Dunn & Wilson Ltd.
Red Doles Lane
Huddersfield
West Yorkshire
HD2 1YE

"What is a club in any case?
Not the buildings or the directors or
the people who are paid to represent it.
It's not the television contracts, get-out clauses,
marketing departments or executive boxes.
It's the noise, the passion, the feeling of belonging,
the pride in your city. It's a small boy clambering
up stadium steps for the very first time,
gripping his father's hand, gawping
at that hallowed stretch of turf beneath
him and, without being able to do
a thing about it, falling in love."

Sir Bobby Robson

ABOUT

Adam and Rob are the brains behind Magic
Spongers, a football blog they created in 2010 and,
despite universal concurrence that the age of the
blog is dead, they are still running. Under this and
other guises including their own names, they have
contributed articles to When Saturday Comes,
In Bed with Maradona and Run of Play,
among others.

You can find the blog at
www.magicspongers.blogspot.com
and some tweets @magicspongers.

This is their first book as joint editors.

Foreword

This book is a time machine. If you remember your own first giddy discovery of football – the moment when the game transformed itself from a colourful jumble with an inexplicable power to make adults shout at the television into something with shape and intention, something that *made sense* – then you will recognise these stories. You've already lived them. You, too, have been a nine-year-old poring over match programmes or almanacs (or, if you're a little younger, the Internet), sorting out the heraldries and histories of clubs you're encountering for the first time. You, too, have gone to a stadium for the slightly overwhelming experience of your first live match and fallen desperately in love with something you saw a player do. You, too, have hung up posters, memorised starting XIs, and – if you're anything like the writers collected here – had your heart stolen by one unforgettable team. It's remarkable, once football starts making sense, how quickly it seems to make more sense than anything else.

The stories in this book are all our stories. It's the details that differ, and the details are what make many of these essays so absorbing. There's Sam Macrory's memory of sitting in the family stand at the old Manor Ground in Oxford with his dad 'quietly reading his *Guardian*' and his mother leafing through *Good Housekeeping*. There's James Young's gripping and funny account of watching football in Northern Ireland with a father who belonged to the RUC: 'Linfield were losing and my father was going to break somebody's legs. Things looked bad.' There's Greg Theoharis's reminiscence about falling for Cameroon during Italia '90 on a black-and-white TV at his aunt's house in Cyprus. For my part, I grew up in America and didn't discover the game the rest of the world calls football until I was already an adult – but I vividly remember standing on my toes in Stillwater, Oklahoma, watching Barry Sanders run with a different kind of football, and feeling the same oh-my-God-what-is-this exhilaration that many of these writers describe.

But that's kind of the point, isn't it? Regardless of our particular circumstances, one of the things sport does for many of us is to keep us in touch with the childhood selves that first fell hard for it. That is, as kids, football can seem like a port of entry into adulthood, maybe the first experience we share with our dads without either of us having to feign enjoyment. As adults, it's a way to preserve a sliver of our lives that's wholly devoted to play – because for all that we pride ourselves on our grown-up cynicism toward the transfer market or our world-weariness toward the media, what keeps us bound to the game is the promise of the next beautiful move, the next big win for our club, the next astonishing goal. And when it comes, the sudden crazy thrill is pretty much the same as it was when we were 12 years old.

Is there anything else in life of which you can say that? I can't listen to the music I liked when I was 12, and while I still love the books I read then, reading them today is a totally different experience. But watch an athlete do something mesmerising and 12 is 25 is 50. What I find so delightful about this book is that it shows how much we have in common in the pursuit of this daffy obsession. Football is a strange language in that it's always transporting us back to the moment we first learned to speak it. And as this book shows, what unites the speakers is a shared grammar of emotion – one whose first word is joy.

Brian Phillips

Introduction

It's easy to talk of high water marks. It's arguably more difficult to encapsulate what made a period of time so special. When we decided to stop merely ranting about football in one of London's many watering holes (usually a Sammy Smith's) and commit fingers to keyboards in 2010, little did we know what a fantastic journey we were about to embark upon. *Magic Spongers*, our blog, was at once our saviour. A release from the drudgery of (paid) work, and suddenly also a medium by which we could interact with a wider audience. That some hardy souls seemed to like what we wrote was a bonus. And being listed as one of *The Guardian*'s Top 100 football blogs on New Year's Eve 2010 was a highlight and a pointer that we were on the right track.

In hindsight, what strikes us is how the period between 2010 and 2012 represented a sub-culture brimming with talent and vibrancy. Our peers, blogs such as Twisted Blood (Andi Thomas), Dispatches from a Football Sofa (Greg Theoharis), Twohundredpercent (Ian King), In Bed With Maradona (Jeff Livingstone, aided by Dave Hartrick, Ryan Keaney and Chris Nee), The Two Unfortunates (Lloyd Langman and Rob Langham), The Seventy-Two (Dave Bevan) and the sadly defunct Run of Play (Brian Phillips, whose foreword we are so grateful for) became our first port of call for the best in football writing and it became easy to get lost in a wonderful tangle of sites that all seemed to have appeared from nowhere. Thankfully, they're all represented here.

Being part of all this was exciting. And that we could hold our own in such esteemed company was humbling. Not only that, but on the odd occasion we made it to award ceremonies or the marvellous Socrates football bloggers meet ups, we found engaging, like-minded souls who cared enough to write for the love of it.

It was these experiences that led us to stumble across an idea, not least because all these talents – and in part, the existence of their websites

– were borne of a faint, but growing, disillusionment with modern football and all its gaudy bells and whistles, This, naturally, made the pair of us a little introspective, as while we had found a readership through raving about the visual and print media's lowest common denominator coverage, our enjoyment was increasingly restricted to the lesser reported exploits of lower and non-league football.

Nevertheless, football at the highest level has, and always will, retain the ability to delight. Watching Barcelona annihilate Real Madrid 5-0 in November 2010 was almost like seeing another sport. Watching Bilbao tear Manchester United a new one at Old Trafford in March 2012 was similarly evocative. These were new ways of applying old rules, framed by the fact we'd never seen anything like it before.

It was through this mindset, and some rose-tinted glasses, that we began to share stories of how our lifelong affairs with the sport had been forged in the first place, when that sheer open-mouthed excitement was the result of a genuinely compelling experience, not a reaction to one of the big boys getting an unexpected shoeing.

Tales of swapping Panini stickers in the playground and before that, Pro Set football cards, started to bounce to and fro. First live game, first televised tournaments, cup finals, favourite players, goals scored for school and Sunday league teams, even goals and players recreated with varying degrees of accomplishment in the garden or down the park, all quickly followed in a barrage of heartfelt recollection.

Of course, as men of a certain vintage, some teams were particularly resonant. *Football Italia* and indeed Italia '90, for example; USA '94 and the original Dream Team; and the start of the Premier League, though it now appears a distant, different era. For us, though the Moss Rose and Bootham Crescent became more spiritual homes, we were weaned onto football elsewhere, on grandiose stories from far-flung international tournaments deemed important enough to be on the telly – when live coverage really was an occasion – and from poring over the only other media available in those days: *Shoot, Match, World Soccer* and our sticker albums.

But despite these shared foundations, our experiences were completely different and, on the surface, completely inexplicable. One of us found football through the successes and then failure, as it was seen, of an

Italian legend, Roberto Baggio, in the 1994 World Cup final; the other by the exploits of a thrilling Nigerian side that lit up first that tournament and later the 1996 Olympic Games on their way to a gold medal. And yet neither of us particularly cares for those teams now, despite an ongoing affection for Andrea Pirlo, our favourite wizard since Gandalf.

We knew we wouldn't be the only ones with these stories. And so we compiled a series on the blog which, though it involved a modest 11 contributors in all, saw the publication of three of the ten most viewed pieces we've ever had. The *Daily Mirror* even made Alex Douglas's naïve recollections of the 1993 Sheffield Wednesday side, beaten in both domestic cup finals by Arsenal, one of their football stories of the week. Reminiscences, some truly emotional, were added to comments sections from a number of different countries, continents and age groups.

It was quickly obvious that certain themes were universal and that by tapping into those – and the myriad abilities of the blogging community – we could create a real collection of similar gems, a book that could contain scribblings by our favourite bloggers and writers, be a platform for new ones (and nostalgia) and cover eras, teams and experiences far beyond the scope of us doing a bit of research and turning the blog into a glorified *Wikipedia* service about the great international and club sides of yesteryear.

What has made this book such a joy to put together is the personal touch afforded it by each and every one of the contributors. The words "addiction" and "love" have continued to crop up in the chapters we received – often unrequited in the case of the latter, but seemingly always unconditional. From teams as mighty as Manchester United and Milan to the lowlier Linfield and Lewes, it doesn't matter – though the stories are different, their traits are reassuringly familiar throughout.

It's easy to talk of high water marks. It's arguably more difficult to encapsulate what made a period of time so special. What this book has done in some small part, we hope, is achieve that.

Adam Bushby & Rob MacDonald

Cameroon 1990

Greg Theoharis

If I were being really lazy, there would be only two words required for the essay you are about to read. These two words would unlock a wealth of memories if you happen to be in your mid-thirties or upwards. If you are younger and have even a slight passing interest in football, you'll have heard about and seen footage of the feats undertaken by the team about which I'm about to rhapsodise. I could significantly reduce the process of summoning up the requisite vocabulary and self-editing that is the chosen purgatory of the frustrated wordsmith. My word count would be drastically diminished, much to the annoyance of the editors of this book. Those words would immediately render redundant the need to even partake in this business of writing, because by committing the words 'Roger' and 'Milla' to print, my work here is more or less done.

I bet you can see it all before you now: the goal-scoring adventures of a man of dubious age, the wiggling at the corner flag, the scything tackles executed on players of bigger name and even bigger ego. Cameroon's Indomitable Lions of 1990 were the first African nation to reach the quarter-finals of the World Cup and they were the team that definitively made me give my heart to football.

I've deliberately avoided watching highlights of that glorious summer years ago for the purposes of this piece. Memory is at best an unreliable witness to events, growing hazy as the years merge into decades and the embellishments expand with repeated tellings of the story. What's more, if I were to apply that most curious of twenty-first century obsessions with pass completions and possession percentages to this tale, then much of what makes that Cameroon team so enduring would be diminished. The facts, for instance, would tell you that Italia '90 was a dog of a tournament. Record sendings-off and an overreliance on defence abounded, leading

FIFA to make significant changes to the format and rules of the tournament four years later.

This is what the facts would suggest. But for a twelve-year old schoolboy, it will always be remembered for Irish penalties, Gazza turns, Colombian hair, a wild-eyed Italian marksman and a team of unknowns from Africa who turned the footballing world on its head in the space of five games.

My family were in the process of re-settling in Cyprus when the tournament began on June 8. I was already sensing that I'd be very much considered an outsider by my peers. I spoke Greek in a fragmented, anglicised way that made me stand out for ridicule. Where I had been used to twice weekly instalments of EastEnders, I would now have to settle for those heavily stylised, rinky-dink variety shows so beloved of Southern Europe which everybody around me seemed to look forward to and obsess over. And as for football, I was swapping White Hart Lane for the modest surroundings of the Makarion Stadium in Nicosia, then home of both APOEL and Omonia. Although I didn't know it at the time, I was every bit Robert A Heinlein's *Stranger In A Strange Land*.

So on that Friday evening, as I sat in front of my aunt's black and white television (yes, even in 1990), having to grapple with a commentary I could barely comprehend, I was blissfully unaware that the subsequent ninety-odd minutes would be the greatest display of outsider culture I have ever witnessed and continues to resonate with me to this day. World champions Argentina were to begin the defence of their title against a rag-tag team of no-hopers. There was a sense that the match would be yet another exhibition of Diego Maradona's imperious skills, openly mocking the snobbery of the Milanese in their own stadium.

Standing in their way were a team resplendent (as I later discovered) in the garish green, red and yellow of their national flag, comprising names of such sing-song exoticism as Omam-Biyick, M'Bouh M'Bouh and N'Kono. Looking now at my complete *World Cup '90* sticker album (the one so memorably hawked by Brian Clough imploring us to "watch out for it"), I distinctly remember committing many of these players to memory before a ball was even kicked or a player hacked in anger. At that point I'd never even heard of 'The Cameroons' as they were labelled in the sticker template, which began to fill as I spent whatever pocket money I had on the 12p packets at any available after-school opportunity. Yet despite the other-worldliness of some of the squad, there were others whose names could easily have fitted in with the hustle and bustle of England's first division at the time. I'd managed to convince myself for instance that Cyrille Makanaky (a name so elegantly and prosaically pronounced by the ubiquitous commentating genius of Barry Davies – Ma-ka-na-keeee, if you will), was somehow distantly related to Aston Villa's bulldozing centre forward Alan McInally despite the obvious differences in both name and genetic make-up.

I only digress to that *World Cup '90* album because there was one glaring omission from the line-up provided and when he made his entrance, he not only took this anorak-in-training by surprise but everybody else in the football world too. Roger Milla was not meant to be at the World Cup. He only came on board by personal request of Cameroon's president. But more of him in a bit... back to Argentina.

It wasn't meant to play out as it did, but I think most of us agree that it was one of the most stupefyingly audacious upsets in the history of the game. Cameroon held off the defending champions brilliantly and then Omam-Biyick rose to score one of the softest headers past Nery Pumpido in the second half. As the ball trickled out of the goalkeeper's grasp and behind the line, there was a distinctive sense that the footballing order was about to be turned upside down forever. If only they could just hold on.

Enter Benjamin Massing who executed one of the most bone-crushing tackles you're ever likely to see, virtually shearing off Claudio Caniggia's legs as the Argentines threatened to equalise. He was inevitably shown his marching orders but if ever you want to understand what 'taking one for the team' means, you should immediately refer to Massing. There was no respect for ego, no deference to supposed superiors and it sent out a message to the rest of the competing nations. Cameroon were not going to be patronised and they weren't going anywhere. Yet.

A win against Romania followed with Roger Milla bagging two goals and debuting that famous corner flag celebration. Despite being thumped by the outgoing Soviets, Cameroon were through to play Colombia in the second round. A largely forgettable game came to life in extra time with Milla once again taking centre-stage.

What the match is largely remembered for is Colombia's self-destructive and extravagantly coiffed goalkeeper Rene Higuita having his hubris pricked by Milla, who stole the ball off him so far upfield that his extravagance was more or less the downfall of his team. Within that lay the moral of Cameroon's adventure. It could easily sit alongside some of the greatest myths of Ancient Greece as this team time and again defied the odds and the footballing gods.

And so to England in the quarter-finals. I'm not ashamed to admit that I was split down the middle for this one. I think most of us were. We all know how it played out and in hindsight I guess Cameroon's luck eventually ran out, however much they outplayed England. Paul Gascoigne had his own date with destiny in the semi-final, but sometimes, when I reflect on that summer, I always feel that an African team taking its place in the final four might have had greater significance for football in the long run. It might have also saved Gazza from himself. And once in the semi, who knows what Cameroon could have done? But that's all conjecture. The reality is that they fell gloriously to the clinical finishing instincts of Gary Lineker, but nevertheless their achievements, though later matched by Senegal and Ghana, have proven to be the high watermark of African performances at the World Cup thus far.

Shortly after the tournament, I briefly had a pen-pal from Cameroon's capital Yaounde (that's the kind of thing pre-teens did in the nineties before the advent of the internet). Why do I choose to bring this piece to an end with that nugget of trivial information? Because, what Cameroon did for broadening peoples' horizons in 1990 ran far deeper than any football match. It shows that football can do more for education than any text book. And because of the sheer audacity of Roger Milla and his mates, a young boy from London was able to face the problems of living in another country with confidence and courage.

In 1990, we all became just a little bit more Indomitable. And I lost my heart. All I ever needed to say was Roger Milla and you'd have understood.

Barnestoneworth United 1922-23

Daniel Gray

I'm a Middlesbrough fan, which is probably why I seek out escapism. You may never have heard of Barnstoneworth United Football Club, especially as they do not exist. They appeared on television for less than half an hour in 1979 and yet they encapsulate, and indeed have shaped, so much of what I feel about the game. Their fictional 1922/23 season is mentioned only twice in those 30 minutes and yet it hangs in the air, a distinguished past reference point and a hallowed marker to judge everything else by. It is the type of re-imagined halcyon phase that we as mere followers of football spend our entire supporting lives harking back to and wishing would be repeated.

Barnstoneworth appeared in *Golden Gordon*, an episode of Michael Palin and Terry Jones' *Ripping Yarns*. Its eponymous lead character was Gordon Ottershaw, a United obsessive who slept in his red and white scarf and hat, and named his son after the team. 'He's got another name', Ottershaw says during an argument with his wife. 'Yes,' she replies, 'UNITED.'

United the team play at the Sewage Works Ground, a rare bit of flat land in a 1930s Yorkshire mill town of incessant rain rebounding off dark cobbles. It is football in a tin pot ground sunk like a steel and stone amphitheatre among a smoke-belching terraced town. In other words, perfection.

Shrill whistles blow and hefty balls are thudded in the valley below as Barnstoneworth United Ottershaw emerges from the family's two-up two-down. Dad is down at the match, Mum is ushering him out of the house and dispatching him to buy a block of lard for tomorrow's dripping. "But Mum," he says, "I'm learning the Barnstoneworth United team of 1922... Dad said he were going to test me." Not pausing for breath his Mum begins "Hagerty F, Hagerty R, Tomkins, Noble, Carrick, Dobson,

Crapper, Dewhurst, MacIntyre, Treadmore and Davitt... Davitt scored twice in't last three minutes, and Frank Hagerty saved a penalty."

Gordon's obsession – and that is not a strong enough word – has permeated family life, the first of many themes dear and familiar to my own existence. It is there in the son trying to impress his Dad, and there in the wife's learning through reluctant osmosis. Like a million wives before and after her, Mrs Ottershaw knows there are three figures in her marriage, and one is a football club.

By the 1935/36 season in which all of this takes place, Barnstoneworth United are dire on the pitch and destitute off it. They have fallen down the Yorkshire League and seen players suspended due to 'indecent exposure in a bakery' or injured by 'boils' and 'a cold sore.' Few now stand alongside Gordon on the terraces of the Sewage Works Ground. Then one night amidst the dark brown panel walls of the Social Club, the club's chairman speaks lines that dagger through his soul, similar lines to those we as fans fear, even if they are suitably droll in this outing:

"We have therefore decided, as from Tuesday next week, to sell Barnstoneworth United Football Club, its players, premises and ground to the Arthur Foggen Scrap Corporation for redevelopment. They have assured us that the name of Barnstoneworth United will not be forgotten and have kindly consented to name one of their steel scrap crushing mills after the club."

His heart shattered, Ottershaw cycles to Foggen's mansion and finds a stubborn businessman and scrap metal fetishist. At first, Foggen is unwilling to hear Ottershaw's pleas that United must be spared. Then, though, our hero mentions the 1922/23 season. He runs through those magical names: Hagerty F, Hagerty R, Tomkins, Noble, Carrick. The scrap man becomes hypnotised, interjecting with "now *he* were a player" and purring in reminiscence. His eyes sparkle: he was there that year, there against Barnsley Reserves in the cup, when Davitt scored with the back of his head from 28 yards.

"There must have been ten-thousand folk down there...", Foggen muses.

"10,118", replies Ottershaw, a man in possession of the unavoidable, Tourettes-like correcting tendency I too am afflicted by in these matters.

Foggen's wife rouses him by throwing a steam train's wheel onto a pile of scrap by the log fire. "Then's then and now's now" he says as he shows Ottershaw to the door. And yet, if you have that feeling, you just have that feeling... when Saturday comes, Foggen is there at the Sewage Works Ground, cheering on 1922/23 Barnstoneworth reunited, the old XI rounded up by Ottershaw, grey but still good enough to batter Denley Moor Academicals 8-1. We never find out if Foggen's steely heart undertakes a change of direction, but it never really matters: Barnstoneworth United and that 1922/23 season survived and are alive and well.

They are alive in the habits, values and customs displayed by so many of us fans. Barnstoneworth United symbolise the preposterousness of betting your heart on a football club, of letting its unalterable course determine how good your mood or week is. Watch Ottershaw's ferocious destruction of his own home after a defeat, and his orgasmic delight after that final win. To employ a recent fad in hashtaggery, We Are All Gordon Ottershaw. They and he encapsulate our bat-blind faith in a club, a feeling always underpinned by the warm glow of better days gone by and a belief that they will be repeated. This is what it is like to belong to something, and we would not change it for the world.

Here's the bit for the psychoanalysts. Barnstoneworth United and that 1922/23 season are a cement pillar of the relationship between my Dad and I. Football has long shaped what we are and how we are. He first took me to Middlesbrough and then stood and sat next to me through two decades of season tickets, Ayresome Park to the Riverside, crumbling terrace to plastic seat. I did not live with my Dad for much of that time which meant I saw him far more in the football season than out of it, a winter father. Similarly the frequency with which we now speak on the phone is far greater from August to May than in June and July. Above this, though, we had and have Barnstoneworth United.

Dad first showed me a VHS tape of *Golden Gordon* when I was 10, in 1992. It was about football and contained comic violence, which immediately hooked me. Sitting down and watching this recording simply became something we did, a habit and a hobby. Given the choice of a new series on telly or the BASF tape with a sticker that had *Howard's Way* scribbled out and 'Gordon' written underneath it, there was only ever one winner. Very quickly, I knew Hagerty F,

Hagerty R, Tomkins… as well as I knew Pears, Parkinson, Cooper, Mowbray, Pallister. Sometimes, particularly if Boro had recently suffered a pasting, I even told the other lads at school that I supported Barnstoneworth United.

When Dad moved away and we no longer had precious telly time, we still communicated in Ottershawese. Why address difficult teenage feelings through the split of your parents when you can phone your Dad and say "I love scrap, I've always loved scrap" and hear him laugh himself silly?

This has continued down the years. If I could find them all, I don't imagine I'd have a single birthday or Christmas card from my Dad without a reference to Barnstoneworth United in it. This could be a picture of a football match where one of the players has had the name 'Davitt' added to his shirt, or a snowman doctored to wear a red and white striped hat and scarf like Ottershaw. Still now, at least one in three text messages between us contains references to "long shorts or short shorts" (in fact, we have a brick at the Riverside with a related message engraved) or our wishes that Boro would sign "another Neville Davitt, another Frank Hagerty". My only hope is that we are slightly more functional than Gordon and his son Barnstoneworth; at least my father took me to the match with him, and I hope formative years spent coaxing me by the sidelines have taught him that, unlike that young lad, I can at least kick a ball straight.

In recent seasons I have rambled among the lower reaches of Scottish and then English football. Ostensibly this has been by way of research for two books, *Stramash* and *Hatters, Railwaymen and Knitters*. Across both countries I have seen homely clubs like Barnstoneworth and met besotted fans like Ottershaw. I have felt honoured to be enslaved to the same game as them, and realised that while we all still belong to it in this manner, existence has at least one purpose. Our nostalgia should not be dismissed as a wet concept but embraced as something that swells our sense of identity. While those of us that hold football dear can still hark back to seasons gone by and dream on about ones to come, the game will always have a soul. These days we just have to look a little harder to see it.

Leicester City 1991

David Bevan

My route into a love of football was the A50. It was also Italia '90, Kettering Town and George Graham's Arsenal, but I came to view the A50 as my route of pilgrimage. Of course, we all now know it as the A5199. Who can forget the day the transport authorities declassified that stretch of the A50 between Northampton and Leicester? To cut a long story short – there I am, sat in the passenger seat of my Dad's Volvo 340 as it climbs the brief incline in south Leicestershire that presents, upon ascension to its peak, a brief glimmer on the horizon. I sit up a little straighter. Filbert Street.

And I'm right back there in an instant, winding my way between the terraced houses. Brazil Street. Burnmoor Street. Filbert Street. Five pounds for adults, two pounds fifty for children. My dad buys a programme. It says "CITY" in faded light-blue stencil lettering, with "LEICESTER" clamped awkwardly over the top in royal blue. It resembles a home shirt – that same royal blue with a thin red and white striped outline. In the same way that I will soon read papers – flicking straight to the sports pages – I eagerly head to the back. "Mitty of the City" is a difficult concept to translate, but if you can imagine a Roy of the Rovers rip-off with every achievement fuelled in some tenuous way by a packet of Walkers Crisps then you will be somewhere close.

Those four lattice floodlights, just tiny specks in the dim distance half an hour previously, now loom over me – each provides a reference point, sectioning off a small part of the city from its surroundings. This is where the magic happens. This is where the jinking Scottish winger Tommy Wright casts a spell over me. I can see immediately that they're not as good as Arsenal or England or Melchester Rovers, but they seem like they're mine. Few people outside of these walls care about Tommy Wright, which makes him feel like my own personal discovery. And all of a sudden, they're not them anymore. They're us.

I'm standing on the far right of the Members' Enclosure at the front of the Main Stand, propped up against the thick white wall that runs the length of the pitch. I'm there when Tony Spearing takes throw-ins a yard or so away. I'm there when Ian Ormondroyd nods Derby County into a sickening early lead. I'm there when we play Port Vale and it's either 0-0 or 1-0 to them and I feel sick for the entire game. I'm there, staring across the angle of the pitch to my right and the Kop. Not THE Kop, perhaps, but our Kop – where I want to go and stand when I'm old enough.

I'm not just there, of course. I'm other places as well. I'm in a huge hangar-like sports hall somewhere in Leicester, in a queue with a load of other kids just like me. At the other end of the queue, Tommy Wright stands with a football. I can't help myself and I'm turning round to look at my dad, open-mouthed in joy and disbelief. I'm also at Southend in the blazing sunshine and Brighton in the pouring rain. I don't remember the weather at Notts County – all I remember is that wire mesh pattern imprinted on my cheek from when a gate was opened to my left and a surge sent me hurtling towards the front of the terrace. We won at Southend, we lost at Notts County and the match was abandoned at Brighton. All of it is teaching me something – how to celebrate success, how to cope with defeat and how to understand that a car full of people can come to travel over 250 miles in one day for no real reason at all.

It's definitely taken hold now and I've forgotten about Paul Merson and Ian Wright, until they turn up in September 1991 at Filbert Street. The programme costs a pound and Ian Wright has just cost Arsenal two and a half million of them. He scores, but so does Steve Walsh. This is one of the few games in which Steve Walsh is not sent off. He is sent off every other week, usually for headbutting a striker with whom he has tussled all game. He misses alternate games through suspension. He is not the quickest, but he gives it everything. He's from Wigan, but he's Mr Leicester City. He runs like my dad, but he's a pretty good footballer. In this way, Steve Walsh is teaching me something too – anyone can view Ian Wright as a hero for his hundreds of goals, but Steve Walsh runs like my dad. In three years' time, Steve Walsh will score two goals at Wembley to ensure City are promoted to the Premier League. This will teach me that anything is possible and never to give up on my dreams, but is all still to come. At this stage, we are bloody awful.

Results are everything and nothing. They matter enough to dictate my mood on a Saturday evening but defeats won't keep me away. The football is mostly terrible, but even when things are going badly, there is still something to captivate me and I've been held captive ever since. Things get so bad at one point that an aeroplane flies over Filbert Street trailing a banner displaying the words "Pleat Out Shipman Out". Soon, both manager and chairman will leave and things will get better. But before that can happen, there must be a defining moment.

11th May 1991. Leicester City need to win. *We* need to win. If not, we are relegated to Division Three for the first time in the club's 107-year history. This is where it starts to become important. This is where it stops being nice. It isn't even exciting. It's just 90 minutes of nerve-shredding agony. I am six years old. The goal comes halfway through the first half, poked into the Oxford United net from close range by defender Tony James. For over an hour, life becomes solely centred around the need for the ball not to cross the line guarded by Martin Hodge. When the final whistle is blown and Oxford haven't managed to score, this is what I want to do. This is me. This is all I need. And I really do need this, in the summer between Turin and Dahlin, Brolin, Dahlin, Brolin. The formative years of England hurt punctuated by a day when Leicester City make it all worthwhile by escaping from the jaws of misery and offering a glimpse of what actual success would feel like.

As you will have noticed, the memories don't come in the right order these days. They come in eras and this was the beginning. A year on from Oxford, it was Wembley. A year on from there, Wembley again. A year on from there, Wembley. These were what you might imaginatively title the Wembley era, during which Leicester City visited the national stadium seven times in eight years. I just thought it was what we did. We haven't been back since. Heroes – Julian Joachim, Brian Little, Martin O'Neill, Neil Lennon, Muzzy Izzet – came and went.

Up and down divisions we went, and into the third division for the first time in our history 17 years after Tony James and Oxford. Back up again and back into the division where it all started for me. But divisions aren't things you can reach out and touch. League tables exist, but there's nothing physical there. They are just the order of things. Filbert Street is just a block of flats now. Our stadium is named after a duty-free company from Thailand. So I'm at the King Power Stadium instead these days. But not really. I'm not really there.

Croatia 1996

Andi Thomas

I suspect, deep down, it was the shirts.

Euro '96 was the first tournament that really hit me square between the eyes. Having come to football slightly late, Italia '90 and Sweden '92 largely passed me by, John Jensen aside, and I recall USA '94 more as series of moments – Diego Maradona's boggle-eyes; Paul McGrath's magnificence; Bebeto's cradle-rocking; Leonardo's elbow; Roberto Baggio doing a Diana Ross – than as a tournament of narrative or character. But Euro '96 was different.

Euro '96, of course, lives in popular memory as the tournament in which Football Came Home And The Sun Was Shining And The English People All Had Fun And Everything Was Amazing. Hindsight, that miserable bastard, suggests that this wasn't quite how it went; Rob Smyth, writing in the Guardian, recalls a "diabolical tournament, full of negativity, fear and, as Franz Beckenbauer described France's approach during the group stages, 'lily-livered football'," and goes on to blame the whole shebang for "the long, long winter of [Tim] Lovejoy". Still, for a 12-year-old international football neophyte it was glorious, and England's progress through and ultimate exit from the tournament gave proceedings an intoxicating momentum.

It was Croatia's first tournament as well. Oblivious to the political snafu in the Balkans, my 12-year-old self fell for the nouveau nation's verve and flair; their dash of brutality; their army of devoted and noisy fans; and most of all the personality and personalities of the team. Whereas England were fielding ten profoundly boring men and one morbidly interesting Gazza, Croatia were, front to back, as fascinating as they were exotic. Most enthralling was the midfield, built around two of the finest players of the nineties: the brooding, brilliant Zvonimir Boban – who I knew vaguely from Football Italia, and who I had somehow learned once beat up a police officer, but in a good way, whatever that meant – and loose-limbed dribbling genius Robert Prosinečki – who I am convinced bears the blame for my occasional urge to dye my hair blond. It hasn't happened yet.

Along with that, the shirts, obviously.

Up front, there was the charming lethality of Davor Šuker, about whom two things stand out above anything else. The first was my stepdad saying "he looks like Lyle Lovett", which, while I had no idea what he was talking about at the time, is a pretty good spot. The second was that goal against Denmark, to round off a 3-0 scalping of the defending champions. Not just for the brutal, satanic geometry of the finish – an angle and weight so pure and malicious that it lifts the finest goalkeeper in the world high into the air, before depositing him in a helpless, hapless heap – but also for the ensuing celebration: one arm in the air, saluting the stadium and accepting the applause. A grin so wide as to threaten the structural integrity of his head. Compelling delight.

Having secured qualification from the group stage with that defeat of the Danes, they were rolled 3-0 by a pretty fine Portugal team, which meant Germany in the quarter-final. Šuker defied the laws of nature to score with his right foot but Croatia, unluckily, lost 2-1. I was hooked. By the time France rolled around in '98 they were my confirmed second team, and what with my first being Wales, there wasn't much chance of a clash of loyalties.

And they had cool shirts.

The France World Cup was, of course, Croatia's footballing apotheosis. Progress through the group stage was more-or-less serene. Jamaica and Japan were dispatched comfortably, before a narrow defeat to Argentina set up a second-round tie with Gheorghe Hagi's newly-blond Romania. Croatia emerged 1-0 victors, Davor Šuker replying to the referee's instruction to re-take his successful first half penalty by blasting it twice as hard into the same corner. While the penalty award was itself a touch soft, Croatia dominated the second half, had the better of the chances and were deserving victors. And waiting in the quarter-finals? A rematch with Germany.

There is, perhaps, something slightly tawdry about applauding a red card, particularly one that doesn't emerge from violence or malice. Sportspersonship, Corinthian values, all that jazz. And yet I don't think I've ever been so happy about a dismissal as when Christian Wörns was dispatched, mid-way through the first half, for clumsily felling Šuker. It was as though the world was shaping itself to my whim, doing everything it could to ensure Croatia's progress. "Football", remarked Gary Lineker, for once not auto-cueing a pun into oblivion, "is a simple game: it's eleven against eleven for 90 minutes, and then the Germans win". But eleven against ten?

Croatia struck first. On the stroke of half-time, Robert Jarni lashed in his only international goal from fully 20 yards, before Tardelli-ing off into a massive Croat man-pile (one of the joys of this team is the utter glee that greets every goal). Back came the European champions: Oliver Bierhoff forced Drazen Ladic into a sharp reaction save; Dietmar Hamann hit the post with a deflected drive. And Germany were pressing again when, in the 80th minute, a misplaced attacking header set Boban free in midfield. He fed Goran Vlaović on the right, who whipped another drive past Andreas Köpke's despairing paw, and slapped the wind out of the German sails. Šuker quickly added a third – as in '96, he used his right, a foot that apparently only functioned in the presence of German defenders – and, somewhere in Milton Keynes, a lank-haired teenager went quietly ecstatic.

The semi-final against France is overshadowed as a game not only by the overriding story of *la France qui gagne* -- more fun with narrative there -- but also by Slaven Bilić making a spectacle of himself and a suspended man of Laurent Blanc. Shortly after Thuram's second, as Zidane stood over a free-kick deep on the left flank, Bilić and Blanc tugged and grappled with one another near the penalty spot. Blanc pushed out at Bilić, and may even have caught him on the lower jaw; he certainly didn't poke him in the eyes or punch him in the nose, which is what Bilić's agonised descent would suggest. Over came the referee, out came the red card, and off went the Frenchman. Outrage. Calumny. A heck of a lot of whistling.

Bilić's defence is interesting. In *Behind the Curtain*, the Croatian explains to Jonathan Wilson that the whole thing was the fault of Alessandro Costacurta, sort of. He says: "I loved Billy Costacurta as a player, and I'll always remember that in 1994 he missed the

Champions League final and the World Cup final because of being booked in the semi. So, I thought to myself before the game, 'Don't do anything stupid ... Don't do a Billy'." And so, when it came to Blanc: "He didn't hit me like Mike Tyson, but he gave me a push. At that moment I was panicking, because in nine out of ten situations like that the referee goes yellow, yellow to both players ... So I thought, no final, no third place whatever, so I went down."

Make of that what you will. The referee – Señor José Maria Garcia Aranda, of Spain – did have a fussy manner and a fastidious moustache, though he had been relatively sparing with the cards. In any case, it might not have mattered: while most of the replays make the push look fairly benign (and so the collapse look utterly dastardly), the most important -- that from close to the referee's angle -- is worse for Blanc. His back is to the referee, and so the official can only really see his shoulder and arm coming round. It doesn't look like a punch, not quite. But it definitely looks like a push to the face. And as the Big Book Of Things To Say About Football will tell you, if you raise your hands, you're asking for trouble.

Whether you're minded to accept Bilić's defence or not – and it does feel an awful lot like another piece of retrospective storytelling – it is important not to forget just how unlucky Croatia were to lose. The first half was the kind of half that commentators might call "cagey" or even "probing" but the rest of us, under no obligation to sell the thing to anybody, are free to call dull. France were largely restricted to long-range efforts, the majority from Zinedine Zidane but the best from Stephane Guivarc'h. Yep, that one. Croatia, meanwhile, spent most of their time either watching Zidane shooting, or clipping long balls towards Marcel Desailly. They did muster a brief spell of pressure towards the interval, and had perhaps the best chance of the half, but having worked himself a yard of space inside the France penalty area, Aljoša Asanović managed to kick the ball with one of his feet while trying to kick it with the other. The shot screwed wide.

But if the first half was nothing to write home about – "Dear Mother. The Mexican wave began on 16 minutes ..." – the second was proper, taut, nervous knock-out football. It's amazing what two goals in the opening two minutes will do. Croatia took the lead, Asanović making the French defence look all Arsenal-like for Šuker to net his fifth of the campaign. But less than a minute later, Boban, the genius playing the fool, executed a quick pirouette on the edge of his own box, then dallied. France pounced. Lilian Thuram scored. And then twenty minutes later, rumbling up the right, he exchanged quick passes with Youri Djorkaeff before curling the ball into the side of the net, as sweet a wrong-footed strike as you could ever hope to see.

A fun fact about Lilian Thuram: his given name is "Ruddy". Another fun fact about Lilian Thuram: he played 142 games for France. A final fun fact about Lilian Thuram: he scored exactly two goals. Those two goals. That's how unfortunate it was; downed by a non-scoring right-back, a French Tony Hibbert, if you will, having the best of all possible days at the office.

The complete, utter, and total bastard.

It's also worth noting that France easily could have gone down to nine men with around ten minutes to go, as Thierry Henry committed three bookable offences in quick succession. First he went flying through a defender at horizontal high-speed, then he managed to handle the ball while simultaneously elbowing Robert Jarni in the head, a double-foul of admirable efficiency that removed the Croatian from the pitch for five minutes as medical staff attempted to stop his head leaking. With Boban only able to play for a hour, and Prosinečki unable to manage anything other than a tiny cameo at the desperate end, it's hard not to conclude that things just weren't falling their way.

This is not to say that Croatia were robbed; that would be a step too far. This is to say: Croatia came second in an exceptionally tight game, as a result of Lilian Thuram doing something unprecedented twice, if that makes any sense. It's a questions of ifs and buts, of what if this and that and t'other, and ultimately it doesn't mean anything. Šuker picked up the golden boot in the third-fourth playoff (denying Gabriel Batistuta the prize, and Adam Bushby, co-editor of this volume, £70 in winnings), and Croatia took the bronze.

It's tempting to push the hypotheticals a bit further, to look forward to a prospective final against Brazil. It's even more tempting to conclude that Croatia's quality and spirit would have given them a real chance against what turned out to be a demoralised Brazil led by a shellshocked and barely conscious Ronaldo. And yes, I'm just making things up now, and yes, if my auntie had balls she'd be a juggler. It wasn't to be; it wasn't meant to be. What came next was failure to qualify for Euro 2000, and the resignation of maverick coach Miroslav Blažević. By this time Boban had already gone; Prosinečki, Šuker and the rest would never hit the same heights again.

In terms of quality, it would be unfair to put this side on a par with the other great unrequited World Cup sides, the Dutch team of 1974 or the Hungarians of 1954. But in terms of charm, well, they were the glorious nearly-men that I fell in love with; a seductive, ridiculous, happy team that nearly had everything, but fell short through a combination of ill-fortune and their own capacity for cocking about on the edge of the penalty area like a berk, Zvonimir, like a berk. Tragedy allied with buffoonery has an allure that crass, simple triumph can never hope to match.

Plus, those shirts. Those checks. About ten minutes from the end of the semi-final, the television cameras cut to the box of the great and good. Michel Platini sat watching, surrounded by the rest of the interchangeable parade of men in suits; men seemingly only employed to gaze protectively over any high-profile football match, an inescapable reminder of who the game is run by and for. But in amongst the suits was sat a woman, remarkable not only for having a completely different chromosonal arrangement to the rest of this most masculine of cabals, but for wearing a bright blue tracksuit top with red-checked sleeves. Hilariously out-of-place, yes, but ineffably and irresistibly cool. A bit like Croatia themselves, then.

AC Milan 1990

Musa Okwonga

Although my lifelong love is Manchester United, the team that will forever turn my head is the AC Milan side of 1990. Milan's squad was so good that season that, it was said, their second XI could have won Serie A and their first XI could have won the World Cup. This was a special year. A year when Luciano Pavarotti made sobbing at an opera acceptable to the masses; and a year when Adidas released the Etrusco Unico match ball, 20 panels of majesty, which remains the best of its kind that I have ever seen or sidefooted.

A special year then, 1990. I was 11 years old, a time when, due to Roberto Baggio, everyone was about to fall in love with Diadora boots. But, before Diadora, there was the Lotto. Not just anyone could wear the Lotto, for two reasons. First, they were narrow as stilettos, which immediately ruled out the flat-footed among us. Secondly, they were worn by Marco van Basten, the greatest pure centre forward I have ever seen.

I say "pure" for good reason. Van Basten wouldn't actually get into my all-time World XI – he would lose the lone-striker role to Brazil's Ronaldo – but if aliens stumble upon the remains of our long-departed civilisation many millennia from now, van Basten's highlight reel will be the most graceful illustration they will find of the centre-forward's art. Where Ronaldo's skill levels were bewildering, he could at least turn to the more prosaic qualities of brute force when needed. But van Basten's game was all elegance and cool intellect. He rose to greatness by touch and touch alone. To buy a pair of his Lotto boots – had they fit me – would have been an act of unparalleled arrogance. They weren't the most expensive range, but I still saw few boys who dared even attempt to emulate him.

Alongside van Basten in that 1990 team, completing the famous trio of Dutchmen, were Ruud Gullit and Frank Rijkaard. Gullit, of course, was the one you noticed first, and that's probably how he wanted it. His dreadlocks swayed out at you from the pages of *Match* magazine, and at the start of each game he strolled onto the pitch with the swagger of a rapper. Gullit was the Carl Lewis of football: a man of overwhelming aura, which was largely the result of his exceptional athletic ability. For a man of such imposing physique, he carried himself with a surprising lightness, not so much sprinting as skipping carefree over the turf.

Behind him, Rijkaard did the dirty work. If it was Gullit who feasted on helpless defences, then it was Rijkaard who set the table. While he did so in unfussy fashion, there was elegance in the economy with which he used the ball; and though he often played the humble role of waiter, he could also be the chef when called upon. It was, after all, his strike which won the European Cup at the end of that season, his goal giving AC Milan a 1-0 victory over Sven-Goran Eriksson's Benfica. There's something about the manner of his goal that was typically Rijkaard; the way in which he ran on through midfield late in the game, finally tired of deferring to the attackers who had toiled fruitlessly up ahead of him, moving gracefully through the gears and beyond the offside trap. His laconic flick into the bottom corner was a finish that van Basten would have been happy to add to his catalogue.

Of course, these three Dutchmen were the foreign icing on a quintessentially Italian cake, a team built upon the exceptional central defensive axis of Franco Baresi and Alessandro Costacurta. If it is forgivable here to draw an analogy with *The Godfather*, then while Baresi was the Michael Corleone of *calcio*, Costacurta was Sonny. "Billy", as Costacurta was often known, was vigorous and impetuous, his temper eventually costing him suspensions for both the European Cup and World Cup Finals in 1994. Costacurta was the instigator, the first to stir up hostilities with the opposition's forwards, while Baresi proceeded in a state of calm that was often somewhat menacing. If a striker found that either the ball or his balance had gone missing, robbed from him by a well-placed toe-poke or trip, it was rare for Baresi's fingerprints to be found at the scene. At a time when English defenders were typified by their execution of endless sliding tackles, Baresi made it the fashion to end the game with a clean pair of knees. His was defence not as thunder, but theft.

To either side of Baresi and Costacurta were full-backs from two very different stylistic schools. Mauro Tassotti, on the right, was all brash tenacity and blue-collar bustle, while on the left Paolo Maldini looked more like someone who'd been kidnapped from his final year of fashion college. Tassotti's appearance was reassuringly brutish, with the kind of features you might expect to find at the bottom of a bar-fight, whereas you could imagine Maldini playing the game with a silk scarf flailing over both shoulders. Maldini, as it would turn out, was deceptively dandyish. He was no figure of fragile beauty, and would last eight seasons longer in the Milan first team squad than Tassotti – 25 to 17. What's more, his trademark, ironically enough, was very English: the immaculately-timed sliding tackle, with which he would whiplash many a stray ball safely into the stands.

The team was completed by three artisans: Giovanni Galli in goal; and Alberigo Evani and Carlo Ancelotti in midfield. Dependability was their watchword; and, in Evani and Ancelotti, Sacchi found the perfect practitioners of the pressing system which would see AC Milan retain the European Cup, the only team to do so in the modern era. Ancelotti's apprenticeship in a team with such gifted players, it seems, was fine training for his career in management, which would see him take Milan to the final of the UEFA Champions League on three occasions in five years, winning it twice (in 2003 and 2007).

The 1990 team was an easy one to love. They showed that you could have your cake and eat it: they proved that you didn't have to sacrifice grace for graft. As much as anything, they had not one but two of the best kits in sport: their all-white away strip channelled the angelic air of Real Madrid, whilst their home shirt was an arrogant banner of broad black and red stripes, with "MEDIOLANUM" emblazoned across the breast in emphatic white capitals. By the time I reached university, I had long since done away with the humility of my pre-teen years: and, finding that our college fortuitously had the same kit as the 1990 Milan team, I made sure to snatch the number 9 shirt, my own small homage to van Basten and his successor George Weah.

It is a mark of the greatness of the class of 1990 that they are the only team in the modern era who could conceivably have given Pep

Guardiola's Barcelona a run for their money. The 2011 side which Guardiola managed to victory over Sir Alex Ferguson's Manchester United – a 3-1 scoreline not doing full justice to their dominance – featured the core of Spain's World Cup-winning side at their formidable best, and in the end might just have trumped Sacchi's magnificent orchestra. Of the two, though, it is the three Dutchmen and their band of brilliant brothers who will linger first, if not longer, in my affection. I have had other footballing loves since they glided into view, but they will remain the first truly great team that I had the privilege to witness: and, as an introduction to this sport's unique beauty, I could not have had a finer one.

South Korea 2002

Michael Hudson

Everyone remembers their first love. Newcastle United, seasons 1992 to 1994: Pavel Srnicek, Peter Beardsley, David Kelly, Brian 'Killer' Kilcline, Robert Lee, Gavin Peacock, Lee Clark, Malcolm Allen, Alex Mathie and Andy, Andy Cole. Did any of us imagine that things would never be so good again?

How about 1995-96, you ask? The football was better but the atmosphere was already withering, the crowd older and less raucous, and the joy of going to the match was already on the wane. Kenny Dalglish's New Model Army football coincided with me graduating from university and needing to find a job. I ended up in Daejeon, South Korea, five and a half thousand miles east of St James' Park. The local team played on sand and caked mud at a roofless municipal stadium with a running track and a few thousand fans. Soon I found other things to do with my Saturday afternoons.

And then came the 2002 World Cup. I'd bought my tickets the previous year, when nobody really expected either host nation to progress beyond their first three games. In Seoul, the mood was downbeat, the last remaining hope being to do better than Japan. In the space of 12 catastrophic weeks, Guus Hiddink's team had been beaten 5-0 by both the Czech Republic and France. Ticket sales were dwindling and Samsung hurriedly axed a multi-million pound advertising campaign based on the now widely derided slogan: "Hiddink, show us your ability."

"The players should be well equipped with advanced superior skills and be more than ready for the World Cup by now when the opening is less than two months away. Isn't that what Hiddink is here for?" chafed the *Chosun Ilbo*, who nicknamed the Dutchman 'Mister 5-0'.

I watched the opening game against Poland on a street corner straight after work. The Europeans were plodding and ponderous, the red-shirted Koreans brimming with pace and intensity as goals from Hwang Sun-hong and Yoo Sung-chul set off the kind of celebrations that the BBC compared to "an FA Cup final, the Beatles at Shea Stadium and the Last Night of the Proms all rolled into one – with the volume turned up". Those 90 minutes ignited the entire country; 60,000 supporters in Daegu were joined by hundreds of thousands of others in front of giant outdoor screens for the second group match with the USA. The one-all draw left Hiddink's side needing a point against Portugal. Thanks to Park Ji-sung they got all three, and Seoul stayed up all night.

Winning the group sent Korea to Daejeon, one of the three games I'd already bought tickets for. So had the Portuguese, a few of whom were wandering forlornly outside the ground as my brother and I took our seats among a tumultuous expanse of scarlet bandanas, noise sticks and t-shirts with the slogan 'Be The Reds' splashed across the chest. A giant Korean flag wriggled back and forth; "*Dae Han Min Guk*!" (Korea Republic) reverberated across the stadium, thousands of hands thrusting cards with the words 'Again 1966' into the air at the opposite end of the ground. The only time you ever noticed the tiny pocket of Italians was when they stood for their anthem and walked out, gesticulating furiously, at the very end of the game.

With Alessandro Nesta injured and Fabio Cannavaro suspended, the *Azzurri* had shuffled their starting eleven, Alessandro Del Piero partnering Christian Vieri up front while Paulo Maldini moved across to the centre of defence. The Koreans smelled blood, pressing the Italians both on and off the pitch.

"*Arirang, Arirang, Arariyo*," 40,000 voices wail in unison; "*Arirang gogaero neomeoganda...*", ('crossing over Arirang pass, the one who abandoned me will not walk four kilometres before their feet ache in pain'). Francesco Coco, filling in for Maldini at left back, seems to have walked a lot further when, hopelessly outpaced, he scythes down Park Ji-sung just to the right of the penalty area. Song Chong-gug takes the free kick, Seol Ki-hyeon – later of Fulham and Reading – rises to meet it and is grappled to the floor by Christian Panucci. It's a clear penalty, but a visibly nervous Ahn Jung-hwan places his shot too close to Buffon, who palms the ball round the post.

The crowd goes quiet, but only momentarily. *"Arirang"* segues into a defiant *"Oh, Pilsung Korea*!*"* (Victory Korea!) as first Vieri, then Totti, miss with shots at goal. But then Totti pitches a corner to the near post and Vieri, bending at the waist, heads in to the top of the net, wheeling away with a finger to his lips.

But still the noise doesn't stop. Nor, more importantly, do the Korean players, who have more and more possession as the Italians cede territory, content to sit on their single goal lead. With an hour gone, a cautious Trapattoni replaces Alessandro del Pierro with Rino Gattuso. Hiddink, with nothing to lose, responds by throwing two more men up front. His team literally chase the game, attacking in desperate waves, while Italy recline then pounce on the counter. Vieri scuffs wide of goal with only Lee Woon-jae to beat, and Lee Young-pyo's kneecap diverts another effort inches away from the post.

So far so predictable. Hiddink resorts to pacing the touchline, there are two minutes left on the stadium clock when a looped cross hits Panucci's chest and spins back off his arm to Seol Ki-hyeon. The Korean jabs the ball goalwards, it goes through the defender's legs, bounces twice and beats a static Buffon at his left-hand post. The ground explodes, Hiddink, dark-suited, pumps the air with his fist. In a madcap final couple of minutes, Vieri fluffs another chance and Seol hits the side netting with one half of the stadium leaping out of their seats.

Almost everything that could possibly happen on a football pitch happens in extra-time. Francesco Totti turns Song Chong-gug and tumbles in the box as the defender slides in to retrieve the ball. The Italian looks back, arms raised in expectation of a penalty, only to see the Ecuadorian referee brandishing a second yellow card. Minutes later, Damiano Tomassi is wrongly flagged for offside as he touches the ball around the despairing South Korean goalkeeper. Even on replay, both decisions were borderline, the contact between Totti's left leg and Song's knee followed by a headlong tumble suggestive of a dive. In football vernacular, you've seen them given both ways.

The play takes on the pace and cadence of a basketball game. Hwang heads the ball into the ground and straight up at Buffon; Seol gets into a tangle and Lee, flying to his right, somehow manages to divert Gattuso's rising shot over the bar. We're down to the last three minutes when Ulsan's Lee Chun-soo rolls the ball on to the right boot of Lee Young-pyo. The cross swings in, "Ahn Jung-hwan...heading! Goooooal!" the commentators howl as 40,011 bodies start leaping maniacally around. Ahn, kissing his wedding ring, sprints off in the same direction Vieri took almost two hours before. Fireworks start exploding behind the stadium, and the Korean players are all on their knees as the Italians, dumbfounded, sit silently by the touchline. Ahn leads a lap of honour and, not for the last time that night, I feel a clap on my shoulder and a beer shoved into my hands. *"Dae han min guk!"* roars out again, and this time it sounds like the whole country is singing. It probably is.

The Italians reacted with predictable outrage. "THIEVES" spat the *Corriere dello Sport*, black capitals blaring out from its front page. "It was a scandal," says Francesco Totti, so confident before the game. "The truth is the referee was set against us...They wanted us out". "Korea is a powerful country. It's clear they would have done something. I've never in my life seen refereeing that bad," remarks the head of the Italian World Cup delegation, sardonically. "It was like something out of a comedy film."

They were laughing in South Korea, anyway, where five million people had joyously spilled onto the streets. "Veni, vidi, vici," mocked the following day's *Chosun Ilbo*.

When I moved to Italy a year later, the mere mention of South Korea still guaranteed a boo in class. Their suspicions of wrongdoing seemed to be confirmed in Gwangju, when an Egyptian referee and linesmen from Uganda and Trinidad disallowed two Spanish goals and repeatedly flagged the Iberians offside. Later that year, Byron Moreno, the Ecuadorian referee who dismissed Totti for diving, was banned for 20 games after adding the same number of minutes to injury time at the end of a game between LDU Quito and Barcelona Sporting Club, during which Quito came from behind to win 3-2. In 2010 he was arrested at New York's Kennedy Airport after police discovered 10 bags of heroin strapped to his body. "Six kilos of drugs?" scoffed Gianluigi Buffon. "I believe Moreno had this already in 2002, but not in his underwear, in his body."

The victories in Daejeon and Gwangju turned Hiddink into a national hero. Samsung re-released their marketing campaign, which now had an estimated value of over US$1bn. The Dutchman was given Korean citizenship and had statues, hotels a song and a football stadium named in his honour. More than 200 books were eventually published on what became known as 'Hiddink Syndrome'.

Did the Koreans benefit from favourable refereeing decisions? In Germany and Argentina they'd argue the same about England in 1966, while Argentina wouldn't have won in 1978 without the fix against Peru, and the Germans only made the '82 final after the scandal of their group game with Austria. For me, it's always been a moot point. Tainted as the Taeguk Warriors' achievement remains, that night in Daejeon made me fall in love with football all over again.

Wolverhampton Wanderers 1990

Drew Kearns

In a radio interview once, Robert Plant, rock god and lifelong Wolves fan, was asked to describe the best and worst aspects of supporting Wolverhampton Wanderers Football Club. He paused, thought and replied, "Realising you support Wolves… and realising you support Wolves". The man has sung many lines, but never has he spoken truer words.

My life of turmoil as a Wolverhampton Wanderers supporter was a near miss. Both Liverpool and, inexplicably, Huddersfield Town vied for my affections. The former was due to the verve and swagger of a side winning trophies with players as immensely skillful as Barnes, Beardsley, Rush and McMahon. Huddersfield, however, was an education in the harsh realities of life.

The son of a Dublin labourer, my Dad was born and raised in London before relocating to West Yorkshire. At an early age he had 'chosen' Wolves as his team (which is a different story altogether). Due to ill health, however, he was unable to take me, his first son, to football on a regular basis. But he clearly knew I needed my football fix and living in Ossett, a sleepy old mill town in West Yorkshire, Huddersfield was the closest I was going to get. Dad kindly arranged for a neighbour with a spare season ticket to take me down the old Leeds Road ground every other week, though what this must have felt like for him I never knew, and maybe never will – his son going to watch Huddersfield Town.

Despite all that though, when he was well enough it was Wolverhampton all the way and we'd go to go cheer on the famous Old Gold. And neither the charm and history of the Kop, nor the 'wonder' of the Cowshed end in Huddersfield, could divert my attentions away from Molineux. Once there, my heart wasn't leaving.

My bedroom walls were beginning to be covered in Old Gold before 1990, but it was that year and that Wolves side which made me fall in love for the first time. The autumn of 1990, the season after the World Cup, Bobby's battling boys, Gazza and those penalties. For Wolves it was the start of a brave new dawn. Sir Jack Hayward had taken over the club, saving it from almost certain failure. Molineux was dilapidated, a lopsided ground with only two stands open to the public. The club shop consisted of a Portakabin; facilities were non-existent. But for a seven-year old like me it was everything I could dream of. The smell of the cigarettes and Bovril, the noise, excitement and buzz before a game. Pushing through the turnstiles to walk out onto the South Bank terrace. Nothing in life back then could beat it. Although the ground has changed and the years have passed, very little even now comes close.

The game I remember the most from this year is a 2-2 draw against local rivals West Brom. The passion, heart and soul from players and fans alike was all I needed. I didn't know what 'this' was, but I loved every bit of it. I'm pretty sure I still remember that as a certain winner was disallowed, the energy generated from this mass of people all focused on one moment was powerful stuff. The game was all anybody in the ground and on the pitch cared about for 90 minutes. The world outside Molineux wasn't so much irrelevant, it simply didn't exist. Going to football provides many things to many people, but thinking back, the sheer escapism of it was probably what got me hooked. And I've been hooked ever since.

So what of these golden heroes to whom I owe this lifelong addiction? As was compulsory then, it was a simple 4-4-2. In goal, a true Wolves legend to me, Mike Stowell. A stalwart if ever there was one. The second best keeper I've seen play for us (no one will beat big Matt Murray, who all bias aside is the best keeper I will ever see play the game), but having 'Mickey Stowell in our goal' meant we had a chance of a clean sheet every game. In front of him the most notable defender was Andy Thompson. Unfortunately for 'Thomo', he will probably always be best remembered as 'the other player' to move from the Albion at the same time as a certain Steve Bull. But Thomo was class. A short, moustachioed full-back with fire in his left peg. Great crosses, great effort and almost perfect from the penalty spot.

Into midfield and the names roll off the tongue. Dennison, Birch, Downing and Cook.

Robbie Dennison from Northern Ireland was an old-school winger and scored in that 2-2 draw. His tremendous effort again made up for any shortfall in genuine quality or the ability to beat his man with a trick. Paul Birch, having arrived in January 1991, became the heartbeat of the team. The midfielder you loved having in your side; perpetual movement of feet and brain. Running, conducting and making the play happen around him. Seeking out the ball and using it to full effect. His continual movement was just as well, as you can't stand still for long when you had a curly perm like he did – a sitting duck for the opposition's brutes if ever there was one.

Paul Cook – Cookie – was the laid back 'flair' player in that Wolves side whose left foot was sweet enough to stand out on the muddiest of second-rate pitches. At times, he went beyond frustrating, but boy the lad could pass the ball. In the old Second Division you could forgive the occasional insipid 45 minutes if he could split a defence with 10 minutes to go, and more often than not he did just that. Then there was Keith 'Psycho' Downing, the hard man. My abiding memory of him is hearing, seeing and practically feeling the pain when he dislocated his shoulder away to Barnsley. The man didn't so much as flinch. If it moved he'd kick it. If it didn't, he'd kick it twice to make sure it would never move – awesome in every way. You can keep your Claude Makeleles, give me a Keith Downing every time.

And so to the front two. Steve Bull and Andy Mutch, the ultimate double act. Mutch was the composed, clever forward who could link the play from the rest of the team towards our goal machine wearing the number 9. Mutchie was the kind of player you couldn't play a bad pass to – he'd do something with it regardless. I still vividly recall an impossible 'flick on' he achieved at Bramall Lane. The ball was cleared from Stowell and basically came down with snow on it. Not only did he get his head on it, he deftly flicked it on with one twist of the neck. The ball easily ran on straight into the path of Bully, who didn't even have to check his stride. The fact I can still remember a 'flick on' from all of 20 years ago should tell you all you need to know about Andy Mutch. Bully rightly got the headlines, but Mutch was the perfect player alongside him. An absolute pleasure to watch.

And so to Steve Bull. Many far more qualified people than me have written about the man. I will try, but only do so mindful of the enormity of the task. The story is a great one: signs from local rivals West Brom; spends over a decade scoring goals for Wolves. Statistics don't explain how he played but anybody who scores 306 goals, 18 hat tricks, manages more than 50 goals in back to back seasons and ends an all-too brief international career with a ratio of one in three can't be too shabby a player. As ex-Wolves manager Graham Turner said at the time: "People say Bully's first touch isn't all that good. This may be true. But to be fair, he scores with his second."

Not many players before or since have had a specific celebration for hat tricks. A great regret of mine is never having witnessed a Bully hat trick, complete with aeroplane celebration. Football fans know the name and the hero status he created and now rightly still receives, however, for me, the goals were simply a bonus. As a seven-year-old boy falling in love with the game and indeed Wolverhampton Wanderers, it was Bully who led the way. Literally. He used to sprint out of the tunnel and race across the half way line before every game. I've never seen anyone else do this. But what it did was show everybody that he meant business. He was ready. He wanted it. Just like the fans, the game about to be played was the most important thing in the world for him. It is this absolute commitment to wearing a Wolves shirt that I adored.

Other strikers scored goals, some scored a lot, few scored as many as Steve Bull, but no other team had a Bully. No other side had a player who ran himself to a standstill every single game like Bull did. He played in the gold shirt like everybody standing on the South Bank would have, given the chance. He had his chance and he took it every time.

It's unfair to his team mates to say that in 1990, Wolves were all about Steve Bull. But Bully showed me he cared as much as the fans. He cared as much as me. Nobody will compare for as long as I watch the game. This much I know. It's not to say the current Wolves side want for this. They don't. But Bully was different. When he ran tirelessly down the channels, we ran with him. When he got kicked, we hurt. When he scored, we celebrated together. To see, feel and share this energy from the South Bank as a young lad was very special. I feel incredibly lucky to have been a very small part of it and in debt to my Dad forever for taking me.

I go to Molineux now trying to share in something which could be described as similar. Soon, the stadium will be redeveloped again. When complete it will be the third version of the ground which I have watched my beloved Wanderers play. Maybe one day I'll take my son and see a game from what I will still call the South Bank and from there I'll recount the sight of the number nine sprinting out onto the pitch saluting the fans on the terrace, all bowing down as one chanting 'Ooh Bully Bully'. I'll tell him about Stowell, Thomo, Downing, Mutch. Hopefully the team at the time will inspire, excite and enthuse him, like the side of 1990 did for me. That was 21 years ago, and they all still mean absolutely everything to me.

Nigeria 1996

Adam Bushby

My love affair with Nigeria began in the summer of 1994. My love affair with Africa as a whole had begun four years earlier in Italy, but those memories are hazy, clouded by vague recollections of tears and mimed 'keep an eye on him's. It was Gary Lineker's accuracy from the penalty spot that prematurely ended my fling with Cameroon in Naples in 1990. And then history repeated itself as the similar rapier-like precision of a man nicknamed *Il Divin Codino* did for my affair with Nigeria in Boston. The Divine Ponytail, from the penalty spot at the Foxboro Stadium. Roberto Baggio stole Nigeria from me in 1994. I was ten years old.

I didn't appreciate this at the time, but up until Italia '90, it had been easy to dismiss an entire continent's football output with a sneer, a wave of the hand and a snide reference to Ilunga Mwepu's infamous caution at the World Cup of 1974 for running from the defensive wall and hoofing the ball away before a Brazilian free kick could be taken (for your consideration: the Zaire national side had been warned by despotic leader Mobutu Sese Seko that should they lose by four or more goals against the holders, they wouldn't see out the week), as if this moment of confusion and comedy was all Africa could ever hope to offer.

But what I'd seen of Cameroon in 1990 and Nigeria in 1994 had whetted my appetite for an upset, what with both being taken to extra time in their respective campaigns. Football at the start of the '90s for me was peppered with disappointment. Liverpool losing 2-0 in Genoa in the quarter final first leg of the UEFA Cup and then again, 2-1 at Anfield a fortnight later in the spring of 1992 both stick out particularly, for some reason. As does England sputtering to defeat against the Swedes at Euro '92. Even to a novice, Neil Webb, Carlton Palmer and Andy Sinton were clearly bad cover versions of Paul Gascoigne, Chris Waddle and Peter Beardsley.

And being a York-born lad with a somewhat worsening addiction to football, it had only been a matter of time before I dragged some poor, unsuspecting non-footballing habitué to my hometown club. My first ever visit to Bootham Crescent was the eyeball-searingly bad 0-0 draw between York and Northampton, on a miserable February afternoon in '92. My stepdad would never go back. I'd become a season ticket holder. Funny how these things work out.

I also remember asking my dad to bring me back a Barcelona shirt from his summer holiday in Cyprus in 1995 – the Kappa one sported by Hristo Stoichkov and Romario, two of my favourite players – only for him to inexplicably bring back an APOEL Nicosia shirt – which, somewhat ironically, I would kill for these days.

In the days before Sky and over-saturated media coverage and with the Premier League very much in its infancy, it's easy to forget just how exciting it all was for a boy. When a World Cup or a Euros or a European Cup came around, you got to see players that you had read about in *Shoot*, *Match* or more likely *World Soccer,* but had seldom ever seen, *Football Italia* aside. I was genuinely transfixed by Romario and Maradona in USA '94; blown away by the swagger of Gheorghe Hagi and Fernando Redondo; mesmerised by Stoichkov's brooding brilliance; and captivated by Rashidi Yekini's emotional, net-shaking celebration after giving Nigeria the lead against the Bulgarians in the group stages. I'd never seen players like this before. I'd seen the likes of, Neil Webb, Carlton Palmer and Andy Sinton, but nothing like this.

Crucially, by the time 1996 rolled round, I'd seen the underdog – an underdog I felt invested in – win only once. I was 12 years old and every time I'd rooted for David I'd seen him dispatched with ease by Goliath, save for one balmy September night (my birthday in fact) at Old Trafford in 1995 when I saw York City beat Manchester United 3-0 and reinforce my belief that sometimes dreams do come true. I still remember gawping, open-mouthed, at the fantastical sight of the scoreboard that night, then looking at my uncle who was doing exactly the same.

A year later, my beloved Nigeria were back in the United States for the 1996 Olympics in Atlanta, entering as dark horses at best. Brazil and Argentina had both named formidable squads. For the former,

Aldair, Roberto Carlos, Bebeto, Ronaldo, Juninho, Flavio Conceicao, Rivaldo and Savio featured. For the Argentines, Roberto Ayala, Roberto Sensini, Matias Almeyda, Jose Chamot, Diego Simeone, Hernan Crespo, Claudio Lopez, Javier Zanetti and Ariel Ortega were included.

But with perhaps the greatest collection of talent to emerge from Africa in this or any year, Nigeria's squad was brimming with potential. The names still roll off the tongue after all this time. Jay Jay Okocha, Nwankwo Kanu, Taribo West, Tijani Babangida, Daniel Amokachi, Celestine Babayaro, Sunday Oliseh and Emmanuel Amuneke were the pick of an outlandish litter. As Oliseh (he of screamer against Spain in France '98 fame), talking to SuperSport about his Olympic success in July 2012, explained: "This Nigerian team of 1996 just had to win something. The team was too good not to win anything." If Nigeria were in confident mood going into the tournament, more than four thousand miles away, I was too.

I don't remember much from the group stages if I'm being honest; not like I remember USA '94 or Euro '96, but those are tales for another day. A 1-0 victory over Hungary and a 2-0 win over Japan sent Nigeria through to the knockouts, though a Ronaldo strike in the final group game gave Brazil a 1-0 victory and first place. Nevertheless, the Super Eagles were in the quarter finals and I was beginning to get excited. A 2-0 win over Mexico saw Okocha score his second of the tournament and a 17-year-old Celestine Babayaro net the other.

Okocha was, and still is, one of my favourite players. I'd seen somewhere, presumably on some VHS compilation snaffled from yet another car boot sale stall, this skinny Nigerian lad single-handedly dismantling a defence in the Bundesliga. For those who have never seen Okocha bamboozling the Karlsruhe defence in 1993, it is an absolute joy, especially given he completely takes the piss out of Oliver Khan, turning him this way and that and back again. For me, this was what football was about. Replicating tricks from the school playground in proper games. And that's exactly how Nigeria played their football that fateful summer in '96.

So, my boys had set up a semi-final re-match with Brazil and I was both elated and petrified. 'There's no shame in going out to the reigning world champions,' I told myself, but deep down it was fair to say I feared a shellacking. The Brazil match, I remember vividly, despite the fact that more than 17 years have passed. Funnily enough, the colour of the shirts is still very clear in my mind. The brightness of the Brazil yellow and the Nigeria green in the Georgian sunshine. Like footballing Opal Fruits (I will never subscribe to this Starburst nonsense). For months I desperately tried to buy that Nigeria shirt to no avail. My best mate and I did end up getting our hands on the fluorescent Nigeria shirt of France '98 sparking a bizarre trend at our school which saw about seven or eight pasty white Yorkshire lads in the gaudy green of the Super Eagles that summer.

It's fair to point out that I didn't really care about tactics at this juncture in my life. In the playground, I was used to being deployed in a *trequartista* role in a 1-1-14 formation. What does still stick in my mind so firmly is the utter freedom of the Nigerians. Free-flowing expansive football, short passing juxtaposed with lung-busting bursts through midfield. There seemed to be acres of space for both sides. For a 12-year-old, this was akin to footballing *Eurotrash*. Soft-core porn for the romantics. With such a cavalier approach being adopted by both sides, 0-0 was an impossibility. I expected flamboyance, but what followed was sheer unadulterated attacking bliss.

When Flavio Conceicao's free kick put Brazil ahead in the first minute, all I could hope for was that Nigeria would avoid a thrashing. But then remarkably, they equalised. A lovely bit of skill from Babayaro saw him skin his marker and fire it across the six yard box only for Roberto Carlos to smash it into the roof of his own net. The goals kept flowing and I was utterly enthralled. Nigeria were 3-1 down by the 38th minute. Bebeto added the second and then a beautiful deft chest from Juninho to Flavio Conceicao saw the latter sweep it over the onrushing keeper.

I remember Victor Ikpeba's goal to make it 2-3 being a real treat and researching this piece, YouTube confirmed it. Both sides are going hell for leather, the ball is won in the centre circle and Brazil's defence is carved wide open far too easily. Brazil's right back is hopelessly out of position as Ikpeba supplies a wonderfully accomplished finish from the angle of the penalty area to nestle the ball into the bottom corner.

The equaliser in the final minute was even better. Kanu has his back to goal two yards out when it bobbles through to him. In an audacious display of quick thinking and skill, he then cheekily chips it up and swivels to dink it over the prostrate keeper and past full back Ze Maria on the line. It's delicious. His frankly ridiculous celebration after the goal – limp hand on his waist in what can only be described as a John Inman 'I'm free' impression – contrives only to make it all the more wonderful. Here I was watching Nigeria, my team, drawing with Brazil.

Kanu's winner – a 94th minute golden goal – was even better. Fortuitous in that the ball cannons of Amokachi's back and into his path, Kanu – on his way to Inter Milan after the tournament – finished with aplomb from the edge of the box. Nigeria had beaten Brazil 4-3. With a 94th minute golden goal no less. This was like overdosing on E numbers at Disneyland. All I remember is not being able to sleep that night and then trying out 'Kanus' at the local park all of the next day.

The final is a bit of a blur for whatever reason. I wasn't the fickle pessimist I am prone to be these days and fully expected Nigeria to beat Argentina. Three things stick out from the game. The scary bald ref, I'd later find out was, of course, the inimitable Pierluigi Collina. Ortega's scandalous dive to earn a penalty – I never did like him after that. And the winner, still one of my favourite ever goals. It was 2-2 in the 90th minute and with the game heading to extra time, Nigeria got a free kick on the left hand side of the penalty area. Just a fraction of a second after the free kick is floated in, the Argentina defence moves out, arms aloft in unison. But, hang on. They've cocked it up. They've sprung the offside trap a fraction too late. Emmanuel Amuneke looks for all the world like he's about four yards off. But he's not. It's beautiful. Completely unmarked, he volleys it left footed past Cavallero. Another fiesta of attacking football ended with the Super Eagles emerging as 3-2 winners and, unbelievably, Olympic champions. The Nigerian players are euphoric. The Nigerian bench, likewise. And a scrawny little 12-year-old in York bounces around his bedroom in rapture.

Cynicism surrounding the modern incarnation of football may well be deep-rooted and widespread these days – I'm as guilty, if not more so, as the next fan – but when I take a moment to recall my earliest footballing memories: collecting *Roy of the Rovers* annuals from various car boot sales; memorising the grounds of each and every one of the 92 football league sides back in '93; high-fiving York striker Paul Barnes after he'd just hit a 25-yard free-kick to draw City level at Rotherham when I was ballboy for the afternoon; scoring five goals on my debut for my local cub scouts side when I was nine; and countless other stories of that ilk, there is nothing I can do to stop myself from falling in love all over again.

Heart of Midlothian 1953-54

Ian Guthrie (ghostwritten by Rob MacDonald)

I was totally football daft. I started playing football for school teams in the Highlands. This was when I was about 12 – at the time, my dad was an engine driver and would get free travel for me on the trains. I was a great Hearts supporter so I used to travel down to Tynecastle on a Saturday morning, 12 years old: onto the train straight down to Tynecastle, watch the Hearts. Come back out through the crowds and home again, back on the train in the evening.

It was only because my Dad got me free travel I could go down there and watch senior football. He was fine with it, no bother. We were tough, but it was a safe thing to do in these days. It was different. It pre-dates all the hooliganism stuff.

So I went by myself. It would've been about three and a half hours on the train. I used to stand on the halfway line, a middle of the pitch man, and managed to get in to stand there each week. I pretty much always managed to see when I had to – the people around me were great at helping me up and making sure there was space for me to see what was going on. Tynecastle was busy back then too, there would have been something like 30,000 or 40,000 all standing in there when the place was full, all died in the wool Hearts fans. I was completely in love with it.

Course there are things that are just part of the experience, not just the football. I used to buy Edinburgh rock when I was down there. That was a great ambition of mine, to buy Edinburgh rock from Edinburgh – it was like chalk, like big sticks of chalk. And I would buy the packet of Edinburgh rock and then coming out of the park, coming out of Tynecastle with all the crowds, you didn't know but you were getting pushed and squeezed, and then you'd get back on the train and go back up home. The first thing I always wanted was to open up the Edinburgh rock and celebrate.

The whole thing was powder of course, by this point, wasn't it.

Why Hearts? I just picked them. The name I think... I liked the name at 12 years old, 'Heart of Midlothian'. I thought 'ach, that's a nice name for a football team', you know?

So I latched on to the Hearts: Alfie Conn, Willy Bauld (the King), Jimmy 'Twinkletoes' Wardhaugh, a great Hearts team eventually. Revolutionaries too, they were. It was the early 50s I started going down there and I remember the one big game, Rangers at Tynecastle, and it was three-nothing Rangers, with about 12 minutes to go and like most Hearts supporters, I was feeling a bit dejected, so I decided to leave the park early and as I just come out of the gate, there was a big roar went up, you know, and the word came back, 3-1, and then about three minutes later, I was walking down the road away from Tynecastle... another big roar, and then another big roar about two minutes later. So I've walked from Tynecastle when it's 3-0... and then it's 3-3. A stick of rock couldn't really make up for that. But they were a great side; I should've known.

It was 1953. Ian, who is my great-uncle, has been explaining how his love affair with football was developing in a year that saw the beginnings of a famous Hearts side. Beyond this – beyond the confines of a train ride from Inverness to Edinburgh – it was also an era in which, famously, the sport would fundamentally change. This was the reign of the mighty Magyars.

But more on them later. When you're 12 years old and swashbuckling and goal plundering are your thing, which at that age they normally are, the Hearts team of the early 50s were pretty much the definitive exponents. And Conn, Bauld and Warhaugh were their key men. Nicknamed the 'Terrible Trio' without a hint of irony, they laid the foundations for an unprecedented era of success, blasting Hearts towards seven trophies in the mid '50s to early '60s.

All three were local boys[1]: Conn and Bauld were Edinburgh-born while Wardhaugh, born a mile from the Scottish border, just north of Berwick-upon-Tweed, was raised in the capital. Conn joined Hearts in 1944 from Inveresk Athletic and would make his debut later that year in a 4-0 win over Dumbarton in a wartime Southern League match.

Bauld, who had been playing for junior side Newtongrange Star, joined Hearts in 1946, as did Wardhaugh, who, unlike his new club-mate (loaned straight to Edinburgh City), would feature regularly in his first season at the club. When Bauld returned from across the city, however, he would score a hat trick on his first-team debut, proving an able enough deputy for Wardhaugh who then missed much of the following (1947-48) season completing National Service in Worcestershire.

Modern game intrusion alert: When Cristiano Ronaldo scored a monster header against Manchester United in the Champions' League in 2013, none other than Sir Alex Ferguson invoked Willie Bauld as a player of similar aerial prowess, calling him "unbelievable in the air, fantastic in the air". High praise indeed from a man who has undoubtedly seen his fair share of unbelievable, fantastic players. And Eric Djemba-Djemba. And Bebe[2].

Ian backs this up enthusiastically.

> *Bauld was a wonderful centre-forward, just wonderful. This side was glorious – as far as I was concerned all of them could do no wrong – but he stood out like a sore thumb. He was a wonderful centre-forward, an opportunist, you know. Could score any which way. On the ground, brilliant. Headers, just unbeatable. They were a wonderful team, they all played for each other, you know, but he was the stand out.*

Bauld's club mates were no slouches either – the three were first deployed together after an underwhelming start to the 1948-49 league campaign. Hearts' manager Davie McLean played the trio for the first time in an October date with East Fife, opponents who had routed Hearts 4-0 a

---

1 ⸱ This of course being a time before 'global scouts', 'miniature Argentine geniuses' and 'growth hormones'.

2 BOOM BOOM

few weeks previous. This one ended in revenge: 6-1 revenge. Preferred personnel (and their positions) appeared to have been established.

Sadly, however, McLean would not ever truly see the combinations come to fruition as his untimely death in February 1951 thrust his assistant Tommy Walker, who had joined as a member of the playing staff from Chelsea a couple of years previously[3], in full control of team affairs.

He had, though, inherited a Terrible Trio that had been scoring for fun in the intervening period, with Bauld's customary poise also helping Conn to notch 102 goals and Wardhaugh (the subject of an accepted £26,000 bid from Newcastle in 1952, but one that never completed as he was unable to agree personal terms) 77 in the four years since their first appearance together in 1948. Nevertheless the trophy cabinet remained bare until Ian's first season on the terraces.

Hearts won their first trophy in 48 years – the Scottish League Cup in 1954 – with Wardhaugh scoring six times en route to the final against Motherwell. Bauld, not to be outdone, scored half that tally in the final itself, with Wardhaugh contributing the third goal in a 4-2 victory and adding another piece of hardware to the divisional top scorer accolade he'd secured in the '53-54 season with 27 goals. Hearts had been overtaken by Celtic on the home straight that year, but following Cup final success in '54 they would add the Scottish Cup in 1956 (with Conn scoring in the 3-1 final win over Celtic and Wardhaugh again the league's leading scorer, this time with 28).

As Alfie Conn became increasingly susceptible to injuries, missing the majority of the 1957-58 season with an ankle problem, Wardhaugh and Bauld joined forces with two new accomplices, Jimmy Murray and Alex Young, adding a league title in the '57-58 (amassing a record 62 points and scoring a ludicrous 132 goals in 34 matches[4]) and another League Cup in 1958, in which Bauld scored twice, as did Murray. Conn would leave the club for Raith Rovers in 1958,

---

3   Walker managed a solitary appearance at right-half (A 1-0 defeat to Dundee [insert obligatory 'definitely time to retire' joke here]) before retiring to serve as McLean's apprentice.

4   3.88 per game, stats fans. They also conceded just 29 times. Wardhaugh was again the league's top scorer and again scored 28 times, but split that year's golden boot (were it to have existed) with Jimmy Murray who also netted 28.

having made 231 appearances and scoring 121 times in the league. In all competitions, he would score over 220 times in 397 appearances over 17 years; a quite ludicrous tally in anyone's estimation.

Hearts won another league title in the 1959-60 season and two more League Cups in 1959 and '62. Wardhaugh was on the fringes of the team by the time the '59 League Cup was won and ultimately joined Dunfermline Athletic that year as Hearts went on to the league title. Bauld, who actually also played in the 1962 League Cup final replay, which was lost to Rangers 3-1, would stay at the club, retiring later that year.

Wardhaugh left Hearts having scored 376 goals for the side in 513 games, and a record League total of 208 in 300 appearances, which remained unsurpassed until John Robertson 38 years later. Bauld's record was pretty impressive too – 277 in 414 competitive games. And to think Conn's seemed ludicrous...

One thing that united the trio was their surprisingly minimal exposure to the international setup: Conn was capped just once for Scotland in 1956, scoring in a 1-1 draw with Austria. Bauld, like Conn, burned briefly but brightly for Scotland, scoring twice in three internationals. Wardhaugh was capped twice for his adopted homeland, despite technically being born in England – a beneficiary (or not, depending on your allegiance) of the Scottish Football Association and their English counterparts considering their line of division to be the River Tweed, south of Wardhaugh's birthplace in Marshall Meadows and north of Berwick.

Wardhaugh's Scottish debut was against the famous Hungarian side of the early 1950s in the Hampden Park friendly of 1954. However, it was irrespective of this match – and rather because of those in the early part of the decade – that the football paradigm had already shifted so significantly that Hungary may as well have moved the goalposts literally as well as figuratively. Here was a different approach, one to blow that of all the home nations, until that point considered the game's inventors and experts, completely out of the water. That said, it was the first time Ian would be watching.

The first time I was amazed at football, was, I think, 1954.
Hungary came over to play Scotland, right, and we didn't have

telly in the house then, but they had a telly in the school. And there were plenty of us in the school wanting to watch the game so we were nagging our science teacher for days. Hairy Hugh, his name was. So eventually there were 30 of us all crowded into Hairy Hugh's lab for this game watching Hungary. The telly was about 14 inches, you know, but we all crammed round it.

Ferenc Puskás. Now, that opened my eyes to a whole new world of football. They were just wonderful. And Puskás – I mean he didn't do it on his own, you can't, not even Bauld or any of the Hearts team could, he had plenty of support – but he was just completely different. The control he had of the ball and the way he could move. He just turned up in places no one expected. That altered your idea of football, you know. Such talent.

In front of 113,146, Scotland were beaten 4-2 at Hampden Park by a Hungarian team that had already inflicted a 6-3 beating on England at Wembley in 1953 and annihilated the same opponents 7-1 in the supposed 'revenge' re-match in Budapest in May 1954. Wardhaugh's debut counted for little as far from being interested in establishing a new 'Auld Alliance', Hungary came flying out of the traps against a Scottish side determined to both limit the damage and play on the counterattack. The Hungarians were 2-0 up inside 26 minutes and 3-1 ahead at half time and it looked like the Scots would suffer the same fate as the English had a year before. However, having scored straight after the break, they forced the issue in the second half and were themselves caught on the counterattack at the last to lose 4-2.

People didn't know who to mark, with these five running around up front but with six running forward from the other team, you know. And two wingers from the back if necessary, you know. And we didn't know what we were watching at the time, you know. But it totally changed the way most people thought about football, I think.

In *Inverting the Pyramid*, Jonathan Wilson suggests this stinging education at the hands of continental Europe had actually begun 10 years early, when Dinamo Moscow toured Britain after the end of the Second World War in 1945. A 3-3 draw with Chelsea was followed by a 10-1 dismantling of Cardiff and a 4-3 defeat of Arsenal, before Rangers attempted to salvage some pride and drew 2-2 with the (nevertheless triumphant) tourists at Ibrox Park. The lessons of that tour, Wilson suggests, were ignored – and England and, to a slightly lesser extent Scotland – were flayed anew in their own backyards.

He also quotes Alex James, a former Arsenal inside forward, who wrote in the News of the World[5] that:

"[Dinamo's success'] lies in teamwork to which there is a pattern. There is no individualist in their side... they show little variation... this lack of an individualist is a great weakness."

Mikhail Yakushin, the Dinamo coach, perhaps not surprisingly, was of the opposite opinion. Wilson quotes Yakushin thus:

"The principle of collective play is the guiding one in Soviet football. A player must not only be good in general; he must be good for the particular team... we put collective football first and individual football second."

Similarly, the 1954 Hungarian vintage, managed by Gusztáv Sebes, were much more a team than a collection of individual talents standing around in a certain area of the pitch waiting for the ball to come to them as expected. Observers of games against both England and Scotland commented on their speed, their attacking and defending as a team (unheard of on these shores up to this point) and, echoing Dinamo 10 years prior, the pre-ordained nature of their attacking threat.

If the key was collectivism, that brings us full circle to the combination of talents – those that Ian, despite my constant questions, would always qualify with the fact that they played for each other – of Hearts' famous group of goalscorers: Conn, Bauld and Wardhaugh; the Terrible Trio. Who were, of course, anything but terrible. And anything but ordinary.

The first team in Scotland to adopt the 4-4-2 [Ian tells me, after the Hungarian trouncings, it appears] *were Heart of Midlothian and they won the league that year* (1957), *and that was a wonderful team and a wonderful system as obviously they were playing against the old system – revolutionaries they were. They changed*

5   Back in the days when people actually did 'write' in the News of the World

everything and it was great to watch, the whole difference in formations; that was what was great about them. They played for each other.

There must be something profound about experiencing such an eye-openingly phenomenal departure from the perceived norms of a game. Especially when, as with all football down the years, you can become immersed in the particular style inherent to the club you support. It must be a ridiculous experience to see a sport you grew up thinking had one set of rules and normal practices, turn, with the application of innovation and creativity[6], into something so compellingly brilliant by comparison that you can't understand how it wasn't invented that way in the first place. And if that happens first as a completely alien, other-worldly concept as it was to watch Hungary dismantle Scotland, but then much closer to home as your boyhood team sweeps all before them – well, it's a potent cocktail, to say the least.

As is fitting, and as I would wish it, Ian should have the final word. A fine footballer himself (a right-half in old money), he played in the Highland Leagues as a 20-something and his infectious enthusiasm remains undimmed. There are still some things that ring true down the years and the joy in just seeing a bloody great game of football, as he must have so many times at Hearts, remains one of them:

Watching the football change for the better, watching Puskás, though I didn't know it at the time, makes it all the more sad to see it change for the worse, with all the money pouring in. All I can say about football nowadays and football when I played – you turned out there on a Saturday, on a rain-sodden pitch, with leather boots that would pass for mountaineering, a leather ball, with the lace around the outside… see most people, as I've travelled through life, most people just want to play a game of football on a Saturday. Or in the park, wherever.

I remember when they – when a full-time professional footballer was getting £20 a week. That was full time. It wasn't big big money. It was good money, but it wasn't big money, it was good money then, but… it's show-business now, that's the only way I can

6   And the absence of wall-to-wall television, newspaper and social media coverage

describe it. Money didn't mean a thing Rob. Not a thing. Just a game of football, the excitement of a game of football on good pitches. That's what it was all about to me.

Sheffield Wednesday 1993

Alex Douglas

Bill Shankly once said: 'Some people believe football is a matter of life and death. I am very disappointed with that attitude. I can assure you it is much, much more important than that.' Although I don't wholly agree with the sentiment, I have always thought that football was a good analogy for life. If football is the journey, then the teams that accompany us are our partners. I have to admit that in my early teens, I was a bit of a slag, chasing shirt. I have had exotic romances with foreign mistresses including a dirty weekend in Paris (St Germain) and an ultimately destructive on-off relationship with England. But if Manchester United were to become my life partner then the Sheffield Wednesday team of '93 was my first kiss. It was an affair to remember.

Back in the days before Football Italia, Championship Manager and The Hurricanes, when Ian Wright wasn't a TV presenter and Ron Atkinson was well respected, I became aware of the existence of a beautiful game. I had seen the older boys kicking something round in the general direction of two vertical white lines, and one horizontal, painted on the wall in the playground. After several days watching this curious activity, I worked out that these lads were attempting to imitate something I had seen on television; it was football. I was eventually allowed to play and instantly established myself as an incredibly mediocre goal-hanger. Even though I knew early on that I would never be any good at playing the game, I was hooked. The delight of scoring the winning goal in a 23-22 thriller with a volley on the half turn would establish football as the one childhood obsession that would outlive Scarcroft Primary School's playground. But where would I go from here and whom would I support?

Growing up in a household indifferent to football, with no affiliations or allegiances, I was free to pick my own team. Being too young to understand local loyalties, the world was my apple, but my imagination didn't take me very far. I was not alone in this conquest as my best friend at the time, Alex Fletcher, was also on the hunt. His family were into cricket and believed, like my own, that football was a sport for hooligans. We would discover Sheffield Wednesday together at exactly the same moment.

Although I can tell you much about that side now; at the time I was clueless. I was nine-year-old with footballing reference points that consisted of the trinity of Roger Milla, Escape to Victory and Frank Rijkaard gobbing in Rudi Voller's hair. If you'd have told me then that football didn't consist entirely of 40-year-old Cameroonian men dancing with corner flags in POW camps while people spit into each other's faces, I would have thought you were mad. I actually thought that Sylvester Stallone and Pele were responsible for the fall of the Third Reich. Part of me still does. But my eyes were soon to be clawed open one sunny (in my rose-tinted memory) spring evening when a chance flick of the remote brought live football into Fleggie's house for the first (second) time.

The FA Cup semi-final between Sheffield Wednesday and Sheffield United was under way and the Owls were already ahead. Our first reaction to this was to turn the channel. We had attempted to watch another grown up football match one week before and had given up after 10 goalless minutes. But this was different. Wednesday had already scored. Maybe there would be more. We decided to stick with it and found amusement in the fact that there were two teams from Sheffield. The fact that one of them was called Wednesday was priceless. Wednesday? What could this mean? After initially deciding to take a side each (me Wednesday, Fleggie United) the free-flowing football and thrill that was to come brought us both firmly behind Wednesday in the Steel City derby.

Chris Waddle had put the Owls ahead in the first minute via a free-kick. United equalised after 44 and set up a second half full of tension. I have to admit that I only have vague memories of these games but the fundamentals are what matters. There was a second half. There was extra time. There was a winning goal. It was scored by my first footballing hero: Mark Bright. This goal sent two nine-year-old boys into each other's arms, united behind a team they had only discovered fewer than 106 minutes before. What had begun as mild curiosity had spun on a sixpence into full-blown football passion. I hadn't been this excited since discovering there was an incomplete and unpublished Tintin book.

But before I describe what took place next I should say something about the Wednesday team that year and the context of that season. As I say, my knowledge at the time was limited. I recognised players such as Chris Waddle and Carlton Palmer who were in and around the England squad but I was being introduced to the majority of the team for the first time. This side had finished the previous season in an impressive third place, earning a Uefa Cup spot. In the season I stumbled across them, they made both domestic cup finals and eventually finished seventh in the league. Waddle went on to become the Football Writer's player of the year. Both seasons must live long in the memory for Wednesday fans who have had to witness a steady fall from grace since those heady days.

The team had a quick, wing-based style with Palmer and Viv Anderson moving the ball on to the more cultured players such as John Sheridan and Paul Warhurst. Crosses would come in from the slick and incisive wing play of Waddle and Nigel Worthington, who got forward like a Brazilian wing-back. Up front were the intimidating twosome of David Hirst and Bright, both good in the air and not afraid to get dirty. In fact, Mark Bright's elbows received more head that season than Silvio Berlusconi (yes, terrible joke). It was a strong team with a great chance of silverware.

Next up: the final. We had discovered in the intervening period that Sheffield Wednesday would play Arsenal, another name to induce pre-pubescent giggles. We knew that they had already beaten Wednesday in the Coca-Cola Cup final a few months before. This wasn't going to be easy. Watching the ritual of the FA cup with the teams walking out in unison, led by their managers, was thrilling and gave myself and Fleggie a real feel for how grand the occasion was. Fleggie had bought a Sheffield Wednesday scarf and, sensing that I was jealous, placed it on top of the television rather than round his neck. The next 90 minutes were spent biting our nails and singing our new song, 'Seaman the sailor and Smith with a wart on his nose'. That's right. We actually thought calling Dave Seaman a sailor was comedy genius. Oh boys. The line about Alan Smith still holds up though.

Arsenal went ahead after 20 minutes with Ian Wright scoring a typical poacher's header. Luckily for us, David Hirst got the better of the sailor in Arsenal's goal and equalised in the 61st minute. The next half an hour is a complete blur but the final whistle went without further incident and the game finished 1-1. What next? Extra time? Penalties? Actually, a replay (remember them) would follow five days later.

The days leading up to the replay passed quickly and I was back round Fleggie's in what seemed like no time. It was as if the two finals were being played back to back and thinking about it now, it's no wonder replays were ultimately scrapped. At the time not only were European cup competitions shorter in length, but English teams were rarely making appearances in the latter stages. Nowadays though, you could never get away with a replay and the diminished value of the FA Cup means some clubs view an early exit as a potential blessing.

But in 1993, the FA Cup mattered. This final mattered and it didn't start well. Our bogeyman Ian Wright turned up again, scoring early. Not only was this match a replay it was also a rerun. Wednesday fought back and played some great football before equalising through a deflected shot from Chris Waddle in the second half.

Once again the teams were impossible to separate. This final got nicknamed the 'longest' final as not only had it gone to a replay but would go to extra-time and was only one minute away from penalties. This whole experience wasn't just a footballing epiphany for myself and Fleggie but it was also an endurance test. In that final minute, we would feel that all those hours hadn't been rewarded. Andy Linighan met a Paul Merson corner and put the ball beyond Chris Woods in the Wednesday goal. We were crushed, but found a little solace in adding Linighan's name to our song: 'Seaman the sailor, Smith with a wart on his nose and Andy L-in-hi-gan!.' Clearly our disappointment hadn't stifled our creativity.

This was the last moment Wednesday and I would share together. Fleggie, the better person, stuck with The Owls. I briefly flirted with the idea of becoming an Arsenal fan now they had won and asked my mum for a red and white shirt. I even goaded Fleggie about how we (Arsenal) had won pretending that I had been supporting them all along. What a horrible little bastard. Spending what felt like an entire summer, but actually consisted of just three football matches with Sheffield Wednesday had consolidated my interest in football into something bigger. The drama, goals, highs and lows of that year's FA Cup taught me a lot about football in what were my formative years. Wednesday, I am forever grateful for that fateful summer.

Argentina 1986

Dan Forman

Do you fall in love with the girl next door because she's the prettiest girl in the street or the only girl in the street? Did I fall in love with Argentina '86 or with football while watching Argentina in 1986? I don't know and probably never will, particularly as I lived next door to a hermit-like old man who only ever came out of the house to raid the bargain aisle of the local Tesco two minutes before it closed. I do know, however, that I watched a lot of Argentina in 1986 and that it's from that year that I date my love of football.

I would like to say it was a political rebellion against Thatcher and the downing of the Belgrano, or a contrary two fingers to the blind patriotism and tabloid culture that made me side with Diego Maradona over Bobby Robson's wronged and brave boys. But it wasn't really, at least not at the age of seven. It was because *Hero* – the official film of the 1986 Fifa World Cup was the only football video I owned and therefore the only access to watching football I had. And it is through the prism of *Hero* that all my knowledge and experience of the Mexico World Cup was gained and opinions of it formed. And as it glossed over the hand of God to focus instead on Maradona's beyond-brilliant second goal against England, then so did I.

Actually it wasn't in 1986 at all, but 1987 when the video was released and I first got my hands on it. The World Cup itself I was certainly aware of and can vaguely recall a daily teatime Saint and Greavsie-fronted highlights show on ITV, with an Aztec-themed studio no doubt in a basement nearer Acton than the Estadio Azteca. But the matches themselves would have been on too late to watch live.

By 1987 though, Saint and Greavsie on Saturday lunchtime was no longer enough. I was both hungry for football and a latch-key kid with too much time to kill. But it was my misfortune to be eight years old in a period in which, the FA Cup final aside, there was simply no live football or even Saturday night highlights on TV. So in the absence of Sky Sports News, or Sky Sports at all, of *Super Sunday* or *Goals on Sunday*, of *Match of the Day 1* let alone 2, of Champions League Tuesdays or *Soccer Saturday*, *Football Italia*, *Revista La Liga* or even the Eredivisie on Channel 5, I created my own saturation coverage by watching *Hero* on a near continuous loop interrupted only by school, sleep, eating and recreating its highlights in the back garden.

Hero was all the more influential in that it was not a conventional football highlights package nor a documentary. It contained highlights, but not all of them. And it does tell the story of the tournament, but not with any great behind-the-scenes access or retrospective interviews. Instead it was more akin to a motivational film played at the start of a corporate conference showcasing the highlights of a company's past 12-months. It was the story of the triumph against adversity of Mexico itself in managing to host the tournament so soon after a major earthquake and of Maradona – not Argentina – in winning it. While M People were yet to record 'Search for the hero inside yourself', the producers commissioned the next best thing in a Rick Wakeman soundtrack full of drama, suspense and soaring melodies. And adding to the emotion was a Michael Caine voiceover that made clear this all had far greater significance than a mere football tournament. This was about euphoric highs, devastating lows, pride, nationhood and the pinnacle of mankind's achievements, shining a laser beam on the very heart of the human condition. Or at least it felt like that at the time.

Twenty-five years later I may, just, understand that this might have been a tad overblown, that it was a good if not great tournament skilfully edited to a VHS-friendly length with a few tugs on the heartstrings to increase the effect. To the eight-year-old me, however, it was as persuasive as those TV adverts for board games that made you feel as if you really could enter a lost valley of the dinosaurs and have fun with all the family, as opposed to the cold reality of cheap plastic and cardboard and a sister and parents who were always too busy to play. As if I needed any more persuading that football was the most important thing in the world, here was all the gravitas of Michael Caine reaffirming it for me. And if I needed any more evidence that Maradona was the best player in the world, in the best team in the world and therefore the most glamorous and heroic man in the world, well here was Deep Throat, a smoking gun and a grassy knoll all rolled into one. Your honour, with this piece of Fifa-endorsed propaganda, I rest my case.

So this is what I fell in love with. Not the reality of the tournament itself but the story of a semi-dramatised version of it. Not Mexico's one world-class striker trying to drag his home team beyond their abilities, but national hero Hugo Sanchez returning from his millionaire lifestyle in Madrid to bring hope and happiness to his suffering people. Not the mundane predictability of three out of four quarter finals going to penalties, but the heart-stopping drama of the France-Brazil shoot-out edited in the style of Alfred Hitchcock directing a 21st century teen horror flick. And not the albeit already incredible story of Argentina's campaign to win a World Cup, but of Maradona's one-man mission to fulfil his destiny and ascend from best player in the world to the immortal status of all-time great and footballing god. And unlike the stories from patronising school assemblies, this was a god I could believe in.

A god of course whose hand played a key role in his team's advancement versus England. It was without question an outrageous bit of cheating to punch the ball past Peter Shilton. Outrageous in that he tried it at all, although he was neither the first nor the last to do so. Outrageous too in his audacity in thinking that – correctly as it turned out – he could get away with it. But outrageous also in that he was allowed to get away with it by the officials, with whom the fault also lies. For all that Maradona was demonised for it is hard to think that even our own golden boy Gary Lineker wouldn't have done the same given the chance, with a little wink to the camera at full time. In the primary school playground we all would have done, having little regard for the rules and if anything admiration for Maradona for daring to do it at all. Handball was almost as common as offside and goals were regularly scrambled over the line in ten-boy scrums with even less protection for the 'keeper than Shilton received. Maradona's was far from the worst example of cheating I would witness in any given week.

As for his second goal, it remains the best I have seen. To do what he did, taking out half a team with a solo run from the halfway line in such a high-pressure game as a World Cup quarter final, under such a weight of expectation from a nation that only a very few can even comprehend, is perhaps the single greatest execution of sporting skill I will ever watch.

So really, for all of its melodrama, *Hero* didn't have this part of the story that wrong. Maradona's performances were extraordinary and, while Argentina was far from a one-man team, his was quite probably the biggest influence one individual has ever had on a major tournament and as worthy of awe as sport ever is. And it was true that his triumph was worth more to the people of Argentina than seven games of football objectively should be.

For me, eventually, as other football arrived on TV and other videos were released, my dependency on *Hero* waned. But I'm not sure its influence did to such a degree. I still struggle to support England as wholeheartedly as I do my club and wonder if this was a side effect. I still find it hard to divorce sport from its social context and treat it as 'just' a game. And I can still recite sections of the commentary, Bryon Butler's "like a little eel" description of Maradona's second goal against England remaining the gold standard of sports broadcasting in my mind.

The danger was that the rest of my sports-watching life could never live up to this Hollywood-meets-Roy-of-the-Rovers experience but in fact it never fails to. Maradona's own life and career was to go through so many more twists and turns that Jeffrey Archer could not have made it up. And football itself was about to go through a media-driven revolution that made *Hero* seem less like hyperbole and more like reality. We are never short of overly-dramatised storylines now.

At the time though, this video was the exception rather than the rule both in its style and in its existence at all. To the eight-year-old me it was revelatory. Had any other team been at the heart of its narrative arc it would probably be their name in the title of this chapter. But it was Argentina and you can't choose who you fall in love with.

Weymouth FC 1987-90

Kenny Legg

"But really, who are your proper club?"

A question that, when I'm asked it, comes complete with a slight tilt of the inquisitor's head and a wide-eyed look of bemused sympathy.

Weymouth FC *are* a proper club. We've got our own kit and a stadium with four walls. We, Weymouth, are the club I've passionately supported since I was six years old.

OK, maybe not passionately since the age of six. At the age of six I was only passionate about *Thundercats* and making fart noises, but something happened while watching the woeful Weymouth teams of 1987-1990 that has turned me into a fan of this 'unproper' football team ever since.

It must have been the first game? You never forget the first game. Well, um… mine was postponed. Our arrival at the stadium gates saw us greeted by a rusty padlock across the gate and a sopping wet piece of paper saying "match postponed". A truly tremendous start. Maybe it was a sign (the event, not the piece of paper. I know the piece of paper was supposed to be a sign. I meant metaphorically). Maybe I should have asked that we turn the car around and speed away from the ground until the land of 'proper football' was reached?

Once I'd finally made my debut at the Wessex Stadium, my pre-match routine was quickly established. Mother Legg and I would pack my bootbag full of chocolate, biscuits, crisps and Panda Pops. I was a fat kid. From 2:00pm, I'd stand in my brother's bedroom, looking out at the front door of our next-door neighbour who would take my Dad and me to the game. He'd never leave the house before 2:20 and I'd spend the 20 minutes waiting time writing score predictions and the occasional motivational slogan using the medium of my own condensed breath and finger combination on the window. "Go Weymouth", "Weymouth 17-0 Sutton", "Weymouth 6-0 Aylesbury". Rarely (i.e. never) did these predictions come true.

When next-door's front door opened I'd sprint downstairs, like the excited little child I was, and harass Father Legg out of the door to ensure we were waiting at the front gate in the 13.4 seconds it took our neighbour to back out of his drive and park outside front gate.

At that young age every trip to the Weymouth's Wessex Stadium represented a whole heap of new heroes, vivid colours, unfathomable noises, the concept of hated rivals, a foul-mouthed crash course in swearing and most importantly, the inexplicable emotions of being a football fan. Every week, Weymouth played teams that seemed to come from another world. A world of giants, of black people (for there were seemingly none in the arse-end of Dorset at the time), of teams in hideous yellow and brown kits (Hi Sutton United) and all arriving in Weymouth from places previously unheard of. Just where is Fisher? Is Aylesbury near here? Just who was the Victoria that Northwich were so keen to name their club after?

Every young football fan wants posters of their football heroes on the wall, my playground chums had Ian Rush and Gary Lineker on their walls. I didn't know anyone who had a moustached, early 30s, Scottish left back for a hero, but Weymouth's Willie Gibson was mine. Primarily as, I now realise, he was the player who operated closest to my position – sat on the gate on the halfway line, guzzling away on a bottle of E-numbers sourced from my bootbag of sugary delights.

One glorious, magical day, Father Legg arrived home with a black and white signed photo of me and Willie. My bootbag and I had appeared in the background of a photo in the local rag, in the foreground of which Willie was embarking on another mid-paced run forward. By some mysterious sorcery, Father Legg had managed to ascend to the higher levels that Willie operated on and got him to write a personalised message to me. Unbelievable. Years later I found out that my uncle worked in the same metal-bashing factory as Willie. This was a more devastating revelation than finding out that whole thing about Father Christmas.

The 1988/89 Weymouth team stank the place out. They finished rock bottom of the league and won only four home matches the whole season. My window-based predictions counted for nothing. Defeat followed defeat but, bizarrely, not once did I beg Father Legg to stop taking me. In those early years I had chance to escape, became a fan of proper football like everyone else, but nope, I stayed. Jeez, I even went to watch the reserves.

I quickly learned that the role of a football fan is to question the birth control methods employed by the referee's mother, query the accuracy of the linesman's last eyesight test and to abuse the members of the away team, while also besmirching one's own players. Every week a barrage of abuse rained down on those on the pitch from behind me, launched from angry men who stood in the same place on the terrace each week to barrack Weymouth towards another defeat. I tried to join in. I like to think of it as an attempt to connect with my fellow fans through my high-pitched insults. It was on this terrace that I received an obscenity education. My first ever utterance of swear word came during this season when my brother was called "a bastard", during a heated argument at home over a biscuit. I had no idea what a bastard was, but I'd heard useless defender Gavin Sandrey use it in anger during a match so it must be good. I got sent straight to bed, without a biscuit, soon after.

I also learnt the importance of having a hated rival, albeit one that is hated for no other reason than their temerity to be based in geographical proximity to Weymouth. The visit of Yeovil in January 1989 was greeted with louder noises, new levels of insults and a tighter grip on my hand by Father Legg. After a 2-1 defeat at home I knew I should always hate Yeovil. Weymouth were relegated at the end of the season and have not played them in the league since that day. I check the results every Saturday to ensure Yeovil have lost.

In the 1989/90, season Weymouth played in the Beazer Homes League and, again, it was a season of misery. Sixteen points by Christmas, on-pitch protests against the directors, the appearance of 41-year-old Frank Worthington for four games, an FA Cup defeat to lower league Exmouth and attendances down to just above 200. Quite what part of this appealed to eight-year old me remains a baffling mystery.

On January 13 1990, Weymouth played Barnet in the FA Trophy. Barnet were at the top of the Vauxhall Conference, the league we had just been spectacularly relegated from, and even my usual optimistic window-based score predictions foresaw a defeat.

As Weymouth battled hard against the yellow-clad giants from Barnet, the crowd broke with tradition and roared encouragement. We even took the lead – then halfway through the second half the ball bobbled just outside the Barnet penalty area and our captain, the diminutive midfield battler Steve Pugh, thundered the ball into the top corner of the net. We, Weymouth FC, were 2-0 up. I can see the goal now. I can hear the celebrations behind the goal. I can recall the feeling that something special had just happened and that all those other defeats didn't matter as we were winning today.

To this day, that victory made me realise that Weymouth were my team and would always be my proper team. These seasons provided me with a sense of the indescribable feelings that being a football fan encompasses, whatever team, at whatever level you support. Feelings of unspeakable passion, of fated heroes and hated rivals, of dispiriting lows and unexpected wins, and of treasured memories formed by those representing your proper club.

Italy 1994

Rob MacDonald

Like many kids' stories, there was a hero and a villain, but unusually, the same person appeared in both roles. The tale of Roberto Baggio and Italy, compressed and intensified into the month-long World Cup of 1994 was an intoxicating and fundamentally addicting story for a boy who never really *got it* until that point. At the end of the final on July 17 1994, as the hero-cum-villain's fateful penalty kick sailed over Claudio Taffarel's crossbar and the injured Baggio's tournament crumbled before me, I got it alright.

The crucial point is that it *was* a kid's story. I was never going to fall in love over the course of a nine-month season (it was all well and good to go to the football, I thought at age eight, but every week? The concept never even registered). But the sporting planets aligned for that summer month in 1994 and I finally understood: recurring characters; gladiatorial combat; victory from the jaws of defeat; the agony and the ecstasy.

It hadn't started quite so dramatically. In fact, it started with precisely no drama at all.

The first football match I ever went to was a goalless draw between Manchester United and Chelsea on November 25th 1989. I don't remember much about the experience. The fact that it was 0-0 and presumably devoid of anything remotely resembling entertainment or indeed football could well be the reason. It was so bad that in school the subsequent Monday morning, I was only able to offer up as my 'This Weekend I...' story a picture of a stick man in blue falling over, or at least horizontal, about two feet off the ground, with two stick men in red in close attendance – a pretty dreadful drawing of a doubtless dreadful scenario.

According to dusty programmes in boxes, a return trip to Old Trafford at some point that season for a 4-1 win over Luton Town followed.

From there the 1991 European Cup Winners' Cup final in Rotterdam is my next clear memory. I still wasn't particularly bothered, clearly, despite the majority of my peers falling in love with the game by virtue of England's campaign at Italia '90, at which point I was living in Scotland and so relatively, if not completely, protected from the later stages of the tournament. And every one since. The sum total of my football awareness was probably 'Mark Hughes likes volleys' and 'England are decent', married somewhat bizarrely with a mild form of terror at the sight of Ronald Koeman. How times change.[1]

Hughes and United had nevertheless made the loudest claims to my early affections, the former by virtue of smashing in the second against Barcelona from an incredibly narrow angle in the aforementioned Cup Winners' Cup final of '91. United's first two Premier League titles following my return to live in the north west of England were then my main introduction to football as a spectator slightly more aware of exactly what the hell was going on.

I also won a competition in a 1994 issue of the (now sadly defunct) *Funday Times*[2] to go and see United play Southampton in the penultimate home game of the season. As another measure of my then-disaffected state, though, I remember only Mark Hughes's goal (not a volley this time, unfortunately), a free meal in the Salford branch of competition sponsor Pizza Hut and the fact that their representative at the time, while apologising for the training session with the then-Champions I'd also won now not being part of the prize – and trying to make up for the fact that he'd mistakenly forecast the presentation of the Premier League trophy and got my hopes up – bought me some peanut M&Ms. As an aspiring footballer then turning out for my local cub scouts, I was, I think, understandably disappointed at missing out

1   I am still quite scared of Koeman.

2   The Funday Times was the kids' section of the Sunday Times, whose competitions rarely centred on football, but often centred on really easy questions. They, like so many of their daytime television descendants, usually had three potential answers, at least one of which was patently ludicrous. The choices in the teaser in question were something like a) Bryan Robson, b) Michael Jackson, or c) Alex Ferguson – I believe the correct answer was c). I'll leave you to deduce the likely question, but it was clearly a simpler, more innocent time for a number of reasons.

on a training session with the Premier League's first generation of celebrities. As a 10-year old, I was appeased by free chocolate.

These early football experiences, therefore, don't conjure up particular players, or the score, or goals. They're of the more primal aspects of being at a football match, particularly one at night. Under lights, there's something much different about how green the pitch looks when you get up those concrete stadium steps. Old Trafford, back then, at any rate, was noisy. It was the first time I'd experienced that extra shift in sound that marks the noise of a crowd as a singular entity out from the noise of a collection of blokes stood on a terrace calling someone a twat. And that was before any goals had been scored.

I was moved, clearly, but still not hooked. It was an experience, but it wasn't a story. I remember that team fondly enough now (my favourite player, mystifyingly, was Lee Sharpe, who to my eternal shame has since been on Celebrity Love Island and starred in adverts hawking sheds on YouTube by hammering footballs at them with no particular degree of accuracy), but I couldn't quite muster the same sense of involvement as everyone else.

As surprisingly to me as anyone else, the thunderbolt that woke me up to football proper came from the Italian national side of USA '94. A mystifying scenario indeed. I can only (in the best traditions of amateur psychological self-diagnosis) assume my primary experiences needed a context or narrative and the microcosm of summer tournament football, in which the tale of a whole team can be written in the space of a few short weeks, came along at just the right time to provide it.

The tournament, whether by virtue of disparaging comments made in the build-up to the state of the game in the US, or by appearing as a strange and bewildering interpretation of football in a country thousands of miles away, initially came across as something of a farce. In reality, this was just the oddities of the opening ceremony, which wasn't helped by Diana Ross missing a staged penalty, only for the goals to fall apart regardless. These days I like to imagine that Harry Redknapp, watching at home, sent wife Sandra round the block for a run to 'get warmed up'.

The Italian team seemed disoriented and stunned at first as well, as if everything was passing them by outside of their control.

The famous 1-0 defeat at the hands of Ireland in their first group game – which I was presumably watching only as a result of Ireland being the only British representatives to have qualified for the tournament – is bit of a blur. Images of a sweaty Jack Charlton, looking faintly ridiculous in a baseball cap and short sleeves have proven difficult to shake for a few reasons, similarly too those of Paul McGrath's heroics and, following Ray Houghton's goal, wondering why on earth Terry Phelan looked so hell-bent on trying to hug so many of his team mates when his arms seemed so short.

The Italians' propensity for a) erecting a large mountain in front of themselves and b) attempting to climb it armed only with firstly a wing, and latterly a prayer, would recur throughout the tournament, but the group at least provided two more chances to issue something resembling statements of intent. I must have thought they would be provided, as my attention was held. The games themselves, unfortunately, were scarcely a reward for this fledgling, arbitrary act of dedication and did more to suggest the only journey Italy would be going on would be back home, rather than marching on into the knockout stages.

There was at least some drama to pique a 10-year old's interest – a win against Norway looked easily attainable in the opening 20 minutes of the second group match, before Gianluca Pagliuca was sent off for handballing outside the box. Nevertheless, a flying header from Dino Baggio on the end of a brilliant Beppe Signori free kick put Italy ahead before a barrage of Norwegian long throws and corners had them clinging on for dear life at the end. The cost of the red card was minimised, eventually, but it wouldn't be the last of them.

The Italy goal in the 1-1 draw with Mexico taught me my first footballing clichés – Daniele Massaro gave the Azzuri the lead just after half time with what can only be described as an 'emphatic volley' from a gorgeous 'lofted pass' from Demetrio Albertini. Marcelino Bernal equalised less than ten minutes later, but the rest of the game, though it included a disallowed goal for Mexico before the break, was desperately bad. Airbrushed from my memory, but thankfully not the internet, it contrived (and maybe this was the reason for the tense and dispiriting performances) to leave every team in Group E in the unprecedented situation of having won, drawn and lost a game each, with goal differences of exactly zero. These were still the days when 'best third-placed' teams qualified for the knockout stages, though, and behind Mexico who had scored three, Italy and Ireland went through having scored two each to Norway's one.

So far then, there was absolutely no reason for me or anyone else not Italian to take any interest in the Azzuri whatsoever. Somehow, the Brazilians and the Nigerians sashayed through without turning my head. The incredible achievement of Saudi Arabia, defeating Morocco and Belgium, left me likewise and mystifyingly unmoved. The sensational Argentina side and the Dutch team that lost a scintillating quarter-final, 3-2 to Brazil, were also ignored. It seems that rather than being affected by the romances of minnows or traditions of superpowers, I was much happier convincing myself that Roberto and Dino Baggio were brothers and believing that if a remarkably unremarkable Italy gave the ball to Beppe Signori, who was quite quick, they'd score a goal.

The Italians met everyone's second favourite team, Nigeria, in the last 16. The Super Eagles took the lead through Emmanuel Amunike in the 25th minute and Italy's woes – unconvincing, under-achieving Italy, looked to be returning fast. They needed to do something. What they categorically did not need was another balls-up.

Gianfranco Zola might have been 27 at this point, but it was the first time I had ever seen him. Standing on the sidelines at 65 minutes, about to go on, he looked nervous and small. Of course, only one of those was true – he was tiny – but my totally unfounded discomfort with his introduction (at 10 years old, I don't know where it came from) did in fact prove to be founded as he was sent off – extremely harshly – ten minutes later.

At this point, it's perhaps pertinent to note the egocentricity of being ten years old. I had no idea this was Nigeria's first World Cup, that they were overachieving or even that, nearly 20 years after this afternoon in 1994, hopeless football romantic and co-editor Adam Bushby would still take it quite so personally. What I certainly did work out was the illuminating drama of Italy equalising in the 88th minute in a knockout game, especially having seen the Nigerians celebrating as Zola despaired and departed 15 minutes earlier.

The quality of Roberto Baggio's goal ultimately doesn't matter, but the way it slid along the side netting made the whole thing so measured and precise that it looked like a work of genius. The build-up was quite scrappy, the connection didn't even seem that great, but in it went. Italian delirium everywhere. Salvation from the jaws of defeat and an improbable result achieved with just 10 men for the second time in three matches. A goal from nothing, again. And the World Cup suddenly had a new hero.

Italy's extra time penalty, given away by Augustine Eguavoen – the man Zola had 'fouled' to earn his early bath – was unerringly dispatched by Baggio, visibly gaining in confidence. Watching replays years later shows that Nigeria somehow failed to reply moments after, when the ball found its way to THREE men spare at the back post, but I don't remember that because I was now transfixed by the man they were calling *Il Divin Codino* – the Divine Ponytail.

If Baggio had been crap in the next game, this would likely be a different story. But every time I heard the name 'Baggio', I started expecting a goal. In the quarter final against Spain, though, it was Dino on the scoresheet first, firing an absolute bullet past Andoni Zubizarreta from the edge of the box. Bizarrely and unusually, Italy were in front at half time. Unfamiliar territory alright. It didn't last either as Jose Luis Caminero – by virtue of a deflection that I'm fairly sure I told my Dad "shouldn't count" – drew Spain level on the hour.

Two flying saves from Pagliuca in the last 10 minutes made me sort of want to become a goalkeeper before the 88th minute arrived again, dragging along with it Roberto Baggio, again. Italy broke, Signori knocked the ball into his path and as he went round the keeper it looked for all the world as if he had gone too far, too wide. But a last heroic effort twisted his body round the ball and fired it into the net, millimetres in front of Abelardo Fernandez, trying desperately to get back. Italy were almost too spent to celebrate. It was getting exhausting, but to me, each win and each goal was becoming more exhilarating than the last.

In Bulgaria, Italy faced another surprise, romantic package in the last four. Did I care? Did I bollocks. The Divine Ponytail was on fire now[3]

3   Not literally.

and a supporting cast of his 'brother' Dino, Demetrio Albertini, Nicola Berti and Roberto Donadoni had me hooked. Two quick Italian goals in the first 25 minutes completely broke with tradition and inevitably Baggio scored them both. That was it. He was unstoppable – the first, two sublime turns from a throw in and ANOTHER finish that only just touched side netting; and the second, a beautifully timed run and volley into the bottom corner. Unerring and compelling. And thereafter, a rearguard including Alessando Costacurta and Paolo Maldini enjoyed the extremely unfamiliar luxury of being not only ahead, but by more than one goal and for more than three minutes, to (as I remember, at least) assuredly see Italy through.

We're all well-versed with what happened in the final against Brazil. The now-fabled 88th minute came and went without heroics. Italy, who had never looked in control of their own destiny throughout the tournament, held out for 120 minutes for a goalless draw. A penalty shootout followed, the first in World Cup final history. Italy had a chance. An injured Baggio would take Italy's fifth penalty, not to win the trophy, but once again to keep them in the tournament, a feat he had already pulled off on what felt like countless occasions. But injured, he put the spot kick over the bar and Brazil were world champions. My heart sank with the number 10's shoulders – and in the background what looked like the rest of the team sagged to their knees.

Baresi and Massaro missed in that shootout too, but Baggio's is notorious, purely for the way he illuminated the knockout stages only for the light to flicker just when Italy needed it most. As an infatuated ten-year old, convinced he was utterly invincible, it was hard to reconcile his miss with the fact that in my soul I knew he was brilliant, but in the end it didn't matter. The very fact I was questioning what happened now this part of his story was now over and the fact that I had been party to Italy's unconvincing, desperate, brilliant, glorious and ultimately unsuccessful month in the USA, was more than enough. They kept coming undone, but they kept coming back, *Il Divin Codino* to the fore each time.

So it was the pure intensity and improbability of the Italians' World Cup adventure in 1994 that really sparked my interest in football. Every game was played at progressively higher stakes and as the price for losing became dearer, so Baggio became more and more prominent. He might have fallen from hero in the traditional sense, but my journey into football was complete. It wouldn't be the same game without both the agony and the ecstasy and if you are going to lose yourself to it, you might as well get used to experiencing both in quick succession.

Bournemouth 1988

Chris Lines

Luther 'Missett'. That's what they used to call him in his Watford days. But as an eight-year-old in the late 1980s all I knew about Luther Blissett was that he'd played for AC Milan and scored an England hat-trick. Consequently I deduced that he was probably pretty flippin' ace.

My bedroom wall back then was plastered with dozens of blue-tacked posters from *Match* and *Shoot*. Any old Luton left-back could get on the wall so long as they had a nifty haircut. But Blissett was top drawer. And now he was about to make his home debut for my team, AFC Bournemouth. I could not wait. The opposition (Hull) barely seemed to matter – all eyes were on Bournemouth's new No.11.

One reason this was all so overwhelmingly exciting was that it would be only my third game as a Bournemouth supporter. I'd made my debut in Dean Court's crumbling F Block with my dad just 17 days earlier and was instantly smitten as a classy Bournemouth side featuring the likes of Ian Bishop, Sean O'Driscoll and Gerry Peyton won me over with a display of zippy passing, comfortably seeing off Crystal Palace 2-0. Bishop in particular stood out with his rockstar hair and a knack of apparently having all the time in the world whenever he got the ball. He was effortlessly cool and I was utterly hooked.

We went back for more the next weekend. But – disaster – seating for home fans had sold out. We had no choice but to muck in with the away support, soon finding ourselves among a cluster of inflatable bananas as Man City won a close game 1-0.

Defeat was hard for this eight-year-old to take in only his second game. Surely Bishop and company were too good to lose to anybody on their own ground? Or so I thought. At one point City midfielder

Neil McNab did a pointless and flashy backheel, to the guffaws of the City fans around me. The slight red mist that descended served only to bolster these partisan feelings I was suddenly experiencing. McNab had slighted my boys and I wasn't having that, least of all from a ginger short-arse with a stupid 'tache.

There was only one thing for it. We would just have to come back every week forever until Bournemouth showed the world what I'd already figured out – that we were the best at this football lark.

Or maybe not? Maybe in a month I'd get distracted by Airfix models, *Thundercats* or building dens in the woods? Football still had the potential to be merely a passing fad for a child with wide eyes and a worryingly short attention span.

Then Blissett signed and I was done for. Football and I would be in this for the long haul.

And so it was that dad decided I could stay up late and attend Luther's first appearance at Dean Court on a damp Tuesday night. He'd scored away at Barnsley on debut and there was much anticipation among the crowd during his warm up. Even limbering up he looked like a proper athlete – lean, powerful, quick.

After a rainy and lacklustre first half – during which he missed a sitter and had fans nervously wondering if they should've listened to his detractors – Blissett went on to plunder four goals in the second half with a ruthless display of finishing. This was exciting.

Or at least it was for those who'd made it that night. A good number of fans missed the game in favour of taking in Barry Manilow's performance at the Bournemouth International Centre. In the days before mobile phones, they'd have only found out what they'd missed once Barry had milked the applause at the end of his third encore. Ouch.

Blissett scored in his first five appearances in a Bournemouth shirt and in my eyes he could do no wrong. He was even brilliant off the pitch, forever attending events, visiting sick kids in hospital and generally being an impeccable ambassador for the club. And when he moved into a property, which as a result of the previous occupant's dispute with the council bore the name 'Far Corfe' on its gate, Blissett decided to keep the name and was pictured grinning next to it in the local paper. What a guy.

Bournemouth were by no means a one-man team though. Manager Harry Redknapp had, with typical cunning, guided Bournemouth to the Third Division title two seasons previously, grabbing players on a free transfer here or a nominal fee there and combining them into a team that played with panache and determination.

And his wily transfer market ways continued once Bournemouth were into the second tier. Canny signings from non-league included Shaun Teale and Efan Ekoku, both of whom went on to have fine Premier League careers. Teale was a tough but graceful defender; all left foot, but rarely beaten on the ground or in the air. Ekoku meanwhile, far from the stocky handful he later bulked up into, was like a leggy gazelle when he arrived from Sutton. Lacking stamina, Redknapp would save him for the last twenty minutes, when he would immediately tear into the opposition defence at frightening speed, a flash of bandy legs.

On one occasion in 1992, before the Rumbelows Cup Final at Wembley, there took place a competition to determine England's fastest player. The Rumbelows Sprint Challenge saw Ekoku make it through the heats to the final, where he'd be competing alongside the likes of Reading's Michael Gilkes. A cool ten grand was up for grabs for the winner, but sadly Ekoku didn't do himself justice. He finished sixth in the final (Swansea's John Williams won it), but we knew how quick he really was. In truth, he'd already started to bulk up a little by then. If the race had taken place 18 months earlier Ekoku would have stormed it. Nevertheless imagine my childish wonder at knowing we had the sixth-fastest player in the country. I had ample confidence that this was a pretty cool thing.

There were some tremendous games in my formative months as a Bournemouth fan and some moments that will stay with me forever. Mind you, not all of them relate to victories, goals and glory. Some are just oddballs; weird footballing curios that never leave you. On 11 March 1989 Bradford were the visitors to Dean Court. Their combative midfielder Mick Kennedy got himself deservedly sent off, a move that annoyed his employer sufficiently that he was sold to Leicester. Suspension served, who were Leicester playing by the time

Kennedy was able to make his debut? You guessed it. And didn't we give him a warm welcome every time he touched the ball, something he appreciated so much that he threw all his energies into earning himself another early bath. To this day any mention of his name still makes me smile and the memories of him stropping off down the tunnel for a second time come flooding back.

But putting the silly stuff aside, the best technical player of the Redknapp era did not require our shrewd boss to do any scouting whatsoever. The day 16-year-old Jamie Redknapp made his home debut it took my dad about eight minutes to start heralding him as a future England captain. He made playing the game look completely effortless and had every attribute required to be (ahem) a top, top player. For a 16-year-old to be immediately bossing the midfield in the Second Division was almost incomprehensible. We knew we had to enjoy Redknapp Junior while we had him.

Alas, we only got to enjoy his near-flawless displays a mere 13 times before Kenny Dalglish caught wind of his talents and made signing Jamie one of his final acts as Liverpool manager. But those fleeting glimpses made quite an impression on me, to the extent I was never able to laugh at Liverpool's 'Spice Boys' era with quite the same glee as most. This was because I knew just how blessed with talent their floppy-haired central midfield pin-up really was. Were it not for his dreadful luck with injuries, he probably would have captained his country a few times. It will be a very good day if we ever see anybody as special as him in a Bournemouth shirt again.

While I am not afforded the luxury to rabbit on about any other great players from Bournemouth's finest era here, if I just offer up a Best XI from 1988-92 you'll get the general idea. It's quite possible that this team could have held its own in the Premier League without too many problems – Gerry Peyton; Mark Newson, John Williams, Shaun Teale, Paul Morrell; Sean O'Driscoll, Jamie Redknapp, Ian Bishop, Gavin Peacock; Efan Ekoku, Luther Blissett – if only they could have competed at that level in Bournemouth colours.

Harry, Luther and the rest of the 88/89 crop came closest, flirting with the playoffs from early January until late March before ultimately falling away. It was thrilling to be watching a team that we thought might be on the cusp of promotion to the top flight. Bournemouth had spent almost their entire history in the bottom two divisions; promotion to the First Division was beyond fans' wildest dreams. And yet with a bit more luck we could have got there. Maybe we still will in my lifetime – our fans live in hope.

The Harry Redknapp era ended in the summer of 1992. That same close season saw Bournemouth sign a relatively unknown 20-year-old Hartlepool striker by the name of Steve Fletcher. A few eyebrows were raised in amusement when Fletcher praised the excellent set-up at the club in his first interview after signing – how dire must the facilities be up at Hartlepool, we wondered.

Fletcher would go on to make over six hundred appearances in a Bournemouth shirt, endearing himself to fans with his relentless will to win and unbreakable spirit. He is probably the most iconic player in the club's history, even ahead of Seventies goalscoring legend Ted MacDougall. Unfortunately Big Fletch signed after Blissett had moved back to Watford. Now that would been a strike partnership to be reckoned with.

But those early games in the autumn of 1988 were what got me hooked on football, hankering for good times while supporting a team that doesn't get many. It's mostly Luther Blissett's fault, and for that I thank him.

Australia 2006
Max Grieve

My father's semi-professional football career – he was paid to play, he says – was cut short on three separate occasions by injuries to his knees that required two reconstructions and several arthroscopies. I retired from the game at the age of six, a severe lack of both interest and skill being the major contributing factors to my decision to leave the Majura Pee Wees and take up Lego construction on Saturday mornings instead.

All the way up until 2005, by which time I was 11, it wasn't hard to be completely blind to football, or "soccer"; as it is still widely known in Australia so as not to confuse it with any of our three other football codes. Harry Kewell and Mark Viduka were ruling the Premiership while the Australian National Soccer League died. International football was mostly made up of relatively low cricket score victories over island nations followed by a tragic loss in some intercontinental playoff or other. Nothing was going anywhere, and it didn't seem to matter.

I can't really say that I cared.

In 2003, billionaire Frank Lowy was charged with the task of resurrecting football in Australia. The A-League had been formed, though this was doing little to trigger a major national interest in the game – what was really needed was for something big to happen in a green and gold kit.

Australia's qualification for the 2006 World Cup finals is almost as legendary as their time at the tournament itself, though I confess that I can barely remember the play-off against Uruguay. Guus Hiddink had arrived in late July 2005 and guided the Socceroos to an 11-1 aggregate win over the Solomon Islands to set up an inter-continental play-off against 'La Celeste'. With the sides tied at 1-1 after three and a half hours split between Montevideo and Sydney, there was to be a penalty shoot-out. It was a little confusing – we hadn't done one of these in ages, and the players looked as though the moon was hanging just above the field, ready to drop on their heads at a moment's notice.

Mark Schwarzer made two extraordinary saves; Kewell, Lucas Neill and Aurelio Vidmar scored; Viduka pulled his penalty desperately wide; and Australia were one converted shot away from the World Cup finals. In commentary, a wildy edgy former Socceroo, Craig Foster, forgot how penalty shoot-outs worked, and lost track of the score.

John Aloisi had, to that point, played 37 times for Australia and scored 21 goals. It is a remarkable record, cheapened perhaps by the fact that he had grabbed 11 in two matches against Tonga and the Solomon Islands. He was the first Australian to play and score in the highest divisions in Spain, England and Italy. With Foster comically nervous, and making the mistake of talking while in such a state, Aloisi scored. There were no words for it, and any intelligible commentary gave way to tears and uncontrollable shouting as Aloisi streaked[1] across the Sydney Olympic Stadium, shirt in hand and teammates in pursuit. I couldn't really understand the relief at the end of 32 years of waiting, but the delirious sense of achievement was palpable.

I knew nothing of professional football and, given Australia's competency in most sporting arenas, the side going to Germany were, if not invincible, then almost certainly perfect. It may have simply been the effect of the green and gold kit, which has been worn by pretty much every Australian who has done something worthwhile in international sport. They were likeable, too – much of the public hadn't yet got to know just how irritating Tim Cahill's celebration was, and there were no expectations to place on players we didn't want in the team. Putting the inevitability of a scoreless, winless campaign aside, there was a real positivity about the Australians.

They had a strong spine in Mark Schwarzer, Lucas Neill, Mark Bresciano and Mark Viduka; the poster boy of Australian football, Harry Kewell, was barely fit, but looked as handsome as ever; and

----

1   Not literally

a few rock-hard defenders of the Australian faith filled the chasms of talent in between. Hiddink's greatest masterstroke, aside from all the tactics and what not, was to embrace the national tendency to be violent, and tone it down to an acceptable level for international competition – Vince Grella and Craig Moore were prepared to enforce a measured brutality.

There must have been a time between qualification and the tournament itself, but very suddenly, it seemed, I found myself awake at midnight watching the Australians, all of 10,000 miles away, walking out against the Japanese in Kaiserslautern. Japan scored first; Shunsuke Nakamura chipped in a cross which dropped over Schwarzer's head as he crashed into Naohiro Takahara in the crowd in front of his goal. It was a foul, but the goal was given.

By the 82nd minute, the Australians were becoming desperate – a loss in the first game, with Brazil still to come, was an entirely undesirable situation. Lucas Neill launched a long throw into the box, and in the sea of flailing limbs Cahill managed to turn the ball into the net for Australia's first ever World Cup goal. Six minutes later, they pushed forward again, and Cahill scored off both posts from 20 yards. There was a glorious pile-on, and Hiddink – or Aussie Guus, as we had taken to calling him – galloped awkwardly down the sideline in a kind of clumsy glee. Aloisi added a third in stoppage time, and we had won.

Brazil, up next, were much better than us, as the rest of the world already knew and, though Australia played admirably in their sartorially glorious navy blue kit, we lost. It was a reminder of the tangible state of things, and I quickly grew to be less idealistic. Elsewhere in the group, the Croatians hadn't yet scored a goal and, having also fallen to the Brazilians, came into their final group match against the Australians in need of a win. We could draw and advance.

Schwarzer had inexplicably been dropped and Zeljko Kalac, whose hair was trying to tear his face off, took his place. It soon transpired that there was no method to Hiddink's madness. Darijo Srna's free-kick caught Kalac out early, before a handball gifted the Australians a penalty. None of the regular penalty takers were prepared to miss, so centre back Craig Moore stepped forward to level the match. Half-time came and went and the entirely underwhelming Kalac familiarised himself with the disappointment of a nation when he allowed a tame shot to hop over his hapless frame into the net – a "shit goal", as he would go on to describe it.

Five minutes later, Croatian Josip Simunic received a yellow card. Remember that.

Australia rolled forward, and Croatia held them back. It was becoming a frenzied mess, with far too much action directly in front of goal to allow for automatically regulated breathing. Tempers, as only tempers can, began to flare. With ten minutes left, Bresciano swung the ball in from the right to Kewell at the far post who brought it down with his left and, fully aware of the danger of his leg snapping off under the strain – it was only held together by string and hope – scored the equaliser on the half-volley. On the other side of the world, in a room lit only by the green glow of the screen, we exploded.

Now chasing a goal, the Croatians lost their heads, and the match descended into farce. Dario Simic was the first to be sent off, with Brett Emerton following soon after. The aforementioned Simunic was shown a second yellow card, but his Australian accent – he was born in the same city as myself – had referee Graham Poll mistake him for his counterpart Craig Moore, and he remained on the field. The match ended, and Simunic, by this time enraged with the universe, received his third yellow card for dissent, and was dismissed. It is to that match's detriment that it will always be internationally remembered for an English referee, rather than a piece of Australian sporting history and one of the great games of that tournament.

We were to play Italy in the first knockout round. By this point there was a sense that we were playing with fire, but we were still having a great time.

I think the 2006 World Cup stopped being fun, for a moment, anyway, in that match against Italy. It can be splintered into a hundred fragments and analysed to death. Italy were a man down for a third of the match. Australia had almost 60% of the possession and should have made more of the chances that they had. Regardless, it was a remarkable effort to hold out such an established footballing nation as long as they did. There was a whole narrative to this match that was killed by a decision at the last.

I can remember only three things about the game against Italy, and each one occurred in all the space of three or so minutes at the end of the 90. I can remember Lucas Neill looking as though the world was crashing in on him after Fabio Grosso, a man who I refuse to like, took unfair advantage of the planet's gravitational pull and flopped over the Australian defender's outstretched leg. I can remember watching Mark Schwarzer squinting into the sun as Francesco Totti waited for the whistle; all the while convinced that the penalty would be saved or missed. I can remember the ball punching the back of the net in a sudden, brutal swipe. The great solar orb scorched Schwarzer's retinas and burned right through the back of his head. He didn't have a hope.

It was all over by 4am on the Australian East Coast. I think I went back to bed.

That we lost to the eventual champions never really meant anything to me. Had Australia managed to make it through extra time and won on penalties, they might have scraped through the quarter final against Ukraine – a very real possibility, given their previous performances – and been in the semi-finals of a World Cup, where they would have been duly beaten by the Germans, as natural order dictates.

The Socceroos of 2006, the majority of whom are refusing to die until 2015 when Australia will host the Asian Cup, sparked within me a wonderful and infuriating fire for football, and an undying hostility towards the Italian national team. The ride was terrifying, wonderful and tragic, though I use that final word with caution and context in mind; the pure emotional spectrum overwhelming.

Above all, it was absurd. The Australian side of 2006 may have opened my eyes to the sport, but it's the enduring dramatic pull that interests me. If football, a game that has given way to external pressures before, falls to complete monotony and predictability, I think I'll stop watching.

Plymouth Argyle 1993

Lloyd Langman

It may be that we've all had to endure the same conversation at least once in our lives.

"What could you least live without" – your partner wonders, light-heartedly – "me, or *football*?"

More rounded individuals than myself will have had little trouble in clearing that one up, gazing dotingly into their loved one's eyes to deliver the necessary response without a moment's hesitation.

Yet for the group of earnest sticklers to whom I belong – at least I hope it's a group – this conversation is always prone to upset given our inability to turn our back on football, even hypothetically.

More precisely, it's Plymouth Argyle who tend to dominate my thoughts every seven seconds; who have the casting vote on whether my Tuesday and Saturday evenings are to be happy occasions; who possess me to involuntarily chant 'Green Army' at myself when alone (I've been caught several times).

It's been this way for as long as I can remember, yet it's ironic that, as my commitment to the club gathers momentum with each passing year, my father's seems to ebb away. For it was my dad who first took me to Home Park; whose money paid for my first kit; whose petrol took me to my first away game; whose Saturday rituals cultivated the most enduring allegiance – parents and siblings notwithstanding – possible.

It's a story often told but, in the classical way, dad and I hadn't really hit it off before Fulham at home on 28th December 1993. There was very little going on in Plymouth at the time and the options for father-son bonding were impoverished: the parks were littered with needles; there was no shopping mall; no multiplex cinema; no ice rink; no bowling alley; no River bloody Café; little in the way of arts. Just one massive dockyard, slowly losing its grip on the city.

For that reason, Dad had to work away a lot – usually shop fitting in London or Birmingham – so the opportunity to spend a whole day with him at the football, bookended by pint-upon-pint of cheap coke in the Britannia and his local – the Wellington in North Hill – was deeply thrilling.

Those who know those two pubs from the early-to-mid-nineties might question whether they were entirely appropriate settings for a boy eight years of age, but I wouldn't want the wool-dying experience of my first few seasons at Argyle to have been any different. I felt something akin to fear at points – not least the time a Reading fan inadvertently showed his colours in a Britannia brimming with wrong'uns – but 90 minutes in a vacuum was not what I was after; if dad was taking me to the football, then I wanted to experience everything that went with it.

I was told to savour the times. "It won't last", my dad said in reference to our free-scoring side one day, as we drove out towards the ground anticipating another win. I had nothing by the way of comparison but even I, with my virtually non-existent knowledge of the game, could tell that the 1993-94 side was special.

In what was to be his only managerial appointment, Peter Shilton had created – for a brief period at least – a team so wonderful that it almost hurts to recall it. I hadn't realised at the time what had come before under England's 125 man – an unsuccessful fight against relegation from the second division followed by a middling season in the third tier – and I didn't have a clue about our manager's playing pedigree or the type of chairman he was working under in Dan McCauley. But I did appreciate that the side seemed capable of scoring at any moment; possessed three of the division's best attacking players in Steve Castle, Paul Dalton and Dwight Marshall; and was backed noisily by big, jostling crowds made up of very happy supporters.

First-hand memories of the team have been cross-fertilised with literally hundreds of viewings of the season review on VHS (I'm not ashamed to admit that I've kept my parents' old player solely for the purposes of playing it), and I'm sure my love for the club – and the game – has developed through this roll of tape as much as the actual experiences of going to the matches.

So, although my season only started on the last game of 1993, I can recall from something like direct experience that Argyle were already in a strong position at the turn of the year. Despite a dodgy start, losing 3-2 to a Kevin Francis-endowed Stockport on the opening day and going out of the League Cup to Birmingham – a tie which featured betrousered Blues 'keeper Kevin Miller performing the most pencil rolls you're ever likely to see via one single save – we gradually picked up some form and were winning more than we were losing by September.

Form on the road continued to hamper progress though. Wins at Swansea and Cardiff early on in the season were glorious – particularly the former given Dalton's exquisite solo goal, which saw the master dribbler slalom through Swansea's left side with ease before drilling one home – but Argyle found it harder to nab points on their travels.

Things would come crashing down in dramatic fashion the following season but, starting with a 2-0 win at Marlow in the first round of the Cup, Argyle would – for about four months – maintain a form so pure and lusty that trips to Bradford, Stockport and Rotherham were made to look like summer evening strolls on Plymouth Hoe. Granted, the odd slip up did occur but by mid-March we were looking fair-set and I – already about nine or ten games down as a real spectator – was getting a bit cocky.

Indeed, highlights were plentiful: the sharp contrast of Fulham's red and black against our green and white stripes and witnessing the classy Ara Bedrossian for the Cottagers on my debut; deciding on my first Pilgrims hero the second Dwight Marshall levelled classily in the Cup against Barnsley, who'd brought a full terrace of red-clad supporters; taking in a thrilling 3-3 draw against rivals Bristol Rovers after which I shared my first post-match analysis session with rival fans (my best mate's grand-parents); becoming a fixture – or so I thought at the time – in my dad's group with little Steve, as quick-witted as my dad was glacial, and Andy, a local petty thief on whose Scouse girlfriend and Wellington barmaid I had the most passionate crush.

We didn't have it all our own way; I listened stoically to my sister's new Sony radio-cassette player as Argyle were knocked out of the Cup in the evening replay at Oakwell; future Argyle captain and public enemy Peter Swan denied us a result with a goal-line clearance during a vital game at promotion rivals Port Vale; and talisman Marshall pulled up with a muscle injury against Swansea which would rule him out for weeks, but there always seemed to be a silver lining. Not least with our first win in an age at Exeter – despite the best efforts of City striker David Adekola ("They call him Pepsi; I wonder if he's put any fizz back into the Grecians tonight?" – Martyn Dean, hang your head in shame) – and a 3-1 home win against eventual champions Reading, during which our rock-hard centre-half Adrian Burrows earned some credit with me, despite being a mere *defender* (which meant he didn't interest me in the slightest), for having his bloodied head sewn up at the side of the pitch.

But then came Cardiff. Fighting against relegation, a pathetic away following reflected how little was expected from the travelling Bluebirds on a marvellously sunny April afternoon. Not that I was there to witness their paltry few myself; because of some long-forgotten misdemeanour – or, more likely, since my Dad wanted a Saturday off from his e-stirred eight year-old son – I was left at home with my mum and sister, cruelly bringing a proud run of consecutive home games to a close. Like his son, Dad had got ahead of himself: without realising it, he'd deprived Argyle of their rabbit's foot and had unwittingly brought about a 2-1 defeat that would set off two more losses over the next 10 days. All of a sudden, Argyle were contemplating the play-offs rather than the top two.

It didn't take long for the Greens to recover; another win against Exeter setting us on our way but – shortly after I'd made my away bow in a Easter Monday 1-1 draw at Fulham, an occasion marked to my dad's dismay by the creation of a truly shoddy 'Come on You Greens' glitter banner at our family friends' home in Hampton shortly before the game – disaster struck again by way of an almost implausible 3-0 home defeat to Cambridge.

We'd go on to win three of our final four games, finishing with an 8-1 win at Hartlepool on the final day, but it wasn't quite enough. Burnley and the play-offs beckoned.

Hastened to bed on spurious grounds just as the Generation Game's cuddly toy was passing the TV screen on Saturday 14th May, I somehow made it to sleep against my will. It was light, just, when I was awoken and Steve and Andy were at the door. We, in Dad's B-reg Mazda 323, were going to Turf Moor for the first leg.

I haven't been back since, but my memory of Burnley itself is grey. Resoundingly so. There were chimneys and fog; it was bitter; the women in the bar were well-bosomed and rosy-cheeked. We seemed to be the only people on rounds of cider (and coke). We were outsiders, but welcome ones.

I remember less of the match, a 0-0 warm-up for the second-leg – remarkable only for having been knocked off my feet by an Argyle fan eager to join dozens of others in jumping up on to the crash barriers in the away end (he said sorry). Back in school the next morning, bleary-eyed, I made out that it was the game of my life.

Just a few days later a bumper crowd gathered at a sun-drenched Home Park for the second leg, which might as well have been in a different country, the grass was so lush. We were wearing a new kit; a rather dashing green and black striped number and Dwight cut a marvellous figure in it, particularly so once he'd given us the lead with a rising rasper. But something didn't feel quite right; possibly unsteadied by those home defeats to Cardiff and Cambridge, we were nervous.

To summarise what followed would be too grave a burden on my still-tormented soul. All that needs to be said is that evening would mark our final game of the season. At the time, I blamed Richard Landon, our most recent signing who I deemed useless from the start for not being Dwight Marshall.

It took a while to sink in, so inured was I to sweet, sickly success. Love wasn't quite what I felt at the time; just an insight into the valuable life lesson that sometimes – actually quite a lot of the time – circumstances are simply out of your control. Players moved on that summer and across the following season we lost both of our first two home games by five goals to one, Shilton left under a cloud, we got crap and I had to resort to being taken to a game by my mum (against Wycombe) once Dad got bored.

Thinking about it, it must have been love.

Canada 1994

Richard Whittall

The summer of 1994 was instrumental in my sporting life for two reasons.

The first reason is this: it was the moment when I realised the Toronto Blue Jays would not win the World Series over and over again off the back of an endless series of stratospheric Joe Carter walk-off home runs.

The two previous Major League Baseball seasons had ended with the Blue Jays' sitting smugly atop the summit of the sport–back-to-back World Series champs–looking down at a host of American pretenders. This had an irrevocable effect on my 13-year-old mind. It made me, for a time, deliriously, impossibly happy, completely in love with sport, and, as it later turned out, forever ruined by the failure of every team I've supported since to live up to the Jays' extraordinary example.

Before that summer, sports for me began and ended with baseball. My father, an Anglican priest, had spent his Sunday afternoons for much of the previous decade lying on the living room couch, stubbing out cigarettes in between cups of stale coffee – and as the afternoon progressed, gin and tonic – watching the Blue Jays cruise through their regular seasons into playoff runs, where, prior to 1992, they would almost invariably choke. Needless to say, the lingering, blue haze above the sofa did not present the most inviting environment, but some success in the Blue Jays' 1989 MLB season encouraged me to join him.

Excuse me: encouraged probably isn't the right word. I was *compelled*. A team, from my country, my *city* in fact, was suddenly, mysteriously winning at the national sport of our powerful Southern neighbour. I laboured through three seasons of playoff agony before jumping out of my seat when Joe Carter caught the third and final out of the 1992 World Series. That I, in my joy, had accidently jumped on my friend's Irish Terrier's paw resulting in abhorrent shrieks for the following twenty minutes or so, barely soured the mood.

When, 12 months later, Joe Carter knocked a famous, walk-off home run to the left side of the concrete and astro-turf atrocity then known as the SkyDome, defeating the Philadelphia Phillies in Game Six and handing the Jays their second consecutive World Series title, I experienced what remains to this day one of the most ecstatic moments of my life. I made a pact with myself then and there (or at least later that night on the roof of a friend's house where I smoked my first cigarette) I would only ever be loyal to the Blue Jays because they would simply go on winning forever.

Less than a year later however, a lazy summer saw the Jays' chances of a three-peat dashed by a dismal mid-summer record, and then in August, a player strike which cancelled the 1994 season. There would be no parades. No impromptu honking of horns. The good things had come to an end far, far too early.

Which brings me to the second reason the summer of 1994 changed my sporting life forever: I watched my first ever football match.

In June while the Jays were running up a losing season, an acquaintance of mine telephoned with a peculiar offer. He wanted to know if I wanted to go watch the Netherlands play Canada in an exhibition game at Varsity stadium, right in the core of downtown Toronto.

"Play them in what?" I probably asked.

"Soccer."

For most Canadian teenagers in the early 1990s, that word conjured up an image of legions of pre-schoolers falling down in ugly shorts trying to kick a gargantuan ball covered with black and white hexagons. I didn't know much about the grown-up version except that Canada couldn't possibly be any good at it. The national team had never graced the front page of my local newspaper for several consecutive weeks. No one ever paraded down Toronto's Yonge Street, flags in hand, because Canada won at the soccer.

When I hung up the phone and asked my dad about it, all he could muster was an "Oh." I'm not even certain we knew there would be a World Cup in the USA that summer. But watching live sports was as prohibitively expensive then as it is now, and the ticket was paid for. My friend promised there would be quite a crowd gathered, and so I went. What I didn't know is that the crowd would be there to support Holland, a team that badly out-matched Canada.

When I think of the utility of time-travel (as most of us do from time to time), I fixate on this moment in my life. I wish that the adult self writing this could go back to that game and sit next to myself, and provide some context on just what I was seeing out there (and also hopefully not creep out my younger self and his friend in the process).

I want to do this because at the time, and for several years after, all I remembered from that game was how bizarre it was that orange was actually some country's national colour. There were thousands of people wearing orange, in public, together. I had no idea why there weren't more people in red cheering for Canada as the host side – a fairly common occurrence in North American sport when the distances that 'away fans' would be required to travel are so vast.

I remember that, and being violently angry that Canada lost the game, 3-0. But I didn't know, and wouldn't find out until later, that the names of the players who scored those goals were Overmars, Bergkamp and Rijkaard. And I had no idea just how well, effortlessly, brilliantly well the Dutch played. I simply had nothing to compare it with. I had no idea who Alex Bunbury was, or that a passer-by had apparently yelled at then-national team coach Bob Lenarduzzi to develop better, younger players, as reported the next day in the national paper, the *Globe and Mail*. This is particularly intriguing because chances are, today, I would be that guy – at least if I was sufficiently armed with liquid courage.

So, no: the game didn't produce a Hornby-esque, out-of-body, epiphanic experience about the fullness of life with football. If anything, it intensified my post-Toronto Blue Jays World Series hangover, which is still slowly receding two decades later. Nothing about what I saw that glorious summer day was intrinsically appealing. It was like seeing David Bowie live before you knew who David Bowie was.

Yet even so, the game's effect on me was profound. For it was because I'd watched Holland thrash Canada that I was curious enough to sit with my uncle barely a week or so after and took in a World Cup game on the same TV my dad used exclusively to watch baseball, and discovered that football wasn't just kids kicking hexagon balls, or humiliating friendlies played at two-thirds speed in my hometown stadium.

I don't remember which game I watched first. It likely featured one of the big teams. Brazil, maybe. Like baseball, football was played on gorgeous, flowerless green, in the sun (and as I'd later find out, the spitting rain). But unlike baseball, it was in constant flux; the play evolved, changed, grew into something promising and then with a single mistake tried to reshape itself again. You began to desperately want these plays to come off, to produce a goal, because for a while you were barely certain goals *could* be scored. The incredible excitement of a counter attack seemed heightened by television, as did the sound of the crowd. There were no ad breaks. And perhaps most importantly, my hometown didn't have a stake in it. Canada didn't either. A glorious sport one could enjoy without the heartbreak of a post-championship season.

I didn't become a fanatic there and then because I was never a "sports person" to begin with, but the seeds were sown. Whenever football was readily available on Canadian TV, I watched it, until I reached the inevitable point where I started to search it out. I eventually learned there were football clubs, like the Yankees and the Brewers, only with less exciting names. I began supporting a club from a place closely tied to my family lineage, in Birmingham. I started watching games every weekend, from every league. Now, somehow, impossibly, I spend my days writing about football.

And I have yet, to this day, experienced in soccer anything close to the ecstasy of those two summers with the Jays. This is not a detractor. Baseball for me is a faint echo of a time I will never get back. Baseball is a gorgeous game, but it's also a reminder of my own mortality, of the impossibility of going home again. With football, however, I've still yet to reach the promised land.

Which would be Canada winning the World Cup, obviously. Part of me hopes I never get there, lest there be nothing but misery on the other side. And if it were to happen in my lifetime (it won't), it would surely be a *nunc dimittis*, a reason to quietly stop and get into chess instead.

Arsenal 1987
Roger Domeneghetti

I can't remember the first football match I watched. A battered copy of Ladybird's *España '82* book partially filled in by a seven-year-old version of myself suggests it was in the early 1980s but unlike, I'm guessing, the majority of writers in this book there was no one 'Eureka' moment or epiphany for me. With little football on TV and an early academic life spent at a private school where rugby was the sport of choice, access to the beautiful game was restricted. So it was that my love affair with football began slowly.

At the time, if Leicester City weren't anchored in the lower reaches of Division One (that's the Premier League in old money) they were fighting their way out of Division Two (that'll be the Championship). Just down the road, Nottingham Forest were still basking in the glory of having won the European Cup (that's the Champions League) twice in two seasons, so for the ever-so-slightly fickle youngster with no father figure on hand to regularly take him down to Filbert Street, there were other, more glamorous, alternatives.

Despite my school's distaste for football, no one was running about the playground pretending to be Dusty Hare or Marcus Rose (former England rugby union full-backs both), so one easy option given the circumstances was to support Liverpool, and that's what a lot of the lads in the playground did. Younger readers might not realise – or perhaps even believe this – but at the time, the Anfield club weren't just good, they were the best of the best. If they weren't winning the League trophy, they were lending it to Everton (yup, they were good too) while sweeping all before them both at home and on the continent.

So when Liverpool faced Arsenal in the 1987 League Cup final, ever the contrarian, I thought: "I'll support the Gunners". It was the obvious choice. After all, Arsenal had won one trophy in the previous eight years while Liverpool had secured the Double the previous year and were making their eighth Wembley appearance in 10 seasons. Liverpool had Ian Rush, who had scored 201 goals for the club and never been on the losing side in the 145 games in which he'd made it on to the scoresheet in the previous five and a half years. On the other hand, Arsenal had "Champagne" Charlie Nicholas who had never scored more than 11 goals in a season since signing from Celtic, although he could boast a brace of drink-driving convictions. Like I said; the obvious choice.

I could pretend that because the match was so important to me I remember every detail like it was played yesterday, but I won't – because I don't. I do remember that, as it seemed with all cup finals from my childhood, it was played in glorious spring sunshine and I can still clearly see each team's sponsor in my mind's eye; JVC for the Gunners and Crown Paints for Liverpool. Ask me who sponsors the teams today and I'd struggle to tell you, but for some odd reason those names have stayed clear in my memory. I remember Arsenal in their traditional red-and-white shirts and Liverpool in an insipid white away strip (possibly the inspiration for the Spice Boys' 1996 FA Cup final suits?). Was the kit a bad omen for Kenny Dalglish's team? Perhaps, but when Rush opened the scoring after 23 minutes it probably seemed more like business as usual. I know that Charlie Nicholas scored twice and I remember Perry Groves skipping past Gary Gillespie on the left wing to cross for the winner, but most of all I remember a sense of vindication; that I had been right for choosing the Gunners instead of going with the flow.

That it was the first game Liverpool had lost when Rush, due to move to Juventus at the end of the season, had scored made the victory seem all the sweeter. I was 12 at the time and didn't understand the nuances and implications of the result. All I really cared about was the playground bragging rights, but equally, football wasn't analysed to death in those days and I wonder how many would have predicted that the defeat George Graham and his young team inflicted on Liverpool represented the first crack in the foundations of their domestic dominance.

The League Cup is sometimes derided these days, but for Arsenal, it was a trophy in Graham's first season in charge and the victory that generated the momentum that would lead all the way to Paris and a Champions League final nearly two decades later. Two years after the Wembley win, in a season tragically overshadowed by the Hillsborough disaster, Graham's team secured the League title in dramatic circumstances at Anfield with the last kick of the season. It was my next personal football milestone; the next game I can actually remember. I watched the end of that game through the window of a TV rental shop on Loughborough's main street and while I couldn't hear Brian Moore's famous "it's up for grabs! Thomassss!" commentary, I didn't need to as the player in question somersaulted across the Anfield turf before using his neck as a spring.

A few months later, on my 15th birthday – which happened to fall, as it sometimes does, on the opening day of the season (August 19, if you're wondering, y'know, for next year) – I got to see the Gunners play live for the first time, at Old Trafford. Rather disappointingly the reigning champions lost 4-1 (for the record, Arsenal went on to finish fourth while United finished 13th, although they did lift the FA Cup, thus saving Fergie from the axe, despite the three years of excuses). But the trip wasn't a total loss. I did get to see some bloke called Michael Knighton doing keepy-ups from the halfway line before volleying the ball into the net in front of the Stretford End. It was a neat trick. It would have been an even neater trick to buy United for £20m, but hey, we all make mistakes.

Despite that defeat Arsenal's success grew greater over the following five years with the team picking up another title, as well as an FA and League Cup double and a European Cup Winners Cup. It was on these foundations that Arsène Wenger built his early managerial success at Highbury – two Doubles and another League title and two FA Cups to boot. The formidable defence of Tony Adams, Lee Dixon, Nigel Winterburn, David Seaman, Steve Bould and Martin Keown helped the likes of Thierry Henry and Patrick Vieira learn to become invincible, a lineage which has long since been broken.

As I grew older and football began its transformation, my desire to watch live matches grew. I made a few trips to the City Ground with my best mate Paddy, a Forest fan (well, nobody's perfect). One game in particular, a 3-1 Simod Cup semi-final win against Crystal Palace, sticks in my mind. The Trent End was packed, literally, to the rafters. We ended up sitting on a concrete lintel above one of the exits at the back of the terrace. It gave us a clear view of the pitch but, more importantly, kept us out of a fearful looking crush. This was less than two months before the Hillsborough disaster.

However, it never felt quite right surrounded by a load of people from Nottingham and in the end I found my football home in the Kop at Filbert Street, the (former) home of Leicester City. I was just in time for an incredible period which saw us reach four First Division play-off finals in five seasons under Brian Little and Martin O'Neill (we won two). O'Neill then also took us to three League Cup finals in four seasons (again, we won two). People laughed when he said he wanted the team playing in Europe, but by the time he left, we had and beating the likes of Manchester United, Liverpool and even Arsenal, for whom I still have a soft spot, had become routine. It's a shame the legacy he left has been squandered. Yet those League Cup wins were high points that give this story some symmetry. It might have been a long road to get there, but as Confucius said, more or less, every journey begins with a single step and that step for me was an April day in 1987.

Aston Villa 1998-99

Jamie Cutteridge

Looking back, many remember the 1998-1999 season in England for some northern team that won a few trophies, but the purists, the romantics, remember it for a team that sold their best player, led the league till Christmas and ultimately collapsed under the weight of the combined egos of both manager and chairman. Ladies and gentlemen, I present you Aston Villa.

Let me give you some context. Being a Villa fan was never easy, a couple of mid-90s League Cups aside, and in my entire lifespan I have only ever ended the season disappointed. Surrounded by Manchester United fans, despite living close to Birmingham, my respite was brief and lasted for the first half of the 98-99 season. For a 10-year old these were heady days and ones that remain stuck in my mind with goals, heroes and memories seeing Villa top of the league at the start of 1999.

The season did not begin with such optimism. Lumbered with an overpriced, misfiring, tabloid-hopping, badge-kissing, Holte End-loving Stan Collymore, Villa's issues up front took a further blow as star man Dwight Yorke left Villa Park to join the eventual champions Manchester United pursued by John Gregory and his shotgun. This left just 'Stan the Man' and a young Julian Joachim as forward options.

The ex-Leicester man Joachim led the line early on as the Villa's now out of fashion 3-5-2 profited from the industrious midfield spearheaded by Ian Taylor and snuck up the table as the early-season favourites faltered. Flair was added to the squad as everyone's favourite borderline alcoholic Paul Merson signed and made his debut in a home game against Wimbledon notable for three reasons. Firstly, both Merson and Alan Thompson missed penalties (Merson knocked in a rebound from his own); secondly Villa's fourth win in a row coupled with a Liverpool draw saw them go top; and thirdly I lost a Villa drinks bottle in the old Trinity Road stand (the first and only time I ever sat in it). Dramatic days indeed.

Villa's good form continued and saw them remain unbeaten whilst competing in the Uefa Cup. A foetus-like Darius Vassell made his debut in a home tie against Stromsgodset coming off the bench to score twice in the final four minutes to scrape a 3-2 win for Villa. In the meantime Dion Dublin was signed from nearby Coventry City which saw him hit the ground running at a pace not seen since sliced bread. His debut saw him link up with Collymore, scoring twice in (another) 3-2 win, this time against Spurs. The following week Villa travelled to the Dell where the Dion hit a hat-trick as Villa won 4-1. It was the first time Dublin had proved good value for money since the 1980s.

Our heroes (because we're all now caught up in this story) then went on a run of four league games without a win, losing their unbeaten record to Liverpool before draws with Forest and Manchester United were followed up with defeat to Chelsea at Stamford Bridge. Villa needed a win and bounced back in perhaps the most notable win and result of my entire football supporting life.

Sometimes life has the ability to throw football into sharp perspective and the second weekend of December 1998 is one such example. Let me cut to the chase. On the afternoon of the 13th December, my brother died. No other way to put it, it was an unmitigatingly shit day. Such tragedies cause the whole world to slow down and I can remember every detail of that weekend, every sodding second, including a football match. Some may consider this shallow, selfish perhaps, but for those of who can't help but love the game, you'll understand. Without going Nick Hornby on you, my life is punctuated by big football games. The day my brother was born (England 1-1 Germany, Germany win on a penalties), my 13th Birthday (Germany 1-5 England), my first night at university (Spurs 1-2 Villa), the interview for my first full-time job (Villa 1-2 Liverpool) and the day my brother died (Villa 3-2 Arsenal).

In the midst of this, Villa had a title challenge to maintain and after their rivals from Old Trafford had drawn the day before, they had the opportunity to extend their lead as they hosted fellow contenders and defending champions Arsenal. Half time not only saw Villa two down but also saw one of the strangest injuries ever seen at a football ground as a parachutist dressed as Santa crashed onto the roof of the ground, suffering an injury that would result in him losing his leg.

I heard the score at the hospital. I felt nothing – the first time a Villa score had barely registered – numbed by pain and the feeling that the entire universe could fuck right off.

The half-time break was elongated, clearly giving John Gregory enough time to sort his team out, and from what I've heard Villa came out a different side. Joachim pulled them back into the game before two goals from new hero Dion Dublin gave Villa an improbable win. The score came through on the radio as we were driving home. I smiled.

For a 10-year old experiencing a less than joyous weekend, football offered a break; a glimmer of hope in a dark situation. The place of football in my life was confirmed as the game once again managed to extend beyond its meagre context to penetrate areas unrelated. This wasn't about football making up for the loss of my brother.. In fact, I can't quite grasp what football did for me on that day, was it escapism, a sign that there was hope and positivity in the universe yet? Or was it just an ounce of good news in a day that needed some? Let's not give football too much credit, it was the last one, but I smiled, and in that moment, it was enough.

Top on Christmas day, Villa's turkey arrived a day late as youngster Adam Rachel was shoved centre-stage to deputise in goal for the injured Mark Bosnich and the sent-off Michael Oakes. Unfortunately Rachel proceeded to make a less than auspicious debut as Villa went down 2-1. Despite taking seven points from the next three games, this game proved a turning point as they lost top spot before going 10 games without a win between January and April, ultimately staggering over the finish line, losing their last three games and finishing sixth.

The season was ultimately a failure. After a bright start, Villa fans knew that this ageing team would never again have a chance at a seat at football's top table. In fact, the team only got older and John Gregory decided to spend Doug Ellis's money on Steve Stone and Colin Calderwood, signings about as inspiring as that anecdote about the bottle in the Trinity Road.

An entertaining run to the FA Cup final the next season ended the same way as the previous season's title challenge in the final showpiece event at the old Wembley, managing to see the old place off with a steaming turd of a game. Gregory didn't get the hint and continued to build some of the dullest football teams ever seen in B6. But this doesn't matter.

It does not matter that Villa played a less than inspiring 3-5-2 with two defensively minded wing-backs in Gary Charles and Alan 'about the same size as Dion Dublin's appendage' Wright. It does not matter that the team was full of ageing names such as Steve Watson and the aforementioned Merson, as well as players whose careers would fizzle out in Mark Draper and Alan Thompson. It does not matter that the second half of the season was such an abject failure, that the team never came close to glory and that John Gregory disappeared up his own rectum. It doesn't matter that the Stan Collymores and Paul Mersons I worshipped as a child were the worst sort of role models or that the signing of Paul Grayson was nowhere near as exciting as I made out. It doesn't even matter that this team failed to achieve anything and is remembered only by me. 1998-1999 was the season that football first made its presence felt in my life. What mattered was that a team shorn of their best player went on a run that made them unexpected title contenders; won games left, right and centre; scored goals; and occasionally entertained - and that they happened to be my team.

For four months they made me proud in the playground and were something to talk about, to boast of, something sadly not seen since. My team made me love football, and football paid me back. Football took over my life, and while at times I hate it for it, and blame Paul Merson for my social ineptitude, I wouldn't have it any other way.

The Arsenal game proved my footballing watershed and as Villa have not pulled off such a comeback against a top team since, part of me still believes that they did it for me, as if the universe works its magic through Dion Dublin. For five weeks in the winter of 1998 it certainly seemed to.

Queen of the South 1980-81
Giancarlo Rinaldi

"Whaur's yer handbag?".

It was a question any player putting skills and style before honest endeavour could expect in the Scottish Second Division in the late 1970s and early 1980s. There was one footballer more than any other who was the recipient of that inquiry at Palmerston Park, the home of Queen of the South, and often from his own support. That man was Jimmy Robertson and I loved to watch him play.

These were my formative years as a viewer of the beautiful game. It seemed to be permanently wet and cold in Dumfries when my father took me to see a match. And a low rumble of discontent or trouble often emanated from the old corrugated iron Coo Shed opposite the main stand.

It was atmospheric in the extreme.

My hometown team, the Doonhamers to give them their nickname, were not very good. Nor had they ever been very good, certainly in recent memory. There was the odd old-timer who could remember them leading the top flight of Scottish football in the 1950s, but most of us were used to more meagre fare. We bade farewell to the 1970s by finishing second bottom of the old Second Division in the 1979/80 campaign. Only Alloa Athletic were worse. Unlike the Maltese Falcon, this was most definitely not the stuff that dreams are made of.

I was 11 years old and my head had already been turned by my Italian roots. The 1978 World Cup had helped me to fall in love with players like Roberto Bettega, Paolo Rossi and, above all, Giancarlo Antognoni. That the elegant Fiorentina playmaker shared my name only clinched the deal. This was how the game was meant to be played.

But I did not live in Italy, I lived in south-west Scotland. And the nearest thing we had to the skills of Serie A was Jimmy Robertson. He was inspirational and infuriating in equal measure but, for me, he was usually what made the game worthwhile. When he was in the mood, he was unstoppable and you could be pretty sure Queens would win.

He was what I think they would now call a cult hero, or possibly a maverick. I seem to remember he smoked big cigars and went by the nickname JR, carrying echoes, whether intentionally or not, of the oil baron who sported the same soubriquet in the TV series Dallas. He had to be just as thick-skinned as his namesake because, one way or another, he usually took pelters during a match.

Opposition fans loved to make him the target of their vitriol but, unfortunately, he was also often criticised by his own support. Their complaint was usually that he tried to do the over-complicated or elaborate when the more straightforward was an option. There were howls of derision when it went wrong. But what delight he provided when he got it right.

He loved to taunt and tease a defender before swinging in a cross or firing a vicious shot towards goal. Where was the sport, he reasoned, in the direct route to goal? Instead, he showed us there were alleyways, shortcuts and more meandering paths towards the net that the rest of us had failed to consider. Some couldn't wait to criticise that approach but for one young lad watching, there was always the hope of some flash of brilliance which would make them eat their words.

Robertson was my idol but it was a time when Scottish football seemed to be littered with such figures. Even the Queen of the South team itself had more than its share of larger-than-life characters. Or at least, at a distance of more than 30 years, it seems that way to me.

The goalkeeper was Alan Ball, who made something like three million appearances for the club. A giant-handed baldy with a broad north east of England accent he was my archetype for how a netminder should be. He used to work in a local garage and I was always a bit awestruck as he and my father haggled over the price of a Fiat Strada.

Another member of the squad was young striker Rowan Alexander, a forward with one of the best leaps I have ever seen, seeming to hang in the air for an age. He would go on to become the manager who took lowly Gretna on their crash-and-burn journey to the SPL. But, back then, he was just a long-haired boy who knew how to bang in the goals.

Even the players' names were redolent of a bygone age. We had a Nobby (Clark) and a Dick (Malone) in the team - you don't get many of those lighting up the Champions League these days. The former won promotion as a player and manager with Queens while the latter had been an FA Cup winner during his days at Sunderland.

I was blissfully unaware of this at the time but we were a club in managerial turmoil in that 1980/81 campaign. The chopping and changing at the top produced mixed results but, in a league with no outstanding side, there was always the chance that a half-decent string of scores could put you in contention for promotion. Why couldn't it be Queens? Especially to a boy of my tender years, there seemed no reason why not.

We started that campaign with former Scotland international George Herd in charge. The records show he produced more league wins than defeats but that they were both exceeded by the number of draws. We sat mid-table by the turn of the year and were within striking distance of promotion when things took a bizarre twist.

Apparently Herd was finding it a strain to travel from north east England to southern Scotland and he announced he was leaving to take a job at Darlington. For a man who had promised to try to make the Dumfries side a big club once more, it was a bit of a disappointment for all concerned. Who would the board of directors turn to in their hour of need?

The answer was, controversially, nobody. In these days where club owners generally like to have a manager in position to take the flak when things go wrong, such a move might be unthinkable. Nonetheless, the directors reckoned they had what was needed to bring the team floating to the top. Incredibly, they were proved right.

Results took a positive turn initially before some further setbacks left Queens on the fringes of a tight promotion fight. It would ultimately come down to the very last day of the season. Queen of the South needed to beat Albion Rovers at Palmerston while hoping Cowdenbeath would not beat Queen's Park. It proved to be an epic Saturday afternoon.

My hero Robertson got two goals and Alexander the other as we sped to a 3-0 lead and then awaited news of Cowdenbeath's result. With eight minutes to play, the incredible happened. Queen's Park took the lead and held it until the final whistle. Nobby Clark waved his arms in the air in delight as the Dumfries crowd cheered. When the result was confirmed, the celebrations could properly begin.

Queens' chairman Willie Harkness could bask in the glory of the achievement. It was an unusual feeling for him as during the rest of the 1980s he would be a figure resented by large parts of the club's support. They accused him of running things for his own benefit, not that of the town and he was regularly lampooned in the fanzine *A Nightmare on Terregles Street*, but – in 1981 at least – he was being hailed as a hero.

But for me he was a peripheral player to Robertson. Jimmy was voted player of the year for the division and finished as top scorer with 20 goals. Considering he did not act as an out-and-out striker but rather preferred to stay out on the wing, it was some achievement. Sadly, it did not bring the rewards I (and he) felt he deserved.

A contract dispute saw him left out of the side at the start of the First Division campaign and it was a loss the club could ill afford. It took them what seemed like an age to get a win and they would never recover from that. Perhaps, looking back, they were not strong enough to survive in the division and their immediate relegation was no surprise. But it still hurt after the joy of the previous campaign.

Robertson went on to write his way into the Queen of the South record books with something like 400 appearances over two spells spanning 11 years. When he finally hung up his boots, in 1993, it felt like the end of an era. There has never been another player quite like him at the club.

If I stop and think about his playing days and those first trips to Palmerston they still have the ability to make me smile. Your heroes were there within touching distance – not broadcast on a screen from who knows where. Your dad was at your side to talk about everything and nothing. And, for a couple of hours or so, you felt part of something that really mattered to the people around you. Not all of that has evaporated with time like Bovril fumes on the wind, but a lot of it has.

Nonetheless, there is still the odd player who can thrill me a bit like Jimmy Robertson used to do. Queens have Danny Carmichael, an old-school dribbler who takes kicks on his shins and bounces straight back up to try to trick his opponent once again. And my other love, Fiorentina, have the graceful Spaniard Borja Valero who glides across the grass. They have the kind of talent which can turn a game and light up a miserable afternoon. And, nowadays, at least nobody feels the need to inquire about any imaginary handbag.

Spain 2002

Ash Hashim

"GO Korea! Go Korea."

With cheeks pressed firmly into the wall and my back fully turned against the TV screen, that was how I 'witnessed' Spain as they crashed out to South Korea on penalties at the World Cup quarter finals in 2002.

As far as I can remember, it had all the ingredients of a spectacularly convoluted football match.

There were three Spanish goals mysteriously disallowed for offside, a generous onslaught of player protests and a delicious dose of Korean 'bias' from Egyptian referee Gamal Ghandour.

If there was a 'Football God', he had simply forgotten to turn up in Gwanju on that fateful afternoon of June 22. At least that was what the 12-year-old version of me – equipped with the conflicted emotions of a fan girl – chose to believe.

In my decade of following the beautiful game, you could say that Spain's rueful elimination at the hands of Guus Hiddink's side of World Cup 2002 has never been far from my mind.

"Go Korea! Go Korea – hey, hey, hey!" my mother, who possessed no cultural or ethnic roots to the country, bellowed into my ears as she clapped her hands and did a zany dance across the living room. Believe me when I tell you that there's nothing more amusing than listening to an Arab speaker mispronouncing the South Korean national football cheer.

Had the neighbours peered into our living room right then, they would have frozen in their tracks (*"Ah, the ones living at 0112 – we always knew they were a little potty inside,"* they would say to one another kindly.)

Finally, I turned my head a little, took a peek from between my fingers and spotted the sweaty armpits of José Antonio Camacho, Spain's coach, who squinted as he examined his own penalty sheet.

A skinny, nervous 19-year-old Spanish bloke named Iker Casillas walked up to guard the South Koreans' first penalty. He was gorgeous and clearly destined for greatness, But if he wasn't going to keep a clean sheet today, did those heavenly cheekbones really matter?

Turned out they didn't.

South Korean forward Hwang Sun-Hong flicked the ball into the young Real Madrid keeper's hands, only for it to fall out of his clutches and woefully float into the Spaniard's net.It's official – Spain were going out, I thought fearfully. The entire stadium clearly despised them and the match, by all accounts, was a triumphant case of the dreaded 'Domino effect'.

I believe that when actions continue to cruelly play out against a team's favour over the course of 90 minutes (i.e. the ball hitting the woodwork, penalty misses and unfair judgments), that team simply isn't destined to win. It's a disgustingly romantic view of football, but it does eat at you from the back of your head, especially when you realise that your own team is a victim of fate.

Now we all know what happened next – South Korea scored all five of their penalties, while Spain missed two (final result: 5-3 to Korea). My mother deliriously leapt onto our family couch to celebrate South Korea's progress into the next round and depressingly, shouts of joy accompanied her from the nearby block.

On cue, the hot tears began to flow from the corners of my eye and down my cheeks – it felt like Ahn Jung Hwan had personally delivered the final blow to me in the form of tattered sheets of origami paper.

Indeed, if there's one Korean name that will stick with me for the rest of my life, that honour goes to Ahn.

Newspaper headlines across the country had been rallying support for South Korea's answer to David Beckham after he scored the golden goal that eliminated Italy.

Even the squad's mastermind, Guus Hiddink, who had admittedly done a remarkable job for the Koreans, bestowed the type of praise upon him that would've made Buddha blush. Ahn's story was fascinating to say the least, because right after knocking the Azzurri out of the tournament, his Serie A club, Perugia, promptly terminated his contract for the 'injustice' he had inflicted upon Italian football.

More shockingly, in two days, all twelve names of Ahn Jung Hwan's former girlfriends were public knowledge, along with stories that the striker was now past his 'playing days' and had settled down with a former Miss Korea. Ahn had also received offers to act in Korean soap opera, and 52-year-old women all around the country – including my local grocer – were desperate to see him naked.

Truth be told, the Korean 'heartthrob' hadn't done much apart from score a penalty against Spain, of course, to have inflicted such pain on my memories, but nevertheless, for crushing a dream, my dislike for him ran far deeper than merely begrudging him a single success from twelve yards.

Despite being a person of mixed Euro-Asian heritage living in Asia, we were force fed the notion of supporting our "brothers" at the World Cup 2002, which was humorous if you look at it from our perspective.

When I asked my Welsh grandfather if he appreciated being a temporary Korean for that week, he laughed it off and simply said "Spain will win" (bless his soul). He later described "Spanish men" in a series of other unprintable adjectives.

It didn't matter that I was living in a country with no roots in Korean culture – there was an unwritten memo that everybody (except me, apparently) had received before dutifully turning into a South Korean that weekend.

As images of Spain getting knocked out of the World Cup in 2002 filled our screens, more tears begin to spill in the apartment we had moved into two months prior. In that moment, I felt truly isolated.

Essentially, that is what happens when you are twelve and football is a painful game of emotions. It strips you down to your raw self and there is no capacity to take in the complexity of 'host-nation politics' and the role a referee plays in it.

That is why many of us stick to the team we supported as little girls and boys – we are attracted to our earliest experiences.

My victims of Spain's elimination were Fernando Morientes, who would not stop crying – and also, to some extent, his tragically injured strike partner and best friend Raul Gonzalez (this was another romantic notion I utterly enjoyed).

Raul had been ruled out of the game because of a groin injury and one of my favourite post-match debates involved the fact that Spain had crashed out because of Raul's absence (which of course, from a purely partisan point of view, they had).

He was the only Golden Boy they had – Real Madrid's favourite son, the symbol of all things '*Madridismo*' and King Juan Carlos's favourite player.

Later on, as a sports journalist staying in the same hotel as the Schalke 04 team in 2011, I discovered that Raul wasn't as highly revered by the Catalans and Valencianos.

"It's not that they hate him," explained my Valencian friend, Miguel. "It's just that he belongs to Madrid." (Ironically, on my maiden trip to Spain, the Raul I had respected as a young teenager was, by some twist of fate, staying in the same building as I was.)

But it was Raul's Spain team of 2002 – the unfortunate ones – who provided the benchmark for their success today.

Ten years ago, Spain were the favourites 'on paper' – a hardworking side with talents such as David Albelda, Gaizka Mendieta and Fernando Hierro, who were unlucky not to have won any trophies.

They were a blank canvas, slowly but surely making their mark on the football world, with glimpses of their promises in the form of Barcelona players, such as Luis Enrique and the terrifyingly young Xavi Hernandez and Carles Puyol, who, as we all know are part of the world football elite of today.

I'd like to think that the real story of Spain is one of a fearful young girl growing into a confident woman – the moment she reaches her peak is in the realisation of her flaws.

The successes of *La Furia Roja* today were only possible when the differences that divided the Basque, Catalan and Madridista players were banished.

Spain's history before 2008 is an essential part of the school yearbook no one bothered to look at and the photos they chose to hide behind the glitz and euphoric celebration from recent years.

And when we reflect on Spain's greatest achievements from the past four years (two European Championships and one World Cup), it is imperative to remember the elements of her past – her insecurities, her painful lessons and ultimately, her redemption.

Ever the wise man, my father has a theory that for the rotten luck Spain suffered in the past, 'karma' has paid back its hefty sum in the form of three back-to-back international competition victories.

Just ask Vicente del Bosque, who was sacked by Real Madrid to make way for David Beckham's arrival in 2003.

We all know who's having the final laugh now.

Rossington FC 1997-98

Glen Wilson

I am unable to recall when or why I fell in love with football. There was no epiphany. No great moment of clarity. Football was just always there; bobbling about eternally alongside grazed knees and episodes of *Why Don't You?* in the goalmouth scramble of my childhood.

In an age before Sky Sports, when John Helm was omnipresent and when come-and-get-me pleas were the preserve of refugees rather than 'want away' strikers, it was the World Cups and European Championships that pushed football onto the kids. Getting them hooked by throwing eccentric goalkeeping, corner flag dancing and alice-bands right in amongst the hose-pipe bans and blue ice-pops of our sepia South Yorkshire summers and hinting that if we stuck with them there'd be much more where that came from. But for me it wasn't like that. I didn't need a quick-fix from a biannual stimulant. For me, football was a constant.

Rossington FC (*nee* Station FC) was my local football team; my dad was their manager. He was also their secretary, their coach, their groundsman, their programme editor and more often than not their substitute too. Football didn't come to me through the television; it already lived in our house. Match programmes were handwritten on the dining room table, advertising boards hand-painted in our lounge, players signed in the kitchen, and a league directory sat by a telephone which rang constantly from Thursday through to Monday.

I don't know the first game I went to; instead I retain a blur of sights and sounds from my formative years. The smell of liniment oil and deep heat, filling the bucket and struggling to carry it back whilst trying to work out what exactly made the sponge magic.

Football as I knew it was swinging my legs from wooden benches in breezeblock dugouts, post-match Working Men's Clubs with cigarette smoke and syrupy coke mix, cheese and onion sandwiches piled up on red Formica tables strewn with Stones Bitter ashtrays, and being told to pick a team from the football card whilst Tim Gudgeon read out the classifieds from a battered old television set on a shelf in the corner.

I was aware of the names being read out on TV, of Barclays League Division One, of Liverpool and Arsenal, and of Doncaster Rovers too, but they were the teams of television, of Subbuteo and the Green 'Un. They didn't exist in real life, not like those on the league tables my dad would carefully annotate in pencil each week. In the real world it was Miners' Welfares rather than Uniteds, Collieries rather than Rovers and teams with much more interesting names in general; Graham Street Prims, Norton Woodseats, Slack & Parr, Derby Carriage & Wagon, Retford Rail and the somewhat oxymoronic Leicester Nirvana.

Don't let anyone tell you that Crystal Palace were the team of the 1980s, nor Aberdeen, nor Denmark, nor anyone else. It was Station. At the start of the decade Station were in the Bentley Sunday League, playing behind a school on a pitch so vast it was referred to by visiting teams simply as 'the airfield'. By 1989, the club were in the Central Midlands League Premier Division, they'd moved to the Welfare Ground, fashioned some dugouts and a covered stand, and begun producing a programme for three-figure crowds as they entertained visiting teams from as far afield as Derby and Leicestershire.

The CML is where my football life began, and for a decade it was pretty much all I knew: welfares, recreation grounds and works fields every Saturday from August to April. There was only a brief half-time break as my parents split up when I was 11; a 'difficult age', I've often been told, a statement which I've since realised is the non-football equivalent of "it was a bad time to concede a goal", as if there could ever be a time to welcome either. But within a couple of months Saturdays as I knew them returned, and the football spared dad and me those awkward forced post-divorce trips to McDonalds or the cinema which befell other children in my position.

Though I would've attended 100 matches before I'd even started secondary school, only a few identifiable memories remain, occasional clarity standing out from the white noise of whistles, of shouts and studs beaten clean on changing room walls. While my memory might fail me, my dad's organisation never will. He kept records from the moment he first took charge of Station and so in a cupboard in his house there exists three decades of football history neatly contained in a stack of green ledgers. Through these I have been able to date the memories which have inexplicably stuck with me.

Monday 6th May 1991
Lincoln Moorlands 2-2 Rossington
(G.Mountford 81, Whittle 84)

The final match of the 1990-91 season, but I recall nothing of the game itself. Afterwards, in the club at Moorlands, one of the players won a crate of lager on the raffle. At a red light on the way home, dad opened the back doors of the mini-bus[1] to throw a few cans to the lads in the car behind. That's it. Most of my childhood spent on football fields across four counties and my earliest true memory comes from a road junction on the way out of Lincoln.

Saturday 17th October 1992
Rossington 2-4 Sandiacre Town
(Nelson 18, Storey (pen) 25)

In the playground as friends talked about Newcastle United winning their first ten matches of the season, I'd excitedly interject to point out Rossington were only a game behind them. The resulting blank stares became a recurring feature; I met them again when I proudly showed off the page in the non-league directory which featured Rossington's team photo before Assembly. Our nine wins from nine did not become 10 from 10. In front of another three-figure crowd on the Welfare we were beaten by second-place Sandiacre Town.

----

1   Mini-bus' was the optimistic name afforded what was essentially a windowed transit. No radio, no heating, no seat-belts, just two long bench seats down either side, backs to the windows, bags, balls and bucket piled up between our feet. Every trip would see a dozing player flung across the vehicle as we rounded a sharp bend, every week someone would bang their head with a metallic thud on the unlined roof. It was a death-trap which defiantly passed its MOT out of spite. Still, despite the weight load of 14 men, assorted football kit and me, we'd thunder home up the M1 and usually make it back in time for Gladiators.

But it was OK, I told myself, they were a bigger club, after all they were Sandiacre *Town*. A whole town. And they had a fan, a bloke who had a Sandiacre club scarf and shirt. We couldn't be expected to beat clubs who had their own scarves.

Saturday 12th December 1992
Rossington 0-3 Emley

Sandiacre Town had a fan, Emley had supporters. They were the biggest side in the Sheffield Senior Cup at the time and Rossington met them in round three. Over 250 were down the ground and dad roped in two lads from school to film the game via a camcorder hazardously secured to the stand roof. I made a banner for the big game; printer paper daubed in luminous yellow and green with *Come On Rosso!* and taped at each end to a wooden ruler. I took it, sat on the fence behind the goal and held it up as Rossington won a corner. My support even assured me a mention on the resulting match video; the two camera operators audibly acknowledging me with, "What the hell does that say?" "God knows, I can't zoom that far".

Saturday 23rd April 1994
Nettleham 0-3 Rossington (aban. 86 mins)
(Troth 47, Nelson 53, 77)

A gloriously warm day; an ice-cream van in the car park, shorts and sunglasses, folk wheezing on the nearby tennis courts. To begin with. In the second half the sky turned apocalyptically dark and thunder boomed across the Lincolnshire fields. Late on, as dad prepared to make a substitution, the heavens opened; not rain, but huge great hailstones the size of dice. Sub Hayden Feirn clocked one right on the back of his ear as he trotted on to replace Robbie Nelson. Despite being on a hat-trick, Robbie gleefully sprinted off and told my dad he loved him. They soldiered on for two or three minutes before the hail worsened and both teams sprinted for the cover of the metal stand. Dad, Robbie and me, marooned in a tiny wood dug-out could only hear the stones ricocheting off the stand roof; it sounded like we were at a panel beaters convention. Eventually the hail became rain, and subsided enough for the teams to try and restart. It was no use. The pitch, bone dry at kick-off was now ankle deep in midfield, and so with four minutes to go the game was abandoned.

Saturday 6th April 1996
Thorne Colliery 0-1 Rossington
(Henderson)

Towards the end of each season, injuries would begin to diminish the first and second team squads and my dad would reluctantly begin penning his own name beside the number 12 or 14 on the team sheet. At Thorne, a month before his 46th birthday, with one sub Scott Henderson already on, an injury to Steve Racjan meant dad had to remove his tracksuit bottoms with a sigh and a weary shout to the linesman. "He'll probably win this for us, your dad," said Rats as he sat down next to me in the dug-out, and a few minutes later, he did. A perfectly weighted ball between the Thorne back-line onto the toe of his fellow substitute, 27 years his junior, who duly slotted it past the keeper for the winning goal.

1997-98

Enough rogue memories. The 1997-98 season was when it all came to an end between my first footballing love and I. It was Rossington's last season in existence. Though competitive on the field, notoriously hospitable off it and financially sound, they were to be gagged and suffocated to death by red tape. Unable to erect floodlights, or enclose their Welfare field, bureaucracy had long lurked in the wings, but this season it took centre stage and played out a farce as Rossington were ordered to replay a cup tie after beaten opponents Long Eaton United complained about the distracting presence of a fairground beyond one corner of the field. We took the hint. The CML no longer cared for the likes of us and so the club opened talks for a merger with neighbouring Northern Counties East League side Rossington Main, to take effect at the season's end. This was to be it.

By now I was no longer travelling with dad and the team, no longer carrying a bucket or a football to avoid being made to pay an admission price. Instead I was part of the regular travelling supporters, a whole car full; Paul, Gerry, Pete and me. Gerry drove. He had been involved in local football for as long as there had been such a thing as local football, as reflected in a typical exchange on the way to a game at Grimethorpe MW *(lost 2-4; Henderson 2)*;

"I told you, I know where I'm going, I've been here before"

"When was that?"

"Oooh, 1956 I think".

In early December, for a game at Kimberley Town *(won 3-1; Breen, Burkhill and Whittle)* it was just Gerry and me. Gerry had an aversion to motorways which meant meandering tours of long-forgotten north Nottinghamshire roads. On the way back he took a corner a bit too quickly, bounced across a verge, landed on an adjoining road, and just carried on driving without so much as a pause, the Carlos Sainz of the B6463. I think I finally retrieved my finger nails from the dashboard about a mile from home. Four days later, for a Sheffield Cup tie at Worksop Town *(lost 0-5)* Pete took over driving duties for our safety... and proceeded to briefly nod off at the wheel on the way out of town.

In February we went to Heanor Town *(drew 1-1; Sykes)*, but before I could hop in the car I was sent back in the house to get my boots. Dad was away, there was only a bare XI, I was to go on the bench; unused, but an ambition realised. In the changing rooms at half-time Shaun Breen had completed his teamtalk with ten minutes still to kill and as we sat idle one of the players realised that Heanor's own tactics brief was just about audible from next-door. Minutes later the referee stuck his head in the door to find twelve of us lined up with tea-cups pressed against the thin pavilion wall.

There was no fairytale ending for Rossington, the club chalked up just one win in its final ten, but it was a very satisfying victory, a 3-0 demolition of the fairground-fearing Long Eaton *(Nelson, Breen, Lewkowicz)*; their increasingly exasperated manager met with a cutting riposte as he berated an official "The louder you scream the faster we go," from one wag in the stand.

I sold the final club programme at a sombre final home game against Kimberley Town *(3-4; Breen 2, McGrane)*. The wake was held a week later as our regular travelling support of four was swelled by a dozen or so for the club's denouement down the road at Harworth C.I. *(3-3; McGrane, Nelson, Henderson)*. The club's final ever goal was scored by Scott Henderson, 17 years after his father Tommy had started at centre-half in dad's first game in charge. Dad was an unused sub. As he almost always had been.

It's odd seeing a club cease to be. At the end, despite all we'd been through together, everyone just seemed to slope off in their own direction, like the characters in The Great Escape. Of course they all had lives away from football, but not to me. While everyone else knew these men as gas-fitters, or firemen, or postmen, or council workers, to me they were always, first and foremost, footballers. The footballers that gave me the game.

USA 1994
Brooks Peck

When Roberto Baggio missed the final penalty of the 1994 World Cup final, my grandmother cried. She is by no means a football fan and, to my knowledge, the previous hour of that match could very well be all she's ever watched. But her parents had come to America from southern Italy and seeing the players with whom she identified left deflated and distraught after losing in one of the most agonising ways possible, in a tournament that the host nation had suddenly realised was rather important, was too much to bear at dinnertime.

As a kid, seeing an adult you're close to (in proximity and emotional attachment) cry over something that doesn't quite make sense has a way of burrowing into your head. Sometimes it's forgotten with time, but eventually it's remembered and the fact you can now relate to those feelings all too well makes it an indelible moment that can cement a bond with the game.

My first exposure to anything related to football at a higher level than me kicking the shin pads of my fellow 10-year-olds was the generic brown cartoon dog that served as the child-baiting mascot for the '94 World Cup. His name was Striker and he was a cog in the marketing campaign to convince Americans that this event was worth caring about and he was on my t-shirt. Having invested my parents' money into the season's finest children's fashion, I felt personally invested in the tournament.

Before it began, I was confident in the USA's chances, mainly because I was young and therefore an idiot. My only previous experience supporting a team representing the United States was the Dream Team – the 1992 Olympic basketball team that obliterated each set of spectators dressed as opponents by a margin of 30-70 points every game on their stroll to the gold medal in Barcelona. So, following the logic of a kid growing up in 1990s America, that meant that all USA teams dominate in all sports always. I had no idea that the USA had only qualified for their first World Cup since 1950 four years earlier at Italia '90 and lost all three of their group-stage matches. Nor did I know that their World Cup place in '94 was guaranteed for being the host nation. This made the tournament-opening 1-1 draw against Switzerland a bit disappointing.

The crowd at the Silverdome in Michigan for the first World Cup match ever played indoors was appropriately big (73,425 people big, though this was 20,000 less than the then record attendance for an indoor sporting event in North America, set by Wrestlemania III in 1987 at the same building) and loud, but yet still the smallest the home side would play before throughout the tournament. Seeing that physical manifestation of acceptance for a sport otherwise reflexively mocked by large herds of the population was a legitimising moment. It was also the start of what remains the highest attended World Cup in history. Clearly Striker deserved a promotion.

Unlike the Dream Team, which had an entire roster of superstars so god-like that I had and treasured each one of them in action-figure form (I'm just now realising how grossly materialistic I was as a child), the USA soccer team were largely unknown. We had no domestic league (that would come two years later as one of FIFA's conditions for letting the USA host the World Cup) or internet to inform us. Striker Eric Wynalda scored the team's first goal to equalise against Switerland with an absolutely perfect, curling free kick into the top corner, so he became a favorite. Defender Alexi Lalas gained notoriety for his combination of talent and looking like a ginger wizard/the lead singer of the Spin Doctors, so he was cool. And, had I known anything of the men who tend to hold such a job at the time, I would've thought goalkeeper Tony Meola the best pony-tailed nightclub bouncer in the world.

Then there was the denim kit. Oh the denim kit. Though not actually made of the acid-washed jeans they so resembled, the shirt was a garish facsimile with stretched-out white stars across the front and back. Even before grunge, OJ Simpson or my only family trip to Disney World, that kit is the first thing that comes to mind when thinking of that year. For better or worse.

The USA's second group stage match again featured the denim kit and resulted in a 2-1 win over Colombia. The standout moment was, of course, Andres Escobar's own goal. In that moment it was high comedy. It was reason to point and laugh and do a manic dance of ridicule. To my uneducated eyes, it came off so perfectly that it was almost as if Escobar was purposefully finishing Wynalda's cross. Not being one to watch the news over, well, anything, I didn't learn of the tragic end to Escobar's life that soon followed until much later. The thought of a mistake in a game leading to a man being shot to death made the sport terrifying.

After losing their final opening-round match to group winners Romania in a way that I have found thoroughly forgettable, the USA moved to the round of 16 as the third best third place team (narrowly ahead of Italy) in a system that wasn't worth thinking too much about since the desired result was achieved: advancement for the first time since the inaugural World Cup in 1930. This led to a match against Brazil, who some child experts (i.e. me) believed to be the second best team in the competition.

The USA held the eventual champions scoreless for 71 minutes, but reality then set in when a Bebeto shot crawled into the net to give Brazil a 1-0 win and knock them out. It was a disappointing and ultimately frustrating moment as my inflated expectations had been slapped aside like an idiot bug. However, since the match happened to fall on July 4 – Independence Day – there were hot dogs to eat, firework accidents to carelessly avoid and football matches to quickly forget about. My interest in the tournament was over. It was a clean break.

Despite losing my interest, the tournament somehow continued. Brazil and Italy reached the final, which coincided with a trip to my grandparents' house. Up to that point, no one else in my family had shown any particular interest in the tournament, but we had a genealogical connection to Italy and, thus, a rooting interest.

Picking up the only scoreless final World Cup history in its second half, we watched and waited, getting more invested with every missed chance. This was a different kind of frustrating. A kind that felt horrible and prolonged, but in a way that was perversely enjoyable. My grandmother made dinner as the match went to extra time and then penalties, telling us how mean each member of the Brazilian team looked while the Italians were all probably very nice. The confusion as to how Franco Baresi could lift his opening penalty over the bar was tempered by relief when Gianluca Pagliuca saved Marcio Santos's effort. The feeling that the match would never end returned with four straight successful attempts. Then Daniele Massaro's shot was saved and Dunga slotted his in.

All day the commentators had harped on about Roberto Baggio as Italy's consistent savior. He had scored five of Italy's six goals in the knockout rounds and his hair tail only heightened my confidence in him. Then he did what Baresi did and lifted his shot over the bar.

Surrounded by 94,194 people and in impossibly sunny Pasadena, California, the Brazilians celebrated while the Italian collapsed in defeat and a jubilant Pele jumped up and down while wearing an American flag necktie. It was the shots of the Italian plays sinking to the ground and Baggio hanging his head that proved heartbreaking though and that's what transferred the sadness to my grandparents kitchen. And that's what didn't quite make sense. We weren't *really* fans of this sport and had only actively cared about this team for about an hour and half. And yet that was enough.

For years, it was the reaction in that kitchen that I remembered more than any part of the actual match. The more football I watched, the more I realised how that moment influenced how meaningful the game would become to me. It wasn't a win that made me fall in love, it was a loss.

Liverpool 1988-90

Alex Bingle

I admit that I am one of those people who allow a football result to determine my mood for the days that follow. Depths of despair follow a loss while a win puts a grin on my face and a spring in my step. In recent years I have gone from one extreme to the next on a weekly basis, such is the down shot of being a Liverpool fan in the two-thousand and tens. I know fans of not-so successful clubs would scream at me "Despair? You don't know the meaning of despair!" and I accept that I have experienced some highs over the years that other football fans can only dream of. But I also still have those days when I hate the game too and would give anything to feel sheer jubilation on a weekly basis like I did when I set out on my own football journey.

I have recently become a father for the first time and understandably want my son to follow in my football allegiance. I recently dressed him in a Liverpool baby grow and was promptly castigated by a Celtic-supporting family member, who told me that the worst possible thing I could do in my life is to make or force my son to support a certain team. When I think about it, I don't care who he supports when he grows up and I mean that wholeheartedly. As long as it's not Man United. But it got me thinking about how a middle class boy from Cheshire, growing up in a place dominated by part-time prawn sandwich-eating Man United fans, with a Leeds United-supporting father and no allegiance to Merseyside whatsoever, could come to support Liverpool Football Club.

Shamefully, I must admit that my first live football experience was actually at Old Trafford, watching a poor Manchester United team lose 1-0 to Coventry in the 1988-89 league campaign. This experience was more for the benefit of my elder brother who unfortunately, to this day, still supports the wrong team.

I can't tell you much about that day except that it obviously did nothing for me.

My first memory of starting to follow my team was not long after though. Back in the day, when Super Sundays meant a double bill of Sharky and George, I remember going into our living room where my Dad was watching a game on terrestrial television. I've got a feeling Liverpool were playing Aston Villa that day. I was mesmerised by one player in particular and his ability to run at – and past – players had me gripped. I couldn't understand why they passed the ball to anyone else.

I think my Dad knew he had finally connected with me. He was definitely onto a winner when he got tickets for Man United versus Liverpool at Old Trafford not long after for my brother's birthday, and the Liverpool team again featured that marauding winger. I've had the pleasure of meeting John Barnes twice in my life, although both times he was a little larger than the svelte figure he cut that day as he tore through United.

In the end, Ronnie Whelan felt so sorry for United that he decided to do them a favour by lobbing his own keeper from 30 yards (it may not have been that far out, but it was quite spectacular as own goals go). To this day, I still have a small figure of John Barnes (granted he is in his England kit from 1990) by my bedside and I could happily say that no other sportsman has ever had me quite as much in awe as he did in his heyday. Though it wasn't just Barnes – the whole atmosphere of the Anfield club had me in its grip.

The second home game of the 1989-90 season at Anfield is a particularly vivid example. Liverpool put Crystal Palace to the sword 9-0 (Nicol, McMahon, Rush, Gillespie, Beardsley, Aldridge, Barnes, Hysen and Nicol again – yes, I actually remember the scorers and the order in which they scored). At 5-0, Liverpool won a penalty and Peter Beardsley offered to be substituted in order for his soon-departing colleague John Aldridge to come on and score a goal on his last appearance for the club. At the end of the game, Aldridge threw his boots and shirt into the crowd. How generous of him, I thought, before asking my dad "Will he get them back before the next game?"

Despite all that, the day etched firmly in my memory as the day Liverpool FC firmly took over my life was a hot day in September in 1990 – the very day I first visited Anfield, at the age of six. It was the last time Liverpool so comfortably dominated their arch rivals for 90 minutes.

Beardsley's hat trick that day was impressive to say the least as they were all served up on a big juicy platter for him. Ronnie Whelan sat in front of an untroubled defence marshalling the midfield, breaking up anything that came near him. The running from midfield of Steve McMahon – his pace, touch and link-up play was simply immense and got him into positions the United midfield could not pick up. No surprise, then, that he set up the first two goals.

Beardsley himself was untouchable, maybe even forgotten by a defence more concerned with stopping Rush, whose movement into the channels was opening up space for his strike partner and the likes of McMahon and Houghton to run into. Barnes himself played a more disciplined role by his standards and in comparison to the previous season's display of technique, guile and speed at Old Trafford. He sprayed the ball around the park as if controlled by passing extraordinaire Jan Molby and still managed to pick up a goal himself just before half time.

With 10 minutes remaining and 3-0 up, I remember Anfield singing to Bruce Grobbelaar, who had been a happy spectator throughout and was absent-mindedly sunbathing in front of the travelling support: "Brucie! What's the score? Brucie, Brucie, what's the score?!" He started counting to three on his right glove, just as Houghton played a quick free-kick for Beardsley to lob over a distraught Les Sealey and clinch his hat-trick in front of the adoring Kop. Grobbelaar, ever the comedian, realised he had got the score wrong and recounted on four fingers for the nearby United fans' pleasure. He might like to be remembered for his erratic style of goalkeeping and for being an incredible shot-stopper with an agility that was second to none. But among all football fans, Grobbelaar will also always be recalled for the clown-like personality and life he brought to the football pitch.

I could wax lyrical all day about the individual abilities of Rush, Barnes, McMahon, Grobbelaar, Whelan, Nicol, Gillespie, Houghton, Beardsley and Molby. In my somewhat biased and rose-tinted opinion, they could play football together like no team I have seen since. When I think about that day at Anfield in September 1990, I get a little misty eyed. I've been lucky enough to see the likes of Fowler, McManaman, Owen, Gerrard, Carragher, McAllister, Hyypia, Reina, Torres and Suarez who were and are all exceptional footballers that I have worshipped in one form or another.

Unfortunately, none of them have been part of such a successful, football-playing team that on their day, could have demolished any other team in Europe like that Liverpool team in the late 80s. Were it not for the European ban on English teams, Kenny Dalglish would surely have a few European Cups on his managerial CV, but unfortunately it was not to be. I look back to these heady days and wish I was the age I am now so that I can enjoy them properly. To have that feeling of invincibility and belief that we could dominate any team is something I would relish again.

I admit that as I get older, those feelings of despair that accompany a defeat don't endure as a week-long sentence like they used to. I guess new responsibilities in my life make me realise that maybe it isn't all about football after all. But when it comes down to it, I wouldn't swap the feeling of being a Liverpool fan for anything in the world and one day I hope my son feels what I feel every time he puts on his match day shirt.

The Netherlands 1988
Richard Hall

Ruud Gullit, Frank Rijkaard and Johnny Bosman. Yes, Johnny Bosman. At the beginning of June 1988, these three men were key to Dutch hopes of winning the European Championship in West Germany.

At the beginning of the decade, the celebrated 1970s side had faded away, replaced as is often the way in footballing nations with small populations, with an inferior crop of players. The Dutch game was no longer cutting edge, tactically, evident in the subsequent failure to qualify for the finals of World Cups in Spain or Mexico. The 1984 European Championships in France, which was won by a Michel Platini-inspired home team, showed that others had picked up the mantle of sophisticated, progressive football relinquished by the Netherlands after their World Cup final defeat in Buenos Aires in 1978.

That same year, Ipswich Town emerged from the footballing backwater of Suffolk to win the FA Cup. Bobby Robson's team had improved by the time my father took me to my first game, at Portman Road, in 1980. It would be facile to say that my five-year-old eyes were dazzled by the elegant passing of Dutchman Arnold Muhren or that my mind appreciated the tactical control of his compatriot Franz Thijssen. For me, falling in love with football engaged more straightforward senses and emotions. I associated football with the weekend, with family, with leisure, with good times. But watching two foreign players week in week out, and then seeing Town pit their wits against the likes of Widzew Lodz, St Etienne and FC Cologne in a successful UEFA Cup run, raised my sights permanently towards events on an international stage.

As it happened, half-term family holidays coincided with the build-ups to the World Cups of 1982 and 1986. I spent these holidays poring over World Cup previews and rehearsing the action in the garden. I wrote in my holiday diary on 3 June 1982: "We listened to the football. Finland v England. England won 1-4. Paul Mariner scored two and Bryan Robson got two." Clearly I was taking a keen, if not particularly prosaic, interest in England's preparations for Espana '82.

The colour, drama and exoticism of World Cup football were far more appealing to me than English football. By the end of the tournament in Spain I was hooked. By the end of Mexico '86 I was obsessed. No sooner had Jorge Burruchaga scored the winner in Mexico City than I was already waiting for the next major championship.

Sustained by World Soccer magazine and small morsels of Football Focus coverage of PSV Eindhoven and Ajax, I was fascinated by the players who were helping the Netherlands qualify for Euro '88. After emerging undefeated from their qualifying group, in which they scored 15 goals and conceded just one, the Dutch were the only novelties in the eight-strong field. Apart from Jack Charlton's familiar Irish lads, the rest of the finalists had travelled to Mexico two years previously.

As hosts, and World Cup runners-up, West Germany were favourites. But they weren't in the Netherlands' group, and I figured that the Dutch couldn't meet them until the final. Italy were also favoured, but their team was an unfinished piece of work, designed for completion two years later at Italia '90. The school playground was sure that England, West Germany or Italy would win. I wanted to be different. I tipped the Dutch. I didn't know then that their manager, Rinus Michels, had been in charge of the great Ajax side of the early 1970s, or that he took the Netherlands to the World Cup final in 1974. But I did know about Ruud Gullit. And nobody else did. He had been voted world player of the year by *World Soccer* in 1987. But the playground was still reading *Shoot* magazine. I knew about Frank Rijkaard, and thought it strange that he had played so little club football for Zaragoza in Spain, after falling out with Ajax. Struggling for match fitness, his place in the team was far from assured. As was that of Marco van Basten.

At 23 years of age, van Basten had acquired a reputation as a remarkable goal scorer – having netted 151 goals in 172 games for Ajax, and scored the winner in the European Cup Winners Cup final in 1987. Along with Gullit, he won the Italian league championship with AC Milan just before Euro '88, but an ankle problem had limited his contribution. With van Basten injured, his successor at Ajax, Johnny Bosman, had scored four goals in five qualifying matches – and had his five goals in a qualifier against Cyprus chalked off after a bomb incident led UEFA to annul the match. When the squad was announced, Bosman was handed the number 9 shirt, and would start as first choice. And then there was Arnold Muhren.

You may think that I was proud that one of the Dutch team had played for Ipswich Town. Not so. I was mortified that an ageing player that had represented a by now much-reduced Ipswich Town could make it into my Dutch team. "They can't be that good if he can still get in the team," said the playground. But as the tournament kicked off I was confident. I had never seen the team play and, with the exception of Muhren, had not seen any of them play for their clubs, even on TV. But I had faith in the idea. I had read about the 1970s. I had read about Gullit, Rijkaard and van Basten – and Bosman.

But after their opening match reverse at the hands of the Soviets, the school playground seemed to have called it right. Bosman fired blanks, and van Basten came on as a sub to no avail. Now I had a problem. England had also lost their opening game – against Ireland – so when Bobby Robson's boys took on the Netherlands in the next match, the loser would go home. I knew who I was supporting. I was relieved when England twice hit the woodwork with the score at 0-0, then ecstatic when van Basten, selected in place of Bosman, scored a hat-trick in his team's 3-1 victory. The Dutch were second best for much of the game, but the decisive moments broke for them. Van Basten was back and I was vindicated.

Yet progress to the knockout stage was not assured. With eight minutes of the final group match against Ireland remaining, the scoresheet was blank and the Dutch were heading home. Desperation had taken hold when sweeper Ronald Koeman's scuffed effort bounced onto the head of Wim Kieft. Kieft nodded the ball goalwards, and it arced around Packie Bonner, spinning into the corner of his net. It was the type of goal that you would have expected the direct style of Ireland to produce. But Michels didn't care. And neither did I. They were through.

It is a myth that this Dutch team produced just stylish and technical football. Midfielders Muhren, Gerald Vanenburg and Erwin Koeman, along with full-back Berry van Aerle and Ronald Koeman delivered a regular supply of crosses and long balls, looking to exploit the height of van Basten and Gullit. Yes there was excellent possession and build-up play, but they knew how to mix things up. Unlike the 1974 version, this Dutch side would not sacrifice all by sticking to Total Football principles. They were resilient, and did what it took to win.

The next match, the semi-final, was more than just a game. Johan Cruyff's swaggering team had tried to make their West German hosts beg for mercy in the 1974 World Cup final. But they failed to build on a second minute lead, and after Paul Breitner matched Johann Neeskens' penalty, Gerd Muller's winner trumped the Dutch. Fourteen years on, Michels now had the chance for redemption. I was interested just in the football, but it was clear from TV pictures that the atmosphere seethed with a hatred that ran deeper than the game itself. The humiliating German occupation of the Netherlands in the Second World War was, I understood, at the root of Dutch venom. The methodical West German extinguishing of Dutch hope and self-respect in the 1974 final made this worse.

Now, again on German soil, the Netherlands willed victory. This twisting of football, politics and history produced a match unsurpassed in my 13-year-old memory. As in 1974, the teams traded penalties. With two minutes remaining, the Dutch produced a breathtakingly simple winner. Ronald Koeman fed midfielder Jan Wouters, who split the West German defence with a pass to van Basten, who guided his shot between the legs of Jurgen Kohler and into the corner of the net. Revenge, redemption, and a place in the final.

Gullit's header and van Basten's volley saw the Dutch claim the trophy, as they eased passed the Soviets. But it was the semi-final victory which stayed with me most. The controlled, technical skill that produced the winner, amid the Hamburg maelstrom. It turned out to be the second match of a great Netherlands-West Germany trilogy. Drawn in the same qualifying section for Italia '90, the Dutch topped the group, though both meetings between the two teams ended in draws and both qualified. But part three came in the round of 16 in Italy. After three unconvincing draws, the Netherlands and Ireland qualified with identical records in second and third place in a group topped by England. Lots were drawn and, while the Irish went to Genoa to play Romania, the Dutch were drawn against their old foe.

In their San Siro home, the Netherlands' AC Milan contingent met West Germany's three Internazionale players, Andreas Brehme, Lothar Matthaus and Jurgen Klinsmann. While Klinsmann's career-defining performance saw him bag the opening goal, and Brehme curl in the decisive second, the Dutch mustered just a soft penalty converted by Ronald Koeman. They were as listless then as they were vibrant in 1988; as fractious as they were once united and as resigned to their fate as they had been bent on determining it. Van Basten, goalless in four games, epitomised his team's woeful tournament. He would never score a World Cup finals goal.

But I prefer to remember 1988. What is striking now, watching the matches again, is the team's tactical flexibility. Three at the back against England – Rijkaard, Ronald Koeman, van Tiggelen – but a back four, with van Aerle dropping deeper, against West Germany. Switching between the two systems in the same game. Gullit either drifting wide, dragging away defenders, and leaving the space for van Basten, playing through the middle alongside his Milan team-mate, or dropping deep between the lines. They may not have played the pure passing football of today's Barcelona, and were not afraid to mix possession football with the direct approach, but the team retained the watermark of Dutch football – the intelligent use and creation of space.

I didn't understand all this in 1988. But this team started my appreciation of the Beautiful Game, beyond the mud, the fury, the violence, the long ball, the insularity and the tactical straitjacket that characterised English football in the latter part of that decade. It fired my interest in history and politics. And my playground predictions came to pass.

After Euro '88, Gullit, Rijkaard and van Basten combined to help Milan secure back-to-back European Cup wins. Their posters were on my wall. The same cannot be said of Johnny Bosman.

Middlesbrough 1996-97

Dan Clark

Let me get one thing straight. I am not from the North East. I'm not even from the North. I'm originally from South East London and a Spurs fan by heritage with a sprinkling of Millwall added in for good measure.

I am, however, a fan of the team that used to set the imagination of a dreaming 13-year old on fire. That team was Bryan Robson's multi-cultural, swaggering, avant-garde Middlesbrough, a side packed with style and panache with stellar names such as Juninho, Fabrizio Ravanelli (the White Feather) and Emerson. Even Nicky Barmby seemed exotic playing among this lot. And they played with style. Bags of it.

On top of that, this was a side under Robson that managed three Wembley finals, albeit losing ones, between 1996 and 1998. The great tragedy was that they were relegated in the 96-97 season after being deducted three points, bringing the curtain down on one of the most colourful chapters in the Teessiders' history.

This period also sat against a fascinating shift in our nation's political landscape: the boom of the Premier League and its increasing vibrancy seemed to merge with the arrival of New Labour in 1997 and its endless sound bites and spin. I could stretch it as far to say the two were a perfect marriage. On one side of the marital bed, New Labour with its relentless optimism and major investment in public services and on the other side, the Premier League with its growing self-confidence and let's be honest, growing self-importance, fuelled by Sky's cash. This was also the era of media-spun 'Cool Britannia', with the likes of Noel Gallagher and Vivienne Westwood smooching up to Blair and company at Number 10 wine parties. And who could forget that iconic Vanity Fair issue in 1997 proclaiming just that – 'Cool Britannia' – with Liam Gallagher and Patsy Kensit on the front cover?

It was as if the nation was being re-imagined, undergoing a dramatic identity transformation. And this was no different with the national game. Except it was becoming an international game. Britain was finding its voice again and the Premier League was one of its noisiest agents. As the country changed with new cultures and communities arriving through the late 90s, so did the Premier League. The feel and the look of the place changed. Things could only get better, right?

But back to Middlesbrough. The coming together of this outrageously talented team was something to admire. And they had goals in them. They were the highest-scoring team outside of the top seven with 51 goals and yet they were still relegated. Ravanelli smashed in 16 goals, including memorable hatricks against Derby County and, on the first day of the season, against Liverpool in a pulsating 3-3 draw, while Juninho chipped in with 12 from an attacking midfield role.

Yet this team spoke about much more than just flair and football that was easy on the eye. It represented a watershed moment in the Premier League's history, epitomising its aspirational quality. It married the industrial with the fantastical. It said if you want to attract big names and play exciting football then it is possible with ambition and desire. It confidently proclaimed that if you want the monotonous to be extraordinary, the parochial to become box office, then this is the league, this is the country, to do it. It set the tone for a series of flamboyant names to grace the top flight. The likes of Okocha, Djorkaeff and Campo at the Reebook, Di Canio and Berkovic at Upton Park and Dugarry at Birmingham.

The Middlesbrough side demonstrated that the smaller teams of this country could deliver imagination and colour. It didn't matter that a lot of the names were coming to the end of their careers and the medals in the cupboard had come from abroad. No – rather it showed that the Premier League was heading to the top. Serie A at this point was still the big dog in Europe, while La Liga was the home of the purist. But there was no doubting that the Premier League was fast becoming the entertainer's league, where tactic-less, dreamy, end-to-end football was emerging as the norm, rather than the exception.

And it wasn't just the football on offer. Even the stadium had a modernistic, free flowing feel about it. The Riverside, or Cellnet stadium as it was known back then, opened in 1995, looking like something from the future. Executive boxes, all enclosed, curving roofs and stainless steel vistas aplenty. I was a teenager obsessed with stadiums. I even owned a manual called 'Britain's football grounds from above'. I used to get in trouble in lessons for doodling in the back of my textbooks, scratching out a vague representation of Old Trafford or Wembley. So when The Cellnet arrived, it truly seemed like a glimpse into the future. This was a time when new visionary grounds were popping up across the country in the wake of the Taylor report. The Reebok opened in 1997, again, all elegant angles and sloping roofs. Sunderland's Stadium of Light and Derby County's Pride Park also sprung up around this time. Old Trafford underwent dramatic changes with mammoth stands suddenly soaring into the sky. Even Milwall's The New Den emerged not far from where I was growing up. I was transfixed by it all and again, it seemed to marry with the transformation of the political landscape: the country's footballing landscape was changing.

I got my first taste of the Riverside in the 07/08 season when the Juande Ramos Tottenham era arrived to a great fanfare of noise and expectation. But by this stage, so many of Britain's new grounds had taken on the identikit look of the Riverside that there was little charm to the trip. And we could only scrape a one-all draw, setting the tone for a disastrous nine months under the ineffectual Spaniard.

With the analysis of a 29-year old man, the thing that still sticks out about that Boro side was its otherness. From the Brazilian samba swagger to the United Nations identity of the team, everything about it felt forward thinking and revolutionary. And they loved goals: they entertained us all with the second highest scoring match of the season, a 6-1 demolition job on Derby County. For the anoraks' sake, if you really want to know the top scoring match that season, well it was Newcastle United against yes, you guessed it, my beloved Spurs in a rampant 7-1 win up at St James's.

Boro also lost a lot of games; often heavily as well. But they entertained. And this was an era, don't forget, when Vinnie Jones could still be found ripping up the turf down at Selhurst Park and Big Dunc Ferguson was smashing heads up at Goodison. So Middlesbrough's distinctly Latin feel was a breath of fresh air to a still overwhelmingly nationalistic division. And it's not to say there weren't other teams that entertained that year. Middlesbrough's Geordie rivals up the road were banging them in for fun that season, while Southampton and Matt Le Tissier were on fire and Benito Carbone's Sheffield Wednesday weren't shy of the net either.

While the likes of Ravanelli, Juninho and Emerson lit up Teesside, it's worthwhile mentioning the workmanlike players that played their part behind the scenes: The Clayton Blackmores and Curtis Flemings. There was a young Mark Schwarzer learning his trade while the long serving Robbie Mustoe provided a link from the side's recent anonymous past to its sudden thrust into the spotlight.

This was an era when the arrival of foreign talent set the pulse racing. In today's game, the foreign export is as common a sight as seeing a two-bit 'ethnic' tattoo on a Saturday night in Middlesbrough town centre. Torres to Chelsea for £50m? Yawn. The Silvas, Dembeles and Hazards? Minor pulses on the radar. They are now the norm. But back then, the emergence of the sophisticated foreign footballer was new and genuinely caused palpitation. It also helped Middlesbrough's cause that they were backed by an ambitious and wealthy owner in Steve Gibson. The arrival of the Juninhos and Barmbys for around £5m apiece constituted pretty hefty sums of money in the mid-90s Premier League.

But the telling conclusion of this side came in the form of a messy relegation at the end of the '96-97 season. The real tragedy of course, lay in the fact they were relegated on the basis of a technicality. Middlesbrough had failed to field a team against Blackburn at short notice after a flu virus had ripped through the squad. The result? A three-point deduction from the FA, which ultimately sounded the bell for this gifted side. Harsh as it seemed to me as a dreamy 13-year old, in the cold light of day and the even colder lens of a cynical 29-year old man reflecting on these events, the FA had no other choice. That a team which had lavished millions on assembling a squad could fail to field a starting XI was a damning reflection on the true lasting value of the vision projected by Gibson and Robson. It confirmed that the project had shallow foundations and was never built to last.

For Middlesbrough fans, the '96-97 season was the ultimate encapsulation of what it is to be a football lover. The highs and lows, the euphoria of naked ambition and then the sudden, forced removal of your hopes that relegation brings. Throw into the mix two heart-breaking losing Wembley finals in the FA Cup and League Cup and you've got a positively schizophrenic season. In a way, it mirrored Cool Britannia. It wasn't built on solid foundations. It was actually a lot of fluff. But it was also a lot of fun while it lasted.

It would have been fascinating to see how this team could have developed without the relegation as it led to losing the crown jewels of Juninho and Ravanelli. But for one season, I fell in love with the dream of how a side could fashion itself with the backing and the vision, and in this one season alone, Middlesbrough's impact on the Premier League had me hooked.

France 1998

Laure James

France's 1998 World Cup-winning squad only managed to follow up their phenomenal triumph with a limp Euro 2000 title.

It had neither the art of the new, nor the sensational impact of French football truly arriving among the best on the planet, as one might expect when one's nation wins back-to-back tournaments. Two years after the immodest revolution of France '98, David Trézéguet's extra-time winner against Italy instead marked an interminable canter toward mediocrity, which has since only shown withering signs of being overcome.

It may have been short-lived, but it was soulfully long-lasting.

I was 13. I wanted to be an economist, a politician, an opera singer. To think France's World Cup win would give impetus to my slowly improving footballer's technique was logical. The fact it would leave a stinging, creeping interest in football journalism was utterly unpredictable.

Maybe it was their minimalist, crushingly effective style. Far from the most flamboyant team in French history, coach Aimé Jacquet hedged his bets meticulously. His assessment of the opposition was clinically comprehensive, yet his conclusions were straightforward enough to translate into a game plan, sustainable for 90 minutes. He spied Brazil's relative ineptitude when defending set pieces – that was, most still believe, all he needed to do to seal his legacy.

Maybe it was the cultural element. Not the way France swelled with fervent infatuation, not the way this bordered on mania. Not the way France, for the first time, was represented in a multicultural sense.

Instead, the way football was first regarded as soft democracy, how it spurred the country to become supportive of a new France, celebrating heritages and giving immigrant groups, regrettably victimised as a result of *l'integration*, a French identity, as well as recognition of their own.

President Jacques Chirac admitted he wished he had been a goalkeeper, while Prime Minister Lionel Jospin was telling anyone who would listen that he once was. Such was the influence of football on politics, Jospin referred to himself as: "a combination of Jacquet and [Zinédine] Zidane."

Perhaps it was simply the ardour and idolisation of watching the driving 4-3-1-2 formation, along with being stunned at times at how an exceptionally good side carried its one lax striker, Stéphane Guivarc'h, and singing La Marseillaise with slightly better recall each time.

Such was Guivarc'h's ineptitude, he stood out – rather than remained anonymous – and even now tops lists of greatest flops with moderate regularity.

The squad also featured four Premier League players and this was keenly noted, since I lived in England at the time. They included West ham goalkeeper Bernard Lama and Arsenal's supremely consistent Emmanuel Petit.

Then there was Zidane; the Italy-hardened man performing at his peak and tipped to become the star of France, although never the star of the tournament.

He was everything I remember being told I ought to be more of at school; Focused, conscientious and precise, leaving the showboating and drama to those who could only talk the talk.

I would never pretend I achieved this, yet like innumerate teens I emulated him. He had perfected the balancing act of affording great loyalty to his Algerian roots and ensuring every one of France's 58 million people in 1998 were absorbed by the pride he showed in the jersey.

None of his off-pitch qualities were lost, each grasped and valued.

Much of the attraction rested on the passion shown by the players. Having scored the golden goal to take France into the final eight, centre-back Laurent Blanc was dismissed in the semi-final after Croatia's Slaven Bilic fell to ground – protesting he had been smacked in the face. Replays showed any contact was below the neck (who's bitter?), but Blanc's suspension from the final is still regarded as among the most unfortunate of absenteeisms. "It's like having tasted the cake, but not being allowed to touch the cherry," Blanc complained.

Then there was the final itself. Conspiracy theories still circulate as to why Brazil, and Ronaldo in particular, failed to contain France for even a portion of the game. He'd been drugged, some claimed, while others said his turbulent love life interrupted his mind and caused him to be completely eclipsed by Zidane.

The showdown was at Stade de France in Saint-Denis, the very stadium around which France had centred its bid to host the tournament. July 12, 1998, two days before Bastille Day.

To get there, France had cruised through to the group stages with three victories and defeated Paraguay in the knockout stages, on golden goals.

It was nail-biting beyond belief, however, come the quarter finals. Failing to score against Italy, as well-organised as they were, made me fear the worst and depending on Roberto Baggio to miss a penalty was behind-the-sofa viewing.

A win over the recently-formed Croatia had then taken France to the showpiece. The final whipped past in a blur overall, but the moments when the ball went out of play – even after Zidane's first-half brace – were torturously long.

Technically, I remember this game as a full introduction to how to watch football with an analytical eye. It was my graduation from the salt and pepper cellar explanation of the offside rule.

In defence, the offside trap was used effectively in the second half of the final game, and the marking was almost exclusively man-to-man. Didier Deschamps played as the anchorman in front of the defence. There were flourishes of measured and controlled skill; heading, passing, individual technique and positioning. There was great support from the midfield and attack while even goal-scoring opportunities were approached with level heads. There was an emphasis on wing play and in switching the point of attack, particularly on the right side to take advantage of Thuram's advances up the pitch.

Even though I was enjoying a break from school, this was a superb opportunity for note-taking and even now, along with the relics of my first (dreadful) published match reports, filed three years later, I still have these incoherent observations. I tend not to look at them too often.

Camp, misplaced and very, very kitsch, French fans adopted Gloria Gaynor's "I Will Survive" as their theme to sing at both tournaments, but it was boomed by tens of thousands at every game – a clamorous and melodically unruly parade, but paradisiacal for the team who beat the world without a striker and for the teenage girl who preferred cricket to football.

Broadcast journalist Stéphane Meunier's intimate documentary, *Les jeux dans les Bleus*, stirred my new interest in the sport hopelessly deeper. Meunier followed the team's progress through the tournament, creating a Gallic *Friday Night Lights* which showcased Jacquet, the players and backroom staff as beautifully committed, endearing individuals.

Meunier risked his professional reputation, not to mention having to awkwardly negotiate his cameras in the dressing room, in the event of a failure in Jacquet's finely-tuned management, with the film. But it's human, behind-the-scenes qualities made me think carefully about the media's role in football.

Like France's later international performances, Meunier's *Les jeux dans les Bleus 2* was rather prolix and vapid, but by then I was considering whether note-taking, press conferences and statistical homework would represent my career.

Of course, they went their separate ways.

They went on to become scouts, managers, Premier League development chiefs and even jujitsu champions, in the case of left-back Bixente Lizarazu.

As far as I'm concerned, they're no longer a team, either. They're the men who bore new identities for France, and for me.

Juventus 1996
Stefano Gulizia

If, as Velimir Khlebnikov suggests in his lyrics, colour is an unthinkable scandal, why try to think it? Why try to speak about it?

"Colour has not yet been named," Derrida observes in *The Truth in Painting*. What truth, then, can there be in colour?

The first time I saw Juventus playing, at the time of Boniek and Platini, the black-and-white jerseys faded into the sepia Fiat models produced in Poland and into the bright metals of the Lada vehicles (in blue, yellow, and red) that were diffused in the territory of the former U.S.S.R., while the last of the Agnelli monarchs – Gianni: the impassioned self of a true dandy – would imagine himself into a gallery of visible signs: green chair, green closet, green-cushioned stools, all adumbrated in a green garden.

Why isolate the status of footballing colour circa 1990s (indeed the status and colour of one team in particular) and turn it into an object of study when there are so many more compelling objects of study in view, objects like the technical revolutions in Manchester, the consolidation of oil capitalism in soccer, the institutionalisation of the Milan Lab and the expansion of its empire, the reification of "race" as a way of classifying people among hooligans, shifts in the ways sexuality was aligned with gender and nationality? There are two compelling reasons.

The first is registered by Derrida in his observation that "colour has not yet been named." Pharmaceutical disputation in the era of Dr. Ventrone, the man who made Del Piero's veins pop ahead like an Egyptian cobra, is a type of colour that forces us to consider the limits of sport and the extent to which we can say that all meanings and positions on the pitch are textual (or tactical) meanings. Wittgenstein is famous for emptying out the content of colour names in the notebooks he kept while resident at Oxford in 1950. With all of his interests, Wittgenstein did not occupy himself with football. And yet, I wonder, how would he learn the meaning of colour names in the successful run of Marcello Lippi's Juventus? In everyday life, after all, we are surrounded by "impure colours" and yet we have formed a concept of "*pure* colours" and given them precise names.

Take the full-back – one of football's most exacting approximations to a pure colour. Juventus had the utilitarian kind (Pessotto: an instrument for thinking, hidden from the world at large), but also Moreno Torricelli – fierce-looking like Verdi's Attila in the orientalist opera, razing on the right lane like Tamerlane or a dashing Cossack – who was always regarded as all the more powerful by virtue of being aware of his own limitations, as someone to be held at bay, as potentially inimical to the self.

Vialli and Ravanelli, however, would be Wittgenstein's favourite example. Some people consider a striker in football to be a primary colour, located between the lines of defence and midfield like green between yellow and blue, whereas Wittgenstein himself sees blue and yellow as "opposites" so that "green is one special way-station on the coloured path from blue to yellow." But perhaps that seems so only because the schematic colour wheels of the 4-4-2 system tells audiences that Vialli and Ravanelli were opposites, respectively second and first striker, while on the pitch they pushed such questions to their logical limits – always dangerous and always the first to defend, making of an attack an holistic threat. Striker-as-seen and striker-as-named remain two separate entities, the first a matter of sensations, the latter a premature simplification of footballing logic.

Marcello Lippi approached tactics with a similar scepticism about categories. Juventus in Lippi's view is an antagonistic phenomenon which resists in history by virtue of being placed as criticism's usual reference point: accordingly, one can only place the team by placing it wrongly. In one particularly rich area of football, the midfield, Lippi brought together different colours, the major and minor musical scales, utility and warrior types (Di Livio and Conte). To think of a midfielder as a fixed entity or character, to say that a particular player belongs to the minor mode or the major, might have been good for Jugovic, but in general, for Juventus, it would be to make the same mistake as assuming that individual colours have a fixed character independent of their context. The fact that you are using both Deschamps and Paulo Sosa, or both Zidane and Davids, licenses no conclusion about their effect in the overall picture.

What is needed in all these cases is an approach that acknowledges the difference between sensations and the premature simplifications of any passing chalkboard. Juventus's philosophy was never just about *what* it is achieved, but also on *how* one must speak about it – it was a way to begin by learning a method of tackling. The presence of different *foci* of playing in Lippi's squad functioned as several mines under the town: a vast network designed to tap the veins of purplish anthracite coal that spread weblike throughout the Piedmontese county of the Serie A and that had been burning since its inception.

Edgar Davids was the perfect embodiment of Lippi's tactical green thumb, and his predilection for the 3-4-1-2 shape. His skin was made of black honey and yellow resins; he possessed the "playful facility" of demigods in the natural world, and you could see him as the "wine-dark sea" of ancient Greek poetry. Davids set up a model of football perception in which subjects and objects exist in a dynamic, evolving state.

Fewer and fewer players – among them, his teammate Montero – have since been able to play as though they *were actually there*, in each part of the field, and to play detached from all the surrounding as if blind to certain individual colours (as you can see, Davids' glaucoma is not merely a deficiency or an accident). By virtue of his entropic movement, the Dutch player was able to introduce harmonies of colours *into the things themselves*, and these harmonies possess great charm, and an enrichment of nature that football has almost forgotten these days.

As for Zidane, in acknowledging the power of human imagination to transform the world, he simply played to effectively reject Kant's distinction between *noumenon* and *phenomenon*.

The cultural implications of the disjunction between football-sensing and football-naming are vast. The Italian establishment delights in postulating a society in which everyone is red-black or blue-black colour blind or belongs to a totally colour-blind tribe who ridicules normal-sighted people on the stadiums. No less interesting in the period was Arrigo Sacchi, who had a different "geometry of colours" than we do and could only think about players in terms of the shapes in which they are naturally set to occur on the pitch.

Clearly, Lippi's work was a way of confronting the resulting aporia. Do we sense more than we can say? Do we sense only what we say? Such issues point to the second reason for studying Juventus in the 1990s. The *bianconeri* made it impossible to separate subject from object. In part, this happened because the green of the vegetation was in their eyes, or, in other words, because every single player was able to perform as if he was pushing back to the time when Adam started naming things and to the expulsion from Paradise of Adam and Eve (the banishment to a comparatively colourless world).

Every action unfolded like an ellipsis of violet, buttercup, lavender and lime. The result was not just knowledge of a strange footballing object perceived, but rather a blend of joy and fear: pleasure in the sense in which Nietzsche discusses the term *Genuss*–"perhaps it was only in this way that mankind first learned to take *pleasure* in the sight of existence." Shade after shade, it was only in the peculiar stadium ability to distinguish bright from dark, a sensitivity to light rays at 510-570 nanometers (the green-to-yellow range), that Juventus's disquisition on colours forced us to recapitulate, in ourselves, this evolutionary process in football.

Olympique de Marseille 1991

James Longhurst

First, a confession.

I'm a Wimbledon fan. In fact nowadays I'm an AFC Wimbledon fan and Trust member, and when asked to write on the team that made me fall in love with football, it was perhaps naturally expected that I'd plump for the '88 cup final team.

It would be pretty easy to write a piece extolling the virtues of that legendary (in almost every sense of the word) Crazy Gang team, but I was only seven at the time of final and while I remember it clearly, that's probably as much from the amount of times I have rewatched my VHS, DVD and now Sky+ versions of the game as from any contemporary viewing.

And it's also because I didn't watch the '88 cup final live, my mum wouldn't let me. THERE, I'VE SAID IT. It's a horrible confession that I don't think I've ever shared with anyone else.

She wouldn't let me watch the game (we had friends staying over and we went out for the day) and we didn't even go and watch the victory parade through the town centre the day after. To say I haven't forgiven her for it would probably be harsh, but ultimately true.

So this piece isn't about May 1988; that penalty save; Sanchez's header or how hard it is to believe that I once looked up to (literally and metaphorically) Dennis Wise.

For most football fans I know around the age of 30, Italia '90 will probably always be the best World Cup. It was our first real experience of the tournament in all its glory and (forgive the cliché) it's true you never forget your first.

For those who can't remember, it must be hard to imagine how comparatively starved of football we were in the early '90s compared with the fest of overblown delights we get now. Those of us who were nine years old in the summer of 1990 were about to have our tiny minds blown by a veritable feast of football. The team that really made me fall in love with football wasn't the England team of Italia '90 either, though again it would be very easy to wax lyrical about fond memories of Gary Lineker's goals, David Platt's volley, Mark Wright's bravery and Steve Bull's substitute appearances and they certainly helped the process of my ongoing infatuation with the sport along.

Italia '90 exposed this young boy to a world beyond English football (by then I'd actually been to Plough Lane to see the Dons and even stood in the Shed End to watch Chelsea play Stoke in the second division, pink panther inflatables and all). Cameroon vs. Argentina in the opener was a whirlwind of drama, exotic names and foreign football.

Cameroon shocked the world with a 1-0 win and I was hooked. The next four weeks of the tournament were a continuing education of football, geo-politics (It would be the last World Cup for a united Czechoslovakia and a divided Germany) and foreign players.

England's ultimate demise on penalties did nothing to dim my passion. The pain and disappointment (there may well have been actual tears) was magnified by the fact that the England player that had emerged as my favourite during the tournament, Chris Waddle, missed the final pen (in a clearly subconscious homage to Waddle I stepped up to take the crucial penalty in the inter school cup that year and blazed it over the bar too, unfortunately the only footballing lesson I learnt from England's number eight).

The Waddler, along with a few more exotic names, had caught my attention and in that pre-internet, pre-Sky age I now wanted to do everything I could to follow his fortunes.

In 1986, Bernard Tapie became President of l'OM, flushed with cash, political influence (the Major of Marseille helped him get the job) and the experience of leading teams to sporting success (his La Vie Clair cycling team won two Tours de France with Greg LeMond and Bernard Hinault).

Tapie took the well-trodden path to success by buying in big name players and coaches. It is worth remembering in those days that the three foreign players limit was in force in European competitions – the rule which saw Inter recruit the German trio of Brehme, Matthaus and Klinsmann and AC Milan the Dutch legends Gullit, Rijkaard and van Basten – Tapie eschewed the idea of a one country core and brought in a more eclectic mix of foreign stars.

So in 1989, Chris Waddle joined l'OM for a British transfer record £4.5m (which made him the third most expensive player of all time) and joining Waddle in that team were Ghana's Abedi Pele and Yugoslavia's (and my all-time favourite player to be almost named after a mythical beast) Dragan Stojković.

Two of my favourite players from Italia '90 were playing for the same team, alongside a player so good he was nicknamed Pele, so when the 1990-91 season started, a small boy in south-west London became an avid Marseille fan.

For your pre-teenage Londoner with an eye on the south of France there were few sources of European football news. The occasional *Shoot* and *Match* feature on Anglo-exiles and even rarer profiles of foreign stars had to be supplemented with weekly teletext updates of foreign league tables.

The only source of actual coverage though was the weekly smorgasbord of global sport that was the early morning delight of *Trans World Sport*, covering everything from handball to pelota and of course, continental football highlights.

Every Saturday morning while eating my pre-football Weetabix (nutrition being all important to Tolworth Tornadoes' no.3 even at that young age), I'd sit down and watch every minute of footage from France that *Trans World* would bring me. In a season when all-conquering Marseille had a team of superstars with 'Magic Chris' Waddle at their head, there was quite a lot.

The team that Tapie built was managed that season by the experienced Belgian Raymond Goethals and together they had brought together a side packed with talent. Players like the prolific Jean-Pierre Papin (his scoring stats are Steve Bull-esque, between the seasons of '89-92 he scored 38, 36 and 38 goals respectively and in '91 joint top scored with seven goals in the European Cup), Basile Boli, Jean Tigana, as well as a young upstart with an attitude problem by the name of Eric Cantona.

But it was Waddle that set the team, and my passion for them alight as, like a laid-back Lionel Messi, the Geordie former sausage factory worker tore French and European defences apart, scoring eight goals that season and setting up many more for Papin and Pele.

Waddle's initial welcome by the fans at the Stade Velodrome had been lukewarm until, in a game against Paris Saint Germain, he took a high ball into the area down onto his chest, flicked it over the hapless keeper on the half volley and, like a school boy in the playground, back-heeled the ball into the empty net.

From then on the fans loved him (Waddle came second to Papin in a poll of the most popular Marseille players of the 20th century).

As the Youtube footage bears out, Waddle's role was clear: to entertain. In his own words: "I was never expected to defend at Marseille; my role was to make goals for Papin and entertain."

Although Waddle may have taken that role a little too far releasing a so bad it's really, very bad single with teammate Basile Boli: (the only Youtube clip that will make you think Diamond Lights wasn't that ill-conceived).

Watching those occasional clips on early weekend mornings though, with the sights and sounds of the French stadiums (even the name Stade Velodrome was exciting and different) was captivating in a way that watching *Match of the Day* would and sadly now, can never be. Even the oddly remote voiceover (one bloke, one woman, both very posh) that was a *Trans World* trademark added to the mystique.

Waddle scored the crucial goal in the European Cup semi-final second leg against the Netherlands-led Milan team who had supposedly set out to beat the sense out of him. Rumour has it that when asked after the game how he managed to hit the ball so sweetly on the volley, Waddle couldn't remember it. He'd been hit round the head that often by the feisty Milan side he was suffering from memory loss, but the goal is well worth a rewatch; Papin's flick on and Waddle's first time hit nestling in the side netting.

As a foretaste of some of the controversy that was to surround the Marseille team later in the decade, the semi against Milan was odd. Not long after Waddle's crucial goal, Marseille fans stormed the pitch thinking the ref had blown the final whistle and as the fans were cleared, the floodlights went out. Milan refused to play on. Uefa handed the home leg 3-0 to Marseille, who won the tie 4-1 on aggregate.

Marseille were in the final for the first time and for me the best news was that it was being shown live on terrestrial TV in Britain. Finally, an opportunity to see a whole 90 minutes of Waddle, Dragan and Jean-Pierre.

Facing them in the final were Serbia's Red Star Belgrade, from whom they had recently signed Stojković. The Red Star team was packed with talented players who would become familiar names from across the former Yugoslavia like Siniša Mihajlović, Darko Pančev, Robert Prosinečki and Dejan Savićević.

This final couldn't possibly disappoint and I made sure that I let all my friends, who weren't as avid *Trans World* watchers and Marseille devotees as me, know that this was going to be the best football game they had ever seen.

I'd promised them football's juiciest apples, but unfortunately Red Star had other ideas. What actually happened was 120 minutes of Eastern European onions.

Red Star, as I fondly remember the commentator saying, set their stall out to play for penalties almost from kick-off. The game was terrible and ended once again with my team – and Chris Waddle's – losing on penalties.

In the second half of extra time, Marseille brought on Stojković, a penalty expert, but as the teams lined up to take the spot kicks he refused to take one against his beloved Red Star. As I was quickly learning is the way of these things, the Eastern European side slotted their five pens home with ease, while right-back Manuel Amoros missed the first spot kick for Marseille and they never recovered, losing 5-3. The only consolation was that I hadn't had to see Waddle miss a penalty again.

By the time l'OM returned two years later to win the inaugural Champions League final, Waddle had returned to England (the Marseille team that year had a 20-year-old Fabien Barthez in goal, no less annoying as a youngster, and was led by the ultimate *domestique* Didier Deschamps), the Premier League had launched and I had a Wimbledon season ticket, my attention firmly turned to footballing matters domestic.

I'd fallen out of love with the Marseille team by then, but when the match-fixing scandal broke and Tapie's full ref-bribing skullduggery was revealed, it couldn't tarnish the memories of the original cast. The team and players that made me fall in love with all that is exciting and other about football were Chris Waddle's 1991 Olympique Marseille.

Brazil 1982

Rob Langham

My first World Cup was Argentina '78, but as a nine-year old, the more scintillating and noteworthy matches involving the hosts – a delightfully easy on the eye victory over France, a shock 1-0 reverse against a Roberto Bettega-inspired Italy and the still dubious 6-0 shellacking of Peru – took place way past my bedtime.

It was a cornucopia of delights to be sure, and all the more so given that at that time, only the FA Cup and European Cup Finals, plus England v Scotland, were shown live on television in a given year. Nevertheless, my experience of the affair was a half-formed series of impressions backed up by statistical boffinry.

That the Brazilian vintage was ever so slightly unpalatable didn't help. Although more appealing than the grotesque wannabe Europeans of four years earlier, Cláudio Coutinho's tactics and approach still owed much to the old continent. A surly 0-0 draw with a low quality Spanish side and a 1-1 tie with a decidedly pedestrian Sweden in the group stage underlined the caution of the coach, subsequently burned in effigy on the streets of São Paulo.

The pace upped in the second round but the safety first management, the chill of an Argentinian winter and the deployment of a kit manufactured by the Europeans of Adidas seemed to obscure Brazil's true identity.

The international round-up page in *Shoot* had provided tantalising hints at the South Americans' mystique. With most players still home-based, the arrival of the Brazilians at a major tournament provided a touch of the unknown – while Europeans toiled in domestic action until just before the tournament, Brazil were immersed in a month-long training camp, kids on the Copacabana were rumoured to possess greater skills than Kevin Keegan or George Best and the sun-drenched Sugar Loaf provided a fashionable opposite to grey Europe, kind of akin to a second California.

Brazil were impossibly fashionable and they did things differently - so, after returning home from Mar del Plata with a disappointing bronze medal, the rumours coming out of the country in advance of the 1982 World Cup were more encouraging.

The golden-shirted squad holed up for four years, save for racing through a qualifying group that saw them gain a historic victory in the altitude of the Bolivian capital, La Paz.

For Tele Santana disregarded the cultural cringe of Coutinho – why ape Italians and Germans when the world's most skilful men are Brazilian? A 1-0 win in a friendly at Wembley in 1981 featured an outrageous swerved shot by the hitherto unknown winger Eder – a real provocation to wide-eyedness in this twelve-year old.

A year later, I settled down to the Spanish jamboree safe in the knowledge that matches all kicked off before the watershed and that I could gorge for a month. Early scheduling for the opener between Argentina and Belgium clashed with other commitments, so it was the fixture between Brazil and the USSR that finally converted me to World Cup football.

The Soviets were scarcely less appealing than the Latin Americans. In possession of two gold stars for a school project on the USSR – perhaps an early inkling of the political leanings that were to blossom half a decade later – I had never bought into the 'they're the enemy and they're all on performance-enhancing drugs' mantra of our commentators, 13 though I was.

At the time, it was Georgia that provided the lion's share of the *sbornaja*'s more talented players – Chivadze, Shengelia and Daraselia turning out alongside that future Ukrainian national team manager, and previous European footballer of the year, Oleg Blokhin.

The flaws that were to come back to haunt Brazil were evident early on – the tradition for comedic goalkeeping maintained as Waldir Peres spilled a speculative shot from Bal into his own net while the cumbersome and frankly un-Brazilian striker Serginho contrived to miss a sitter – perhaps time travel would have signalled to Santana the wisdom of a 4-6-0.

For the midfield was as sumptuous an array of talents as I have seen – Falcão, Zico and Eder were in turn supplemented by Socrates – still the most excitingly named footballer in history as well as the talisman from the 1978 side, Dirceu.

A feature of those World Cups was the long range goal and just as Arie Haan had thrilled me in '78, the Brazilians turned this match round with two eye-wateringly divine strikes – first Socrates skipping crossfield before unleashing one past keeper Dasaev and then Eder, teed up like a place kicker, thundering the ball goalwards and in. It was all unimaginably entertaining.

Dirceu actually performed disappointingly in that opener – so Toninho Cerezo, suspended for the first fixture, was recalled for the second match against Scotland. Nominally more defensively minded than his cohorts, he was actually about as defensive as Ronaldinho and ditto the two full backs Leandro and Junior, the latter developing a real taste for action in the opposition box throughout the competition.

A Scotland team with as much ability to call upon as at any point in their history – Dalglish, Wark, Strachan, Souness, Robertson, Archibald etc. – had hit five past New Zealand in their first game in Malaga, but the fiesta atmosphere of Seville would prove to be far from fitting surroundings against such venomous opposition, despite David Narey bending in one of *the* memorable World Cup goals to put them ahead.

Brazil roared back – Zico with a peach of a free kick putting them back on level terms before centre-back Oscar headed in. Then Eder was left in isolation to succeed with a ridiculous chip before Falcão made it four. Pundits were likening these Brazilians to their forebears of 1970 and it was clear that we were watching one of history's greatest teams.

A 4-0 victory over the hapless All Whites was an exhibition and Brazil were pitched into perhaps the Group of Death to end all Groups of Death – both Italy and their Argentine neighbours from across the

Uruguay river lay in wait, having stumbled only to second place in their groups. The venue for the three match mini-league was the unlikely backdrop of Español's Sarrià stadium – only a third of the size of the Nou Camp across Barcelona city.

With the Italians having surprised the *albiceleste* in the first match, the stage was set for international football's most fearsome derby and Brazil didn't disappoint. Although a Barcelona-bound Diego Maradona had theoretically strengthened the holders, who already boasted a squad including the likes of Daniel Passarella and an Ossie Ardiles temporarily exiled at Paris St. Germain due to the vicissitudes of the Malvinas, this Brazil were simply too good.

First, another jaw-dropping bender of a free kick from Eder crashed against the crossbar with Zico following up, then the much maligned Serginho nodded in a Falcão cross after a defence splitting pass from Zico, before Brazil's new talisman repeated the trick to set up Junior for one of the goals of this, or indeed any, World Cup. Maradona's sending off for lashing out at substitute Batista seemed a fitting conclusion to the assignment, although some subsequent monkeying around at the back allowed future Oxford United gaffer Ramón Díaz a consolation.

Sadly, that tendency to hang on to the ball and attempt to dribble or pass one's way out of trouble was no isolated aberration – and this lack of ruthlessness and hint of vulnerability were two of the reasons that made this Brazil team so appealing. With the midfield quintet about as interested in defending as they were in that year's inauguration of The Weather Channel, chances would always be afforded – and so it proved against the Italians.

It's still one of the mightiest of all World Cup encounters – Zico's turn and pass to Socrates provoking the immortal John Motson commentary on the summing up of the *Philosophy* of Brazilian football and the veins prominent on Falcão's neck as he brought the *Seleção* level for a second time are memories cast in gold.

But in between, a tyro by the name of Paolo Rossi swooped three times, most tellingly after a suicidally casual crossfield stroke from Cerezo and then once more as Junior decided to sit deep and play everyone onside. A horror of a miss from Serginho compounded the calamity and Brazil were unfeasibly heading home.

History now records that Italian side as worthy winners of the competition as they swept past West Germany in Madrid, but at the time not a soul thought them the best team in the world. Brazil's 1982 vintage may still be the best team never to win the World Cup. I was hooked from thereon in.

Hangleton Juniors 1989-90

David Hartrick

Sitting in my car I was contemplating a thought that has been nagging at me for some time now. Like a skipping record, it has forced its way into my conscience via repetition. Am I, like Danny Glover *in Lethal Weapon*, simply too old for this shit?

I thought this stress fracture on the bone in my heel would have mended itself by now. A few years ago it didn't seem to matter what the injury was, a fortnight off would deal with it. These days the injuries are more frequent, have far scarier names, last longer and seem infinitely more painful. True, I had enjoyed playing for my five-a-side team as ever, but the last 10 minutes had been agony as a Gremlin poked around the sole of my foot with a hot poker.

On top of the pain were the opposition, a team of late-teens with indie haircuts and stylings who had not been alive when the Stone Roses released their second album, never mind their first. At their age I was a washed out Umbro drill top and Puma Kings kind of guy, still am if truth be told, but they have chosen Paris Saint-Germain training equipment and boots so garish they would make Lady Gaga blush. I'll admit that I have succumbed to the whole under-armour revolution but whereas these lads could tell you how the material draws moisture away from the skin and helps muscle movement, mine just keeps me a bit warmer.

"...a bit warmer."

What have I become?

And so there it was again, that thought. Was I now at the point where it was time to stop playing regularly and sate the appetite with the odd 'kickabout' now and then? Not give up altogether *per se*, but accept being part of a team week after week was a slow way to end up walking with a stick.

Where once I would have played at the gates of Mordor in bare feet, now my first thought is to moan that it might rain. Where once I genuinely did a John Terry and played with a broken toe, nowadays I'm thinking twice if my hay-fever makes me sneeze more than twice in an afternoon. Throw in the tiredness, the weird strains, the kids who run past me and leave only a faint 'wooshing' sound and the fact that it's becoming increasingly difficult to just buy a pair of good old Puma Kings without bells or whistles or anything fluorescent, and my time may be done.

Don't get me wrong, I'm not some old pro lamenting a future life away from a game that became my day-to-day, but I have now been playing for teams on a regular basis twice a week for the best part of 25 years. I'm at the point where my knees are basically made of sawdust and Murray Mint wrappers, while my ankles perform a perfect Wilhelm scream every time I walk past the football boots I leave in the hallway. The mind is still just about willing, but the body? I'm just not sure anymore.

Besides the body there's the position. I'm an old-fashioned centre-forward and poacher – just ask Michael Owen how relevant they are nowadays. In eleven-a-side teams I don't work as part of a front three as a fluid and interchangeable forward anymore – and having a front two, even at park level, is so 1990s darling. At five-a-side I can still be a focal point but have to chip in defensively more and more as the teams we play adopt a theory of amateur total football. This means I find myself up front when the opposition attack and then in defence when we have the ball going forward. Pace used to be my strong suit, but now? Not so much.

I'm a dinosaur. To dip into the Hollywood analogy well once more, like John McClane was told in one of Die Hard films (which are in order 'good', 'bad', 'okay', 'hits a jet with a lorry' and 'a bridge too far') I'm an analogue watch in a digital world. I'm clinging on to the last vestiges of a once-passionate love affair with someone who finds me incrementally less attractive with each passing year. When I started playing, these moments felt like they were several lifetimes away but they are, to borrow a song title from a musical hero of mine, right here, right now. Where do I go from here?

How about right back to the beginning?

To be completely truthful, when I first started playing I absolutely hated it. The nub of the problem was that I just wasn't very good. Like Kerry Katona rejoining Atomic Kitten for the 2013 reunion tour, I was enthusiastic for all the wrong reasons and utterly lacking in talent. While Kerry needs the money for myriad tax-related, divorce and advertising-work-drying-up issues, I was following the urge all young boys feel to just 'fit in'. All the people I wanted to be friends with played football, so I had to as well.

By the age of eight it still hadn't clicked. I had long immersed myself in football culture via an addiction to *Roy of the Rovers* so severe I would ask repeatedly for his pineapple chew bar over all other sweet options. I loved *Shoot* and *Match* magazines and covered my side of the bedroom I shared with my brother with posters of the great and the good. League ladders were meticulously kept up to date, football stickers got, got, got and needed as required, but with the ball at my feet I was still pathetically useless. The following year I was finding my place in the microverse of Hangleton Junior School (situated in tropical Hove) but I still looked like a newborn foal walking on ice on the pitch. I was a 'tryer' and the world loves them, right? No, actually. Even less than it likes a nice guy; and my severe lack of talent was holding me back.

At home I was the youngest of three brothers whose main pursuit in the back garden gladiatorial arena was football. When your brothers can consistently leave you on your arse and open to all sorts of pile-ons, it's difficult to improve. At school, my friends had all grasped the concept that a ball can be kicked in a straight line and playground games wilfully passed me by with full lunch hours where I didn't touch the ball. I knew football, I could tell you anything you wanted to know as long as it had been printed at some point in the last two years' worth of *Shoot* magazines, but I couldn't 'do' football. Although I was obsessed I was not in love, but a breakthrough was coming.

By some miracle I was selected to play in a B-team of sorts in a friendly against Somerhill Juniors. When you reached your last year of junior school you could play for the school team and with a summer holiday still to go for me, a couple of these reserve games were played to check the runners and riders for the following term. I can only assume I was picked on the strength of my brothers having attended the same school and one of them making the team a few years previously, but regardless, most of my mates were playing so I gladly went along.

I remember very little of the game other than the moment things changed. I was brought off the subs bench in true 'Arry Redknapp style to run around a bit. With the mighty Hangleton-B leading, the ball broke to me around the penalty spot. I kicked it as hard as I could in the general direction of the goal and true to form, it moved about two feet in the wrong direction. As was the form in these games at the age of nine it was all about chasing the ball, but as it had come to me in the perfect position for the shot, my ineptitude had actually bought me some space. My own awful kick had taken the ball slightly wide when most had turned away or been expecting to block the shot. I chased and made contact with a clear path to goal and a keeper ahead who was watching his mum on the sideline rather then me. With a bobble, a bounce, a trickle and an apology on its way past the goalie, I had scored.

The feeling was incredible. Team mates jumped on me, the eight people watching clapped and I had actually done something worthwhile on a football pitch. The boy with a sheriff's badge of a right foot had scored. There were no action replays, no Scottish sexist saying "tack a boo sun", but this was a moment of bliss, and a moment I've spent the rest of my life chasing.

If that was the moment the love affair began, the following year was the time where I knew we'd be together forever. From the moment the ball crossed the line I was consumed with kicking a football in a glorious honeymoon period. Inside the house I had little foam tennis balls and a various doorways to act as makeshift goals. In the back garden I had mini-footballs, full-size footballs, flyaway petrol station footballs and jumpers for goalposts. Everywhere I went I was kicking a football and luckily, I had parents who indulged my addiction.

I improved through enjoyment. I returned the following school year a changed player, a striker no less, and first-choice striker for that exalted school team. I was always quick but now I was a bolt of lightning who could kick a ball straight. I scored in playground games, P.E., football practice and then my first, second, third and fourth school games. This was a buzz unlike any other, a heroin for the ages without the *Trainspotting*-esque misery attached.

Hangleton Juniors were the only team I have played for where every single person on the team just revelled in the sheer joy of playing. At the age of ten there is nothing to bring you down, even defeat feels like victory as long as you've played well. The exhilaration of playing for that team is the same feeling I'm still chasing the dragon for now. We won the Stearman Cup that year and only lost one game, I finished as top scorer and it was official – I had fallen for football. My last goal was the second of a brace I scored in the final and I can remember it as clear as if it was yesterday. Tim Proudlock picked the ball up in midfield, shifted it to Jonathan Mitchell (a second-half substitute on the day) who knocked it past the defender and then into my path. I galloped through and pushed it past the keeper, wheeling away long before the ball crossed the line with arms aloft and a cup in the bag. We had a team picture taken that day which I have kept, along with another taken at half time as we had a "just keep going!" team talk from our manager Mr Vine. It was a hell of a time and and a hell of a team. A life-changing experience I'll never forget.

At the end of that year, life really did change. The team split as people went to different secondary schools and I was moved with my family some 230 miles north to Huddersfield. The change of scenery was tough on me as a new kid in a big school, but one thing got me through – football. It opened the doors of friendship for me, gave me some sort of status thanks to my residence on the left side of Rastrick High School's midfield, and gave me somewhere to go where I could escape desperately missing Brighton and struggling with life in a new town.

That feeling of release is another reason I'm struggling with the thought of giving up. It is still where I retreat when things get stressful, even to the point of me now keeping a ball under my desk to keep my feet on and knock about when the situation demands I relax a little. On February 5 2011 my daughter Beau was born and as I write this now two years later, I'm pleased to report she has already mastered kicking the ball straight and doesn't throw like a girl. Football runs through my veins and the early signs suggest they're all present and correct in her. I only hope it gives Beau half the good times it has given me.

For many writing in this anthology and for most reading, there will have been a similarly cathartic experience from supporting a team or witnessing greatness. For me, it has always been about playing and always will be, and although I love watching as much as anyone here, given the choice, I will always opt to pull the boots on myself if given the merest hint of a chance.

And so we come back full circle to that thought, the one that had me looking out of the car window wistfully for a moment or two. Is it really time for me to think about knocking regular football on the head?

The weather.

The kids wearing stupid boots.

The injuries.

The dinosaur.

What do you think?

See you at five-a-side next week.

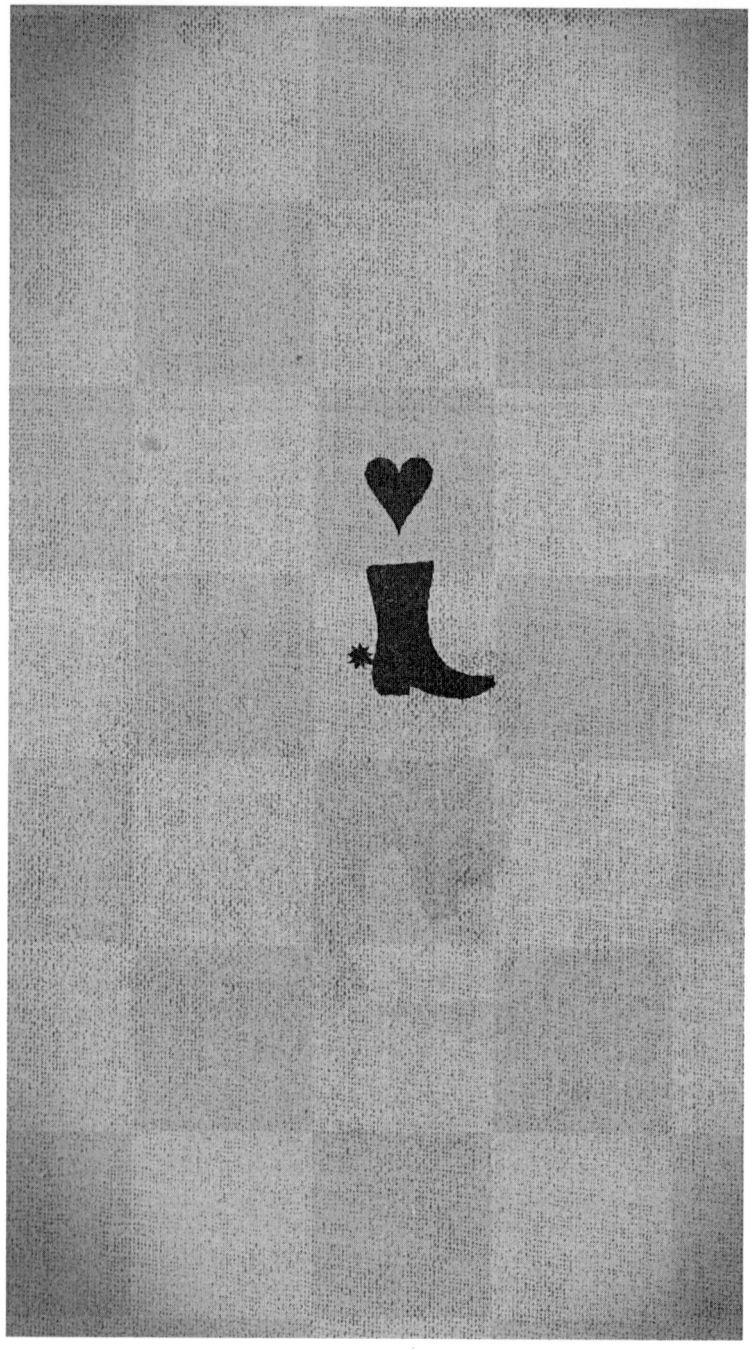

Tottenham Hotspur 1981

Ian King

At the start of the new term at Bush Hill Park junior school in Enfield in 1980, an ingratiating new teacher stood before a class of seven year-olds and called the thirty or so children to attention. "Right," she said, "Who in this class supports... Arsenal?" Thirty or so children kept their arms well and truly down. A couple of children at the back of the class booed under their breath. "Okay," she continued, "Who supports... Tottenham Hotspur?" Thirty or so arms – it might have been as many as forty or fifty – shot up in the air.

Living in Enfield will do that to you. The northernmost borough of London, Enfield is what might colloquially be known as, "Tottenham territory." Bush Hill Park railway station, a handsome red-brick building framed by trees at the heart of north London suburbia, is just three stops from White Hart Lane. Spurs, they may well tell you, is in the blood around those parts, and if it isn't, then it may well be in the genes.

As would be the same with so many other people, the fact that I ended up supporting Tottenham Hotspur was my father's fault. My sister, nine years older than me (and, in terms of playing the long game, it would seem somewhat mentally quicker on her feet), had chosen Manchester United from a very early age because she liked Bobby Charlton. I, however, was somewhat more sluggish in taking up the game and by the time I started to express an interest in something other than toy cars, the London A-Z and dinosaurs, the decision had been made for me.

Even by the age of seven, we hadn't lived in Bush Hill Park all my life. The first five years of it were spent in a block of flats in Lower Edmonton, just one stop on the train from White Hart Lane. We moved in 1977, when my parents' protests that having a teenage girl having to share a bedroom with a child that was clearly no longer a semi-sentient toddler was, well, weird finally gained some traction with the local council and we were moved into a new block of maisonettes a little further to the north. "We could see the White Hart Lane floodlights from our living room window there," my mum is still wont to say when we talk about that flat in Edmonton. I never stood a chance.

Fortunately, 1980 was a better time to be starting to support Spurs than much of the previous decade had been. Following the retirement of Bill Nicholson in 1974, the club had gone into a swift decline and a last day reprieve from relegation at the end of the following season proved to be merely a warm-up act for finishing bottom of the table in 1977. This, however turned out to be the hosing down that the club needed. Promotion straight back was achieved the following season and, under manager Keith Burkinshaw, the club stabilised with three successive mid-table finishes upon returning.

More importantly than this, a new generation of players had come through that was enticingly attractive to watch. Osvaldo Ardiles and Ricardo Villa arrived amid much fanfare in 1978, and they were joined in the summer of 1980 by the waif-like Scottish striker Steve Archibald from Aberdeen and a fresh-faced young forward from Stoke City, Garth Crooks. In addition to this, Spurs had their own one-club man in the form of long-time captain Steve Perryman and a lavish home-grown talent in the form of 'The Man That England Forgot' (which is, as anybody who knows that he won 53 caps for his country over the course of nine years, a myth), Glenn Hoddle.

This wasn't, however, a team without its flaws. By the summer of 1980, Spurs still hadn't successfully replaced Pat Jennings, who had left for Arsenal three years earlier, and had three goalkeepers – Mark Kendall, Barry Daines and Milija Aleksic – none of whom seemed particularly up to the task of helping to get the club back into, say, the top six in the First Division. Furthermore, while the likes of Hoddle, Ardiles and Villa had more than a flash of elegance about them, the same could hardly be said for Graham Roberts, for whom the kindest thing that I can think of to say is that he looks like *exactly* the sort of player who would lose three front teeth during an FA Cup Final and refuse to leave the field of play.

Possibly more important than any of this in my seven-year old eyes, the Spurs of 1980 dressed as if they were from the future. If the Admiral kit with big, flappy collars that the team wore between 1977 and 1980 was the sartorial equivalent of Dr Hook & The Medicine Show, its successor, designed by Le Coq Sportif and unveiled for the first time in the summer of 1980, was Visage, a shiny, minimalist v-necked shirt with the badge placed in the middle, and shorts so tiny that the more diminutive players, such as Steve Archibald, looked as if they weren't wearing any at all if their shirts were untucked.

This 1980/81 Spurs team was inconsistent in the league, eventually mustering a tenth placed finish in the First Division. The FA Cup, however, was a different matter. The fact that 1981 would be the one hundredth FA Cup helped, but the biggest frisson of expectation came from the fact that the year ended with a one. Local heroes Chas & Dave would later immortalise it in song, but it is worth remembering that there was a time when it was indeed lucky for Spurs when the year ended in one. FA Cup winners in 1901, 1921 & 1961 (amongst other years) and League Champions in 1951 & 1961, there was a feeling that there was something in the air that year.

Luck certainly favoured them in the draw, with four successive home matches against Queens Park Rangers, Coventry City and, somewhat improbably for a quarter-final match, Exeter City. They finally had to leave the sanctuary of White Hart Lane for a semi-final at Hillsborough against Wolverhampton Wanderers, where a last-minute penalty for Wolves forced a replay at Highbury in which Spurs finally brushed aside the pretenders from the Black Country with a comfortable win by three goals to nil. By this time everybody already knew that the opposition in the final would be an eminently beatable Manchester City side.

Beatable though City were – and let's not forget that "year ending in one" thing – Spurs themselves were far from invincible at the time. They won just two of their last fourteen league matches of the season, with Barry Daines getting injured and losing his place in goal to the relatively inexperienced Milija Aleksic. On a rainy May afternoon, I sat awestruck in front of the television as the two clubs played out a one-all draw at Wembley in a match which featured the singular feat of City's Tommy Hutchinson heading his team into the lead, before preposterously deflecting a Glenn Hoddle free-kick across his goalkeeper Joe Corrigan and in doing so becoming the first player to score at both ends of the pitch in an FA Cup final.

The story of the replay is well-worn enough to skip over in brief here. Ricardo Villa had been substituted in the first match and, after leaving the pitch in tears, subsequently managed to convince himself that he wouldn't be selected to play again in the replay. With Villa already having scored the first goal of the night, however, Manchester City scrambled their way to a two-one lead before Garth Crooks levelled up before, with fourteen minutes to play, Villa – with Steve Archibald standing on the right-hand side of the penalty area, completely unmarked and screaming for the ball – drifted through the Manchester City defence like a ghost wandering the corridors of a stately home, slid the ball underneath Corrigan and in and brought the FA Cup back to White Hart Lane.

There is a point during one's childhood at which you realise that those matches that grab your attention are the exception rather than the rule. Perhaps, for me, that moment came a year later when Spurs and Queens Park Rangers played out 180 fairly abject minutes as Spurs won the cup again. I was disappointed by my team's lack of elan over those two matches, but perhaps I shouldn't have been so complacent. In the 30 years since then, Spurs have only won the FA Cup on one further occasion – perhaps fittingly, when the year ended in one in 1991 and they chanced their way past Nottingham Forest in a match that is now most remembered for a horrific and self-inflicted injury to Paul Gascoigne after just 17 minutes.

Perhaps Spurs pulled the wool over my eyes by winning two FA Cups in my first two years as a football supporter. Perhaps, though, I pulled it over my own. A cursory read of the history books might have told me that, for Tottenham Hotspur FC, glory comes in a drawn-out series of fleeting glimpses and that the moments which lodge themselves in our memory are all the more special for their transience and rarity value. Throughout the 32 years since that class of school-children raised its arms in unison, Tottenham Hotspur have been occasionally delightful, frequently frustrating and occasionally baffling. It is an irony that perhaps would have been lost on the teacher, whose name escapes me through the mists of time, but the fortunes of that club and of the game in a wider context have taught me more about the nature of life than I ever could have learned in a classroom.

Chester City 2008-09
Richard Bellis

By all accounts, including my own, Chester City in 2008/9 were awful. Relegation from the Football League, despite there being four teams in the division that had been deducted points, was an impressively diabolical feat, but far from a pretty sight. The football was dull and even slightly depressing at times. No-one in their right mind would look forward to that weekly dose of utter ineptitude. Why, then, have I singled out this year over any other?

My brothers. It was their fault.

Family bonding through the medium of football is a cliché, but that's because going to the football is an easy, almost ready-made, way to relate to each other through a mutually enjoyable activity. Every match is a unique experience that you share with those around you and topics for conversation – the pies, the referee's bias to the other team, your striker's horribly coloured boots, oh, and the football – are right in front of you, staring you in the face. After the first few forays to the match, it develops into a habit, a habit that can create and strengthen relationships. The sport is basically a very handy tool for human interaction.

So it was with my two brothers. I have very different relationships with both of them. Neil is my identical twin and so, naturally, we are close (although don't tell him I said that; if he asks, tell him he's a prick). We grew up together and have shared some great experiences together. Gaz on the other hand, is nine years my senior and also severely disabled. While I was growing up I sometimes wouldn't see him for months at a time and it is also difficult to communicate with him unless the room is quiet. It's fair to say these are quite contrasting relationships.

But one thing we all enjoy is the football. Gaz actually introduced football to his little brothers before he was disabled, and my earliest memory is of him teaching us how to play in the back garden. There wasn't any parental influence or indoctrination of football in us boys as our parents didn't like the game. So, growing up in the '90s we were subjected to the growing hype and excitement of the Premiership, consumed without any kind of guiding hand. There were sticker books, making our own league tables, *Sensible Soccer*, pretending to be Michael Owen or Thierry Henry while playing football, France '98, reading *Match* and watching *Match of the Day*. This resulted in us supporting big north-west clubs (no, I'm not telling you which ones) and completely ignoring local football.

As for going to matches, that was an extremely rare treat. Our Uncle Rob has a passing interest in football and took Neil and I to a couple of matches at Liverpool and Manchester United. The visceral experience was amazing, although we were annoyed by the people who kept on standing in front of us, being, as we were, a fair bit shorter than the average fan.

Anyway, so far, so Rupert-Murdoch's-ideal-kind-of-fan. Luckily though, our Dad refused to buy Sky, which meant that we couldn't watch football very often on TV and develop into armchair fans. Instead, as we grew older, Neil and I slowly started to learn more and more about the lower leagues. This is a pretty organic process for all football fans, but it was aided by playing games like *Championship Manager* and watching the early rounds of the FA Cup on the BBC.

It was during the 2003/4 season that I first went to a Chester City game. Neil and I had noticed on *Sky Sports News* (when it was on Freeview) that Chester were top of the Conference and decided that going along to a match would be fun. Clearly, we had a strange idea of fun at the age of 13.

Chester City v Scarborough turned out to be the match that would win Chester the league, and it was mine and Neil's first at the Deva Stadium. Being completely unsure about what the crowd would be like, we arrived too late to get in as the ground was packed to capacity way before kick-off. Not wanting to phone up/annoy our Dad, who had agreed to drop us off and pick us up, and also hoping we would get in at some point, we sat on top of a van parked near one of the stadium's corners so that we could see in over one of the walls. The view was awful, we could only see a sliver of the pitch, but we celebrated when Chester scored and eventually, with ten minutes to go, a steward came out and finally let us in, along with the dozen or so people who were also on top of the van.

Thrilling. That's the only way to describe it. We were stood in the home terrace behind the goal that Chester were shooting towards. The crowd was loud, 1-0 up and singing the league title home. A shot clattered the board right in front of us, just wide. I couldn't believe how close to the players we were. At the final whistle there was a mass pitch invasion. We stayed in the stands for a few minutes, watched Chester lift the Conference trophy and giddily wandered out to our waiting Dad. We decided to go again when we could.

Unfortunately, circumstance meant it was a lot longer than we originally intended. We were attending a boarding school and had been for several years after the death of our Mum. That meant we were away from home a lot and when we did get back our Dad didn't want to ferry us around to the football every week – he had a business to run and Gaz to look after. It was only after a few years when we started weekly boarding (going home on weekends) and got weekend jobs that we were around enough and had the money to start going ourselves.

By this time we had been helping to look after Gaz for a couple of years. Neil and I always thought that he didn't have enough stuff to do, so we decided to take him to the football too, as we knew he'd enjoy it. Little did we know what we were letting ourselves in for.

We went to a couple of matches towards the end of the 2007/8 season, but it was the 2008/9 season that we started to go more regularly. As I mentioned at the start of the piece, the 2008/9 season was diabolical for Chester City. On the opening day of the season we were rogered 6-0 by Dagenham & Redbridge and things didn't improve much from there. Manager Simon Davies guided Chester to just three wins in the first 18 games of the season and was duly sacked for his efforts. The replacement manager was Mark Wright, in his third spell in charge of the club. He had previously won the Conference with City but could do nothing to prevent the slide out of the league this time, especially after the idiot chairman sold most of our decent players in January.

That, however, isn't the point. Yes we were rubbish, but us boys were gradually becoming fans of the club. We were lucky with the matches that we went to, as we managed to avoid most of the tonkings that Chester received at various points of the season and saw most of the team's decent performances. There was Kevin Ellison's early season hat-trick, Paul McManus' equaliser against Shrewsbury, a couple of wins over Christmas, a crazy last-minute equaliser against Dagenham and a desperate win at Accrington – all experiences we brothers all shared.

The best match had to be that draw against Dagenham & Redbridge. It was getting towards the end of the season and it was becoming increasingly likely that Chester would be relegated. For 80 minutes the performance was backing that likelihood up and it looked like the Daggers would be going home with a very comfortable 2-0 victory. But suddenly, inexplicably, Chester started to play well. A few chances were made and squandered before a corner from Ryan Lowe was powered into the net by the head of David Mannix (an awful, awful player). A few quick high-fives were exchanged before the ball was grabbed and escorted back to the middle by City's players – more out of fulfilling an expectation than actual belief they could get the equaliser. But get it they did. Lowe again provided the cross and this time Kevin Roberts nodded in. I was ecstatic, perhaps mostly through the sheer surprise of it all and jumped about like a loon, before nearly tearing my head off when Mannix missed an open goal which would have won us the game. Still, I went home in that euphoric mood that only getting an undeserved point out of a game can provide.

Of course, it wasn't all brilliant. Most football matches have large periods where not that much is going on and it was especially true if you were watching Chester that season. And yet we really enjoyed watching our local team. Slowly, we gathered our little rituals – finding the spot in the stand we liked, taking turns to go in with Gaz (for the free carer ticket), buying the half-time teas, reading *Deva Chat* – and began to become more involved with Chester City, to the point of stopping to care about the clubs we'd previously identified with, but only seen live on a handful of occasions. Neil and I went to our first away match on a cold Tuesday night at Shrewsbury's shiny New Meadow and took Gaz to his in the much more prosaic surrounds of Accrington Stanley's Crown Ground.

Overall though, our support was not enough to prevent Chester getting relegated. The relegation started the frankly stupid chain of events that led to Chester's liquidation around a year after that Dagenham & Redbridge game. But we're still fans of the club. It reformed as Chester FC and is now much more fun to support than it was in 2008/09. The two versions are virtually unrecognisable to one another, but whenever I think of why I support Chester FC, I remember the season we started taking Gaz to the local team. And, whenever I think of why I love football, I think of the local team, my team.

And my brothers.

Switzerland Schoolboys 1982

John Dobson

I'd been aware of football before, of course. It turns out that remembering things from the age of three is odd, but I do remember flashes of the 1978 World Cup. I remember grainy re-runs of Liverpool's epic European Cup quarter-final against St Etienne, which was brilliant and inspired a love of all things French.

Jumping forward and rapidly approaching my seventh birthday, I'd still not actually been to a game. I was aware of the football team in my home town, the perennially unsuccessful York City, whose ground was a 10-minute walk from home and which I used to pass while walking to school. The corner shop barely 50 yards from the front gate was where my younger brother and I would get Panini stickers and sweets on a regular basis. But the foreboding edifice was not one I'd got beyond, so their charms had yet to be spun on me.

My father was not a well man. Born with a curved spine, he was in pain pretty much every day from birth to his death almost four years ago as I type. As such, he was reluctant to go and sit for a couple of hours in a plastic chair inside a stadium that even in 1982 was probably past its best, just so number-one son could finally get the football experience he craved. There was plenty of it on television after all, and with front and back pages full of horror stories about the shenanigans inside and outside football grounds at the time, it was made plain that going to a game wasn't so much out of the question as to be completely insane. I devoured match reports though and even started writing ficticious ones, substituting my schoolfriends for the names of the York players.

By this time, my peers at school were already supporting teams. Liverpool were popular at the time because of their phenomenal European success, a fact which made Manchester United an attractive option being the contrary character I was then and remain today. I tried getting upset when United got knocked out of the cup by West Ham, but it just didn't feel right. I had to get to a game and it had to be at the one place I could easily access – Bootham Crescent.

My pestering paid off. The warm spring of 1982 saw the Swiss schoolboys team pay a visit to York to take on their English counterparts. The hooligan threat did not exist for this one – there had been a lot of trouble following a Hull City visit to the Crescent earlier that year – so my dad's list of excuses were reduced. He agreed and we went.

For a start, my memory is clearly playing tricks on me. I could have sworn it was a 2-0 England win, but painstaking research shows that it was 1-0. I don't know who was playing, I never kept the programme. What I do know is that I was gripped and utterly thrilled at the sight of this visiting bunch of foreign schoolboys from a country I knew only for its chocolate and neutrality in global warfare. The atmosphere was muted, but the very shy kid I was back then mustered enough enthusiasm to pipe up with a brief 'come on England' during the second half. It doesn't matter that I can remember so little about the finer points of the game, the makeup of the two sides and that I had even convinced myself the scoreline was different. This was real, this was football – and international football at that. What matters is that it was played and that I was there.

I often wonder what other details I've missed. Did I see a teenaged Stéphane Chapuisat or Kubilay Turkyilmaz? How many of those England players were in Turin eight years later? My level of obsession with seeming trivialities, which endures to this day, was high back then, so how on earth did I not end up bedecked in Swiss red and supporting FC Basel, Grasshoppers, Young Boys or the now defunct Neuchatel Xamax? Sadly, all of these questions will remain forever unanswered.

The record shows that Switzerland lost to Scotland in Airdrie on the same tour before a loss to Northern Ireland and two wins against Wales back at home – hardly earth-shattering. This isn't a team that will go down in history other than for the fact that they came to the UK in 1982 and got beat. But a skinny lad with bad teeth was incredibly grateful to them for just being there.

The game proved to be my gateway drug and truly was the appetite whetted. Months later, Spain hosted a World Cup with those magnificent Brazilians, a not-half-bad England side and Paolo Rossi, who I once dressed as for a church fancy dress thing, number 20 sewn onto the back of a generic blue shirt by my loving mum. A gangly youth with similarly thick eyebrows, I might have passed for the equally gangly Rossi's much younger brother, but I didn't win and still bear a grudge against the Catholic Church for this oversight. Still, as crimes by the church against young boys go, I got off lightly.

Still I was vulnerable to the curse of supporting a big club, but the deal was sealed a year later. Something was beginning to happen at York as Denis Smith put together a formidable side. In October 1983, my dad and I made our second and last visit together to the Crescent. York raced into a 2-0 half-time lead against Reading, only to see them blow it and draw 2-2. It was an early lesson that this whole football supporter lark wasn't going to be easy. My first game on my own followed quickly, a 7-0 thumping of Gillingham and that 1983/4 season wasn't a bad one to get a local lad hooked as York romped to the Division Four title with a then-record 101 points, the first team ever to break the ton – you can't take that away from us.

That Gillingham game was my first experience of the seething mass of humanity that was a 1980s football terrace, the heady aromas of stale beer, fags and testosterone pervading the atmosphere. Following promotion, Arsenal were beaten in the FA Cup via a dramatic Keith Houchen penalty and the club's fame was never higher. The come-down was hard and lasted almost entirely until 2012 and a promotion back to the Football League after eight years in the Conference.

In between times, I drifted away from the game. It was during my university years that I came back to it; perhaps the geographical dissociation sparking something, perhaps meeting people from all over the country and hearing them talk of their teams, their heroes and their memories brought it all back. Years later, I'd find myself writing match reports again, but not fictional ones. Real ones, for the real team and the club's official website.

As I write this, I realise I am the same age now as my dad was the day we went to the England v Switzerland game. That was the game that did it for me. Everything that has followed stems from that. Yes, my time spent in the Netherlands as a teenager lent me a tremendous fondness for all things Oranje and FC Twente, my time in Germany for Eintracht Frankfurt, but it would have been irrelevant were it not for that first trip behind the concrete wall that separates the Bootham Crescent pitch from Grosvenor Road to see what lay beyond.

Having no children of my own, I'm envious of other 37-year olds who are taking their sons and daughters to their first games and hope it leaves the same impression on them as that day did on me. I know I enjoyed it far more than my dad did and I'm aware he was racked in pain for days after as a result – I was too high on excitement to notice at the time. He didn't have to take me that day. He knew it would mean excruciating pain for him. But he did take me – I assume I was a really annoying child when I wanted something that badly – and for that I will always be grateful, and grateful to the Swiss FA for sending a team over and not objecting when their English counterparts suggested that York would be a suitable venue.

Lewes 2008-09

Stuart Fuller

This is the story of a first love, jealousy, betrayal, divorce and finally finding a new soul mate for life. You see, I'm a simple chap and I like my home comforts. I like things to be just so. I like Yorkshire puddings with roast beef and stuffing with my chicken, and never should the two mix. I like my music in its original version and not the Shep Petibone burglar alarm remix featuring some forgettable minor rap artist. I like my football at 3pm on a Saturday, unless I'm on one of my European jaunts when I want all the games to kick off four hours apart so I can cram in three games in a day.

I like what I like and change? No thank you.

But when it comes to pinning my allegiance to a team, well, let's just say that's slightly more complex. Born into a family of West Ham fans in the 1970s, I rebelled. I wanted to be Graham Rix (not something you really confess to in modern times, I know) and so I supported Arsenal. If people think Stoke City are "difficult on the eye" to watch today then you missed a treat with Arsenal in the seventies. It was pretty torrid stuff. My Dad, forced to take me to a couple of games at Highbury a season, used to dread having to drop my brother off at Upton Park where he'd be entertained by Brooking, Devonshire and the swashbuckling Billy Bonds, before heading to North London to watch Arsenal invariably fail to score.

Then in 1980 he was presented with his golden opportunity. The 10th of May of that very year would see Arsenal play West Ham United in the FA Cup final at Wembley. It was a formality for the Gunners, playing a Hammers team who were in mid-table in Division Two at the time. I was so sure that Arsenal would win I said that if West Ham won I would change allegiance and follow the family to the Boleyn.

Trevor Brooking and his ridiculously low header have a lot to answer for.

Today my father wheels out this story for all and sundry on a regular basis. As I point out to him I would have experienced a few league titles, couple of doubles, four FA Cups and a Champions League Final appearance if I continued to be an Arsenal fan. I console myself with the fact that I'm sure Gunners supporters are still insanely jealous that they didn't win the 1999 Intertoto Cup, West Ham's sole honour since 1981.

I was a man of my word and thanks to that FA Cup win I changed my allegiance. The following season I saw 48 West Ham games as they romped to the Division Two title, took the almost unbeatable Liverpool (how the world has changed...) to a League Cup final replay and reached the quarter finals of the European Cup Winners Cup (ask your Dad, kids). I was now for better and for worse, in sickness and in health, a Hammer for life.

I can still remember major events in my life based on West Ham games and the club itself. Missing an away game at Cambridge because I was a page-boy. Seeing my first ever fight at a football match at home to Sunderland. Fearing for my life in a crush at an FA Cup game at QPR in January 1988 when I have no doubt fans would have died if Loftus Road had perimeter fences. I lost my virginity on my West Ham United bed spread. I proposed to a girl on the way home from a 6-1 win in the cup versus Aldershot and she said yes such was her excitement from the game. I even took my daughter to her first ever match at Upton Park. You never forget those moments.

But things started to change five years ago. The cost of watching the Hammers was spiraling out of control, we were one of the most expensive teams to watch in Europe and believe me, I should know. The football on display under Alan Curbishley was dire to put it mildly, although I'd welcome him back today with open arms. By this stage I had bought a season ticket for my daughter in the Bobby Moore Lower and she was the coolest kid in class.

We had a great little set of fellow season ticket holders around us who would always look out for each other but as the price kept on going up they stopped going, replaced by a new breed of fan who thought every opposing player was a "cunt!". We moved our seats to the Family stand where the only difference was that the kids also thought every opposing player was a "cunt!" as opposed to it coming from just the parents. Reluctantly I knew it was time to reassess my parenting skills.

The Zola and Pardew eras were replaced by Avram Grant's. Dear God, what had we done to deserve this? It couldn't get any worse I thought. On the day our owners appointed Sam Allardyce I knew there was now no return for me.

But strangely I was okay with that, as I had already found a new love. I started dipping my toe into the non-league water when West Ham were away. When Sullivan and Gold rode into town to save us from a fate worse than death I decided that spending the best part of £1,000 a year wasn't going to deliver me any pleasure. Quite ironic when you consider how they have made their vast fortunes. Day one and they publically announced what a crock of shit they had bought and how the club needed the fans to spend more money. No thanks.

My adultery began back in November 2008 when an email arrived in my inbox from Danny Last, he of European Football Weekends fame. It was an invite to come and sample the delights of Lewes FC. Where? I had to look it up, unashamedly admitting I'd never heard of neither the town nor the football team.

The more I learnt about the team the more intrigued I became. Promoted last season to the Blue Square Bet Premier they immediately released all the playing squad bar one player, and then said cheerio to the most successful manager they had ever had. Bizarre to say the least. Just what sort of ambition did this club have? Little did I know where that first trip to watch them win a rare game against Grays Athletic would take me.

From the moment I walked into the Dripping Pan, part of me changed forever. It was so basic compared to what I'd been used to for years. There was terracing where you could stand and not be told to sit down by over officious stewards. And on that terrace people were drinking beer rather than being ferreted away in a cave far removed from the pitch. This was a different world. The players emerged from a strange looking building on top of a hill, walking gingerly down some concrete steps onto the pitch.

I saw a few more games in that ill-fated season as Lewes were relegated by Easter. The following year having given up my West Ham season tickets I became a regular home and away, experiencing football as I remembered it through rose-tinted spectacles, and more importantly how I wanted my young children to experience it. We went on day trips to places like Weston-super-Mare, Basingstoke Town and Bath City. Everywhere I went I met more and more Premier League exiles, enjoying their football more than ever.

Around Christmas 2009 the club announced it was in a spot of financial bother. It seemed the win-at-all cost promotion push a few years ago was now biting the club hard on the non-league-revenue-arse. This looked serious with winding up orders and final demands being the main topics of discussion. Then the magic of Non-League football kicked in, people rallied around, funds were donated and the club was saved from the brink.

That summer, a group of six converts to the game took over the club. Using the model adopted successfully by AFC Wimbledon, FC United of Manchester and AFC Telford, the club became community owned. They appealed for 'Pioneers', people who were willing to invest a minimum of £1,000 to become life members and rebuild the club from the roots up.

A thousand pounds or to put it another way, the cost of two season tickets to watch West Ham.

It was a no brainer. I was now officially a (part) owner of a football club.

The six owners revolutionised the approach to running the club. No one had a background in football, but all were very successful in their respective fields. The sole aim was to put the club back at the heart of the community. Alas, results didn't go the right way on the pitch and the club were relegated to the third tier of non-league football, the Isthmian league. Did I care? Of course not. I bloody owned a football club and I didn't care what ground I would be visiting.

I had been bitten by the football bug again and had fallen hard. Standing on a terrace, beer in hand, watching players who are playing because they love the game and not for the brown envelopes at the end of the rainbow. I even had players offering to buy me a beer after the game. There were people who wanted to hear your opinion, and I was meeting others loaded with similar stories about the good old days like me. No longer was football just about 90 minutes of normally pretty awful sport. For the first time in many seasons my whole weekend mood wasn't dictated by the poor performance of a handful of overpaid primadonnas. Football was making me smile again, I was back in love.

Slowly but surely I got more involved in the club. It started with writing for the programme and helping out on match day and not just by putting money over the bar. The new owners began to engage the wider community, making people realise that there was more to Lewes than just a love of bonfires (Lewes's November 5 celebrations are world-renowned festivals of fire). With the first anniversary of the club's move into community ownership they launched an annual share ownership plan and I was asked to become involved in driving community ownership high and wide. I loved the club so much that I wrote a book about my conversion from the Premier to the Ryman League.

In the club's first season back in the Isthmian, they secured the return of the most successful manager in their history. The return of Steve King certainly raised many eyebrows in the non-league sphere, and optimism was high for the first time in years. I was approached about standing in the first elections the club had held for the board. On a cold night on a work trip to Zürich, I found out I had been unanimously elected. My footballing journey from being a player, a manager, a coach, a fan and a volunteer had been completed. The day I was given my club tie was one of the proudest of my life.

All of a sudden my world changed. I no longer cheered when a centre-back hoofed the ball out of the ground, knowing that if it didn't come back then we were £20 down. All of a sudden I was no longer able to bet on the FA Cup by law. Was it fun? Hell yes and I was more in love with football than ever. Some nights in board meetings at 1am discussing the toileting provisions may not have been as glamorous as planning a trip to the Emirates, but it was far more rewarding.

Of course it wasn't all fat cigars and brandies in the boardroom. I've actually never worn that club tie, preferring to stand on the terrace with my friends rather than with the suits. I'm realistic enough to know that we will never reach the Football League, hoping every year we can have a cup run such as our good friends down the road at Hastings United experienced all the way up to Middlesbrough this season. Would I change our situation? No, although a few more pound notes over the turnstiles from new fans will always be more than welcome.

So that is my journey from falling in lust to falling in and then out of love, to finally finding the girl of my dreams in a small Sussex town. I went from the cathedrals of the sterile Premier League to the rough and tumble arenas of the amateur game. I don't regret walking out on my real love, not once but twice, as I found true happiness on the third occasion. If that was good enough for Liz Taylor, then I'm certain it will be good enough for me.

Sheffield United 1988-90

Ian Rands

Growing up in a two-team city is tough, more so when, for your formative years, your club is the lesser performing of the two. Seemingly in the minority; the playground jibes and hidden envy of relative success combined to make the 9:00 to 3:15 life of a Blades-supporting schoolboy in 1980s Sheffield much less fun than it should have been.

Although, in the first few years of my life, the Blades and Owls were in the same division, it all changed with the 1979-80 season when the other lot gained promotion from the Third Division. After fading away from a top three position at Christmas, United finished mid-table. They were a club on the slide and were relegated to the Fourth Division 12 months later.

A last-minute penalty miss from Don Givens, in the final game of the season, saved opponents Walsall and condemned the Blades to the bottom tier of English professional football for the first and thankfully only time in their history. I was there with my grandparents. I was five. The death of my grandad just a few days later meant that I was to see little live football over the following few years; such experiences reduced to my Dad taking me to midweek games in the school holidays.

Ian Porterfield took over as manager and steered the Blades straight back up as champions. Within a couple of seasons he had United back in Division 2 but, by then, Wednesday were in Division 1 taking on Liverpool, Everton, Manchester United. The Blades plateaued under Porterfield and his successor Billy McEwan fared little better, with United playing some of the worst football in recent memory.

It was following McEwan's sacking that United enjoyed probably the most exciting and successful period of my time watching them. It also coincided with me starting to regularly attend Bramall Lane;

as my Dad's changing working hours now freed up his Saturday afternoons. I wasn't just watching football on the television and attending the odd game anymore.

I loved the buzz of standing on the Kop every other week; stood swaying with crowd, surging forward, meeting the team as they bore down on goal. I was watching positive attacking and successful football. Yet, it could have been so very different.

The appointment of Dave Bassett as McEwan's replacement was not widely supported by Blades fans. He came with a reputation for direct, long ball football infused with a loudmouth barrow boy charm.

His managerial reputation, built steering the Crazy Gang of Wimbledon up the divisions, had been partially undone by a short and unsuccessful spell at Watford. Had he been the right man, with the right ideas, at the right time at Plough Lane and since found out?

Bassett did little to arrest the slide and United finished third bottom in the table, losing a play-off semi-final with 3rd Division Bristol City. United were back in the third tier. Going into the summer following relegation, Bassett tendered his resignation, thinking he had failed in his job. Thankfully, wise old sage Derek Dooley, then a club director, persuaded him to stick at it and bring us straight back up. "We hired you to do a job, I suggest that you go back to your office and get on with it".

Working on a shoestring, Bassett assembled a squad that, on paper, did little to raise expectations or potential excitement levels, but what did we know? What he did with his squad was create a mentality, a team spirit and a passion that was shared on pitch and terrace alike. There was a closeness between player and fan that seems unthinkable today.

Far from direct, United played better football than anyone ever gave us credit for. Bassett had a fondness for wingers and the diagonal ball from full back to winger was often played to perfection; the wingers laying on the chances for newly formed front two Brian Deane and Tony Agana. This was a strike pairing that brought together two players who complemented each other perfectly; one left footed, the other one right; one tall and the other less dominant in the air; both with a seemingly telepathic understanding of each other's movements from day one. Their marauding runs along the frontline pillaging goals not only for themselves, but pulling defenders around so goals were scored from elsewhere in the team. All delivered with pace, power and a fair degree of technical skill.

May 1989, a year on from play-off relegation despair, United returned to the Second Division at the first attempt, finishing runners-up behind Wolves. Bassett again wheeled and dealed over the summer, tweaking the squad where required, but nothing pointed to anything other than a season of consolidation. Again, we were wrong. I remember returning from holiday and hearing on the car radio how we had torn apart a fancied West Brom side at the Hawthorns on the opening day. That one result, not only gave the fans enhanced hopes, but it also instilled a great deal of self-belief in the players. If one of the favourites for promotion could be beaten 3-1 at home, who should we fear?

United challenged at the top of the table all season and entered the final game away at Leicester level on points with Leeds United, but needing a win to guarantee promotion with Newcastle breathing down our necks. The entire focus of Blades fans was on Filbert Street, but little did we know that events back in Sheffield were to make the day doubly special.

I was one of over 7,000 Blades fans at Filbert Street that day, part of a cavalcade of cars, minibuses, vans and coaches carry a human sea of red, white and luminous yellow - the colour of United's ubiquitous away shirt that season. After going one down early on, the Blades attacked Leicester at will, equalising and then racing into a 4-1 lead. Each goal was followed by a pitch invasion of exuberant Unitedites, many in fancy dress, some falling at the feet of the players in praise. A goal apiece in the second half was followed by one final pitch invasion as Blades fans celebrated at 5-2 win.

The fact that Leeds' 1-0 victory at Bournemouth guaranteed them the title on goal difference mattered little; promotion was enough. The joy in that away end was something I don't think I have experienced at a football match since and it was to become greater as news came through that a Wednesday defeat against Forest at Hillsborough, combined with results elsewhere, meant that Wednesday were passing us in the opposite direction. As the local paper headline announced that night: "Blades Glory, Owls Down".

On August 25 1990, I saw my team take on reigning league champions Liverpool at Bramall Lane, as the Blades played top flight football for the first time in 14 years. What followed that game was one of the worst starts to the season by any top flight club, but the passion and positivity never faded. On December 22 1990, with 16 league games played, United took on Nottingham Forest at Bramall Lane. The Blades sat bottom of the league with just four points on the board and not a win to their name. Coming from behind to win the match 3-2 kick-started the season and a miraculous escape from what seemed inevitable relegation was achieved. United, on just seven points at Christmas, eventually finished 13th on 46 points, nine points clear of the relegation places.

In three further seasons, United more than held their own with memorable victories over the big teams of the time; Liverpool, Manchester United, Arsenal and Spurs, the latter on the receiving end of a 6-0 thrashing at Bramall Lane. Wednesday had returned within a season and had reclaimed positional superiority, qualifying for Europe for the first time. But it mattered little. We were not just turning up in dutiful support of our club; we had a sense of pride, topped off by doing the double over Wednesday in the first top flight Steel City derbies in 23 years. Sadly, we couldn't do the same in the all Sheffield FA Cup semi-final in 1993, Wednesday winning 2-1 after extra time.

It all ended in tears. A final day, last minute relegation at Stamford Bridge was followed by an unsuccessful attempt to bounce back to the Premier League. Just over 18 months after relegation Bassett had gone; the initial impetus and impact having worn off. His methods not generating the same results.

People talk about the pleasure of watching the great passing teams and the Spanish tiki-taka, but what really excited me, what made football real to me, was watching a team being built from the ground up, with hard work, a great team ethic and an unrelenting willingness to attack the opposition with pace and power. They generated a spine-tingling visceral thrill as they bore down on goal and the opposition defence. A team driven by a passion to prove that the underdog tag was misplaced. For a while, they took on the bigger teams, the richer clubs with the bigger names and often won.

Those formative teenage years shape your outlook on life and define who you are in a number of ways. Passions start to run high, your emotions fluctuate violently and you experience many new things. You achieve a number of firsts; be it a season ticket, an away game, a gig by your favourite band and... well, I'll gloss over some of the others. As a teenage lad, I got my kicks from girls, music and football. The girls change, the bands come and go (sometimes returning 20 years later), but the one constant love was, and still is, football and my team. Sheffield United FC. Those late teenage years (The Bassett Years) embedded that interest in football as a passionate love of the game.

Swansea City 2000-01

Abigail Davies

Standing in a crowd of predominantly middle-aged men, I can easily recall the first moment I saw their passion, pride and love for 90 minutes, desperately seeking reward for their adulation and finely balancing potential jubilation with, quite often, despair and angst. And even though these sights were initially a little overwhelming, they were ones I soon wished to experience on a regular basis.

Football allows you to escape from your everyday life for 90 minutes; you are absorbed and its almost as if you enter a different world, albeit one, admittedly, where people accept that men can be paid £200,000 a week for kicking a ball.

Many, therefore, wonder why I love football to the extent that I do, with the disparities, let alone the displeasure and fury a defeat can lead to and not to mention the expense and the travelling required, but for me, football is like a relationship. No matter how angry it makes you, however many times you think, "I can't possibly go through that again", there'll always be that one moment where you're reminded just why you do it and think "I really do love you, Swans". More often than not during my first few seasons of watching Swansea City, this moment of spectacular, life-affirming flair was provided by Swans bona fide legend Lee Trundle.

Prior to my first live Swansea match, the majority of professional football matches that I had watched were televised Premier League games and I think that in many ways, this helped me to fall in love with the Swans and the "lovely, ugly Vetch" as it was so often described. It seemed that the more glamorous clubs were more distant from their fans and it was easy to tell instantly that we weren't like those clubs. The fans have a voice at Swansea City with 30% ownership and the understanding and respect of the fans is evident even when going to watch a match.

One of my very earliest memories of watching the Swans is not of a particular game, but is of the aforementioned Trundle. It was in a match of no particular significance, but one that profoundly sticks out in my mind due to the talents and trickery of a player who quickly established the nickname 'Magic Daps' for reasons apparent in an instant. The hush of awe and admiration that descended on the stadium when Trundle was in possession spoke volumes, as did many people's inability to find a superlative to quite acknowledge the supreme talents of a player who was little like the Vetch Field had ever seen before. His control and quick feet were mesmerising and after each moment, each half, each game, would leave you wanting more.

One of the first games that I remember the details of more vividly was in February 2005. It was a Friday night at the Vetch and it was against fellow League Two promotion candidates Southend United. That year, I experienced one of the greatest feelings ever. Promotion. Swansea City were to enter the third tier of English football. The club was seemingly putting behind them the traumatic times and had a good squad of players who were playing football the right way and continually improving.

It still remains one of my proudest moments as a Swansea fan. It may not be remembered as well or regarded as being so significant in our history as our promotion to the Premier League or THAT game against Hull, but it was the first major success I ever experienced as a Swansea fan.

You could see exactly what it meant to players and fans alike. A superb occasion. It was everybody's victory. We had stuck by our side through the most difficult days, seen the club sold for a pound and it felt like this was our reward for persisting and not giving up on Swansea City. It was worth the pain. It felt like we as a football club were able to deal with anything. From abysmal chairmen (Tony Petty) to the football game which would have, in my opinion, seen the club relegated from the Football League forever.

I learned very quickly that 90 minutes can shape your entire weekend and even the week that follows. Victory ensures hours of elation and the overriding emotions of pride and admiration for your club that make you feel like shouting your team's name and chants from the rooftops, whilst pouring a victory endorsed vino and looking where your team sits in the league table. One example of this – and another game that sticks in the memory – is our 1-0 victory over Tranmere Rovers in August 2005.

It was our first competitive game at our new stadium and our main aim for the season was to retain our League One status. We faced a Tranmere side who were looking for promotion to the Championship that season and I remember thinking that we had little chance of victory.

However, one of football's many beauties is that anything can happen in 90 minutes. Therefore, I arrived at the game optimistic that we could, at the very least, avoid defeat. We actually took the lead through new signing Adebayo Akinfenwa and despite Tranmere being awarded a penalty in the first half, remained 1-0 at half time and then, almost before we knew it, at full time too. Although we knew that a long, hard season lay ahead, everyone celebrated and felt proud as the win showed we were more than capable of competing at that level. We were proving that we had the credentials to stay in the division.

Defeats, which aside from making victories that bit sweeter, lead to an overwhelming anger and often a bitter resentment for the opponents and anyone who should ask how the game went, are part and parcel of the job, not that it makes accepting them any easier. But even in defeat, there can be small victories – not least the memorable feeling that you experience after a goal for your club.

To anyone without an interest in sport, goal celebrations are ludicrous and incredibly overstated, but for those thousands of fans inside the stadium, watching your team score produces a rush of adrenaline like no other. Euphoria! You want to scream, jump around, go mad, regardless of whether it was a scrappy goal or a wonder strike. Although not one of the earliest goals I remember, Ferrie Bodde's magnificent strike away at Preston in October 2008 is one of the best Swansea goals that sticks out in my mind.

The Swans had just been promoted to the second tier of English football and everyone was on a high. Preston had not been defeated at home on a Tuesday night in seven years, but Bodde's goal from

40 yards out inspired us to end this record. Bodde is one of the most naturally gifted players I have seen in a Swans top and I still think that had his career not been blighted by injuries, he'd have set the Premier League alight.

Though, as is the way in football, this is often balanced out against the feeling of conceding. Letting a goal in is without a doubt one of the worst feelings to experience. Each time we concede I get a sinking feeling in my stomach, regardless of whether our opponents are Manchester United or Torquay United. Even goals, albeit for very different reasons, are unforgettable – at once the best and the worst parts of any given game.

Local derbies have an equally divisive quality and they too personify many of the factors involved in making me both love and loathe football. Particularly when your rivalry is as keenly felt as that of South Wales.

When in the Championship, the first games to look out for when fixtures were released were Cardiff City home and away. The nerves felt in the build up to and on the day of a South Wales derby are like no other. The want and will to claim the right to state your superiority over your main rivals causes tension which is not eradicated until the 90 minutes are up (and sometimes not even then).

When the final whistle is blown and you have been defeated on derby day, it can initially feel like you've been relegated until you are able to look at the bigger picture. However on the reverse, if you claim derby day victory, there is nothing else in the world that matters. You feel as though you've just won the Premier League. The only negative, of course, is that the intense rivalry can often be taken too far. You can't help but feel football suffers enough these days without its own fans feeling the need to put the boot into each other.

Nevertheless, the turbulent times at Swansea and those first, early memories of watching them during some of their darkest days are what makes our rise through the divisions, envied style of play and recent success so encapsulating and enjoyable.

The familiarity of attending, the family that you feel welcomed into, the big stands and terraces, new grounds that you visit, heated debates and the common ground we can all share of celebrating a goal like a crazy person – all reasons I initially fell in love with football and why the love affair continues.

Linfield 1988-89
James Young

It was all a very long time ago now. And it happened so fast. One game, it feels like, though of course there were others. The goals are on YouTube, just about, but there are no elegiac documentaries, no rose-tinted interviews with those who played, no balmy broadsheet retrospectives about this team. If it felt at the time that a little bit of history was being made, history, it seems, has moved on, left the game and the players behind.

These are footballing memories of a distant childhood in a time and a place which no longer exists, at least not in the same way as it did then.

To begin, a non-footballing memory.

It is after dinner. We are watching Blake's 7. Or at least I am watching Blake's 7. My father, who is in the RUC, a *peeler,* is grouchily rattling the pages of *The Belfast Telegraph*, irked about something or other. In those days, there was always plenty to be irked about. My mother is fussing in the kitchen. My younger brother is pushing his Matchbox cars around the carpet.

My mother comes in from the kitchen.

"There's two men out in the street, Billy," she says.

"Get down on the floor and turn out the lights," my father says, "and turn off the bloody TV too." The paper crumples to the floor. The standard lamp is behind him and when he stands a great shadow is cast across the room.

"No way," I say, "*Blake's 7*'s on. Blake's going mad at Avon."

"On the floor. Now."

There's a tone in his voice of gravel and grit and fury that I know well enough. I get down on the floor and crawl around behind the sofa to where my brother is already hiding. My mother turns out the lights.

Did it really happen? My mother tells me it did. But telling it now, it seems impossible, like something from a film. These things didn't happen to us. We were middle class. We lived in leafy South Belfast. These things happened up the Falls or the Shankill or in Andersonstown or far away in Derry.

In the end, nothing happened that night, or any other night. Whoever the men were, they weren't brash enough not to be worried about witnesses. And they or their bosses were smart enough to know you didn't gun down an entire family in cold blood if you could help it. Bad PR move, that. Although it didn't always seem like it, politics lurked somewhere in the background.

My father went to the phone, called a few of the neighbours. Asked them to go out into their gardens, talk about the roses or the weather or football. They did. The men bottled it, drove off in a screech of tyres.

Probably my brother and I didn't know what was going on. In any event, we didn't really talk about it, not that I remember. The next day we got up as usual, had breakfast as usual, and walked a half mile down the road as usual, before my father came roaring down the street in his battered yellow Volvo to pick us up and drive us the rest of the way to school. We had to walk a bit first, you see, in case there was a bomb under the car.

Everything was back to normal.

Anyway, I digress. Back to the football.

I suppose this story started in Albania. The first football match I went to was Linfield vs. 17 Nentori in a European Cup first round game at Windsor Park. It was the September 29 1982. Linfield had lost the first leg 1-0 the previous week in Tirana, but would surely win the second leg comfortably. After all – Albania? Where the hell was Albania? Somewhere east of France, I knew that much.

My father took me. We didn't pay – my father punched the other *peeler* on the gate faux-chummily on the arm, grinning and saying "let us in there handsome". He was well known, my father, and not always in a good way. The policeman didn't look very happy to see him. But he let us in anyway.

I was 10 and it was very cold and everybody smelt of cigarettes and booze. I think I probably started wanting to go home around the 10-minute mark. I would have been well advised – 17 Nentori scored after 28 minutes, pretty much killing the tie.

When the goal went in my father – who didn't much like Linfield – jumped up from his seat and cheered. "What a load of shite," he shouted, or words to that effect, "come on the wee Albanians!" This was in the middle of the Troubles and also around the peak of the football hooligan years. A few people near us made threatening noises and a big man with a red face stood up and came towards us. My father told him to sit down in a way that let the man know that the alternative to sitting down wouldn't be much fun. The man sat down.

That was my introduction to football. Linfield were losing and my father was going to break somebody's legs. Things looked bad.

Here are some other things I remember about watching football in Northern Ireland in the 1980s (as glorious as that moment in Spain in the summer of 1982 was, it was as fleeting as a bright glint of sunshine on a slate grey February afternoon).

Going to The Oval for Big Two derby games against Glentoran. The games were good at Windsor Park too, but Windsor was bigger than The Oval, and the fans were further apart, especially after they built the new North Stand, which had bright red plastic seats and seemed as shiny and modern as a Gehry museum. The Oval was better, because it was going into enemy territory: three quarters of the ground were a low bank of terracing; the Linfield fans filled one side and the Glentoran fans filled the other, half of which wasn't terracing at all, but was (and still is) just a big lump of grass. Between the two fans there was an empty bit of terrace, fenced off to keep the two tribes apart. Except that was the only bit of terrace with a roof, and under the roof was a layer of chicken wire, so what happened was that young (and some not so young) boys would get lifted up and would climb through a hole in the chicken wire and crawl across the no man's land until they were over the opposing fans and then chuck stones or bottles down at the raging mob beneath them. It all seemed great fun at the time, but then I was 11 or 12 or more or less and didn't know any better.

The songs, which were exclusively about how Roman Catholics (Fenians, in the parlance of the day) were a bad lot, and how great something called The Sash and some battle that took place in 1690 were, and other such gibberish, because Linfield were the best Protestants in the world anywhere and everybody else was Catholic and therefore to be despised, even Glentoran, who were generally all Protestants too, except they weren't as good at being Protestants as Linfield, or something. It is shameful now to remember that I lustily sang along with such tripe, but that was the currency of the times and as I say, I was 11 or 12 or more or less and didn't know any better.

Taking my cousin to see Linfield play Larne at Windsor Park. He was a huge, bearish New Zealand copper, schooled in rugby league and union and other such legalised brawling. We sat mostly in silence throughout a typically joyless top flight Irish League fixture, our hands pressed under our legs against the cold. Afterwards I asked him what he thought.

"It was ok," he said. "Bit rough for my tastes, though."

Tiki-taka, you'll understand, was some way off.

Linfield vs. Donegal Celtic, Irish Cup, 1990. Not necessarily a happy memory, but one that has never gone away. A lower division side, the famed three men and a dog would have represented a bumper windfall at the ticket office for Celtic. But when drawn against Linfield in the Irish Cup, the game suddenly took on a whole new dimension, and 'sympathisers' from both sides came out in their thousands. I've lived in Brazil for the last eight years, but even taking into account South American footballing fervour, nothing can match the madness of that day. Even watching the ITN news report on YouTube today sends a shiver down the spine. *"Jesus there's lads up on top of the floodlight pylons! The Linfield fans are chucking rocks at the Celtic fans! The Celtic fans are chucking rocks at the Linfield fans! The peelers are firing plastic bullets at the Celtic fans! There's a riot going off on the Kop!*

There's a mad Linfield fan on the pitch going after the Celtic players!"

"This could get really out of control," the fella beside me said in the middle of all the carnage, his definition of "under control" presumably being somewhat broad.

Great days.

I was lucky in one way though, for Linfield had a terrific side then. In those days, if you played for Linfield or Glentoran, there really wasn't anywhere else to go, so you ended up staying your whole career and becoming the stuff of local legend. Roy Coyle was manager for 15 years and won 31 trophies. Martin "Buckets" McGaughey played 533 games and scored 317 goals. Goalkeeper George Dunlop also played more than 500 games, and skilful midfielder Lee Doherty spent 14 years at the club. Then there was captain Lindsay McKeown (known as The Elephant Man by opposing fans due to his rugged good looks) and his brutish partner at centre half, David Jeffrey, now the club's manager. A little later, in 1989, young sweeper Noel Bailie made his debut. He would hang up his boots in 2011, a paltry 1013 club appearances down the line. These players, and others like them at clubs across the country, such as Alan Paterson and Jim Cleary at Glentoran, or Felix Healy at Coleraine, would become as much a part of the firmament of the Northern Ireland landscape as the cranes of the Harland and Wolff shipyard or the gable end murals of working class Belfast streets.

It wasn't a very cosmopolitan place in those days, Northern Ireland (a pause here for the reader to compose him/herself after this shocking revelation). McDonald's (that symbol of sophisticated style and grace) didn't arrive in Belfast until 1991 – a year after a branch opened in Moscow, and a mysterious foreigner was somebody up from Dundalk. Occasionally, you'd see a family of black people wandering around the city centre. It was only after you'd seen them a few times you'd realise it was always the same family.

Which, finally, is where we get to the point. In the summer of 1988, Linfield, not always the most progressive, go-ahead of clubs, did something very strange. They signed a foreign player. Weirder still, they signed two. And they were Africans! This, you'll appreciate, was not entirely typical Linfield behaviour.

Antoine Coly, a 24-year-old attacking midfielder, was from Senegal, and had previously played in Belgium for Club Brugge and then the somewhat lesser known Racing Jet Wavre. He had played for the national side 20 times, scoring "six, or nine goals, I forget how many," and was joined by his pal Abdelli "Sam" Khamal. At least it was assumed they were pals – they were both from Africa, weren't they? Sure, they must be mates.

The pair were not the first black players in the Irish League. Portadown's Joey Cunningham, who also played Gaelic football for Crossmaglen and Armagh, was around at the same time. And Ghanaian goalkeeper Tony Wilberforce played for Cliftonville in the late 1950s. There may have been others before him, lost now in the fug of time. But Coly and Khamal were perhaps the most high profile, maybe even the most exotic.

They enjoyed mixed fortunes on the pitch. While Khamal would spend the majority of his time on the substitutes bench, Coly quickly became a key part of a Linfield side hell-bent on retrieving the Irish League title from The Oval – Glentoran had won the league the previous year following a run of six consecutive Linfield triumphs.

Despite their success over the decades, Linfield did not always have a reputation for being easy on the eye. Which is where Coly came in. He formed an immediate partnership with Lee Doherty at the centre of midfield, spraying quicksilver passes through to the deadly, if slightly lumbering, McGaughey, and George O'Boyle, back on loan from Bordeaux, and clearly far too good for the Irish League. It may have been his colour, his European pedigree, just the fact that he was different, but Coly brought a little bit of style to Windsor Park.

As manager Coyle said at the time, "He doesn't have too many peers. He's a different player than the Irish league is used to. He'll do something in a second that nobody else can do in this country. It's a new dimension for the Irish League."

Unfortunately there were, and still are, plenty of people, and not just in Northern Ireland, who weren't great fans of the exotic. The Oval was the worst. At Coly's first game in East Belfast in November 1988 the pitch was dappled with hundreds of bananas, and the monkey noises rose darkly into the night. It would be easy, in a way, to call

Glentoran fans racist here, to pick on an easy target. But it wasn't just Glentoran fans. It was pretty much everybody, at least at the beginning. And had Coly been playing for Glentoran against Linfield, the abuse might well have been a lot worse. This was a disease of a time, and of a society, not of one football club or another.

And if it was worse at The Oval than anywhere else, it was because Glentoran had more fans than any of the others, and because Glentoran were the great rivals, the enemy. Which is why Tony's greatest moment in Northern Ireland could not have been better timed, or come at a better place. An Irish Cup third round "Big Two" derby at The Oval, in March 1989. The Linfield masses huddled at the City End, Glentoran fans on the steps and the muddy slope of the Sydenham End. To add spice to the occasion, if Linfield usually won the league in those days (and still do today), then Glentoran were the Irish Cup kings. The Glens had won the competition the previous four seasons, and hadn't lost a tie at The Oval for 13 years.

There were few, if any bananas that day. Perhaps Coly's novelty value had worn off, or perhaps his performances on the pitch had earned him a little grudging respect, even in East Belfast. Either way, Linfield tore the Glens to shreds. After half an hour, O'Boyle surged down the right and crossed onto the toe of the Belfast Niall Quinn, Stephen Baxter, who swivelled as slowly as one of those aforementioned shipyard cranes that rose like gallows behind the ground, before poking home. Then halfway through the second half O'Boyle (again) planted a perfect cross onto McGaughey's head for a 2-0 lead.

All that though, was just the cheeky little aperitif to Coly's *thieboudienne*. With the light draining from the sky, McGaughey found some space on the left and floated the ball towards Coly, 30 yards from goal. The Senegalese flicked it on to Lee Doherty, who then took a couple of steps forward before feinting and rolling a pass back to Coly, who without blinking hit a languid, spiralling arc, high into the right hand corner of Alan Paterson's goal. The Linfield end erupted, while the Glentoran fans drifted off slowly into the dusk. It wasn't the first time I'd seen someone do something beautiful with a football, but it was the first time that I'd been so close, and the first time that I'd heard it, or rather not heard it – that infinitesimal moment of silence from all present while the brain processes what the eyes have just seen, followed by the unbelieving, throaty roar of triumph. And all these years later, it is still the earliest moment of footballing sorcery that I remember seeing in the flesh.

It is not known how Coly and Khamal found life in Northern Ireland. Maybe they liked it well enough. An Ulster fry every morning, washed down with mugs of tea so strong the spoon would stand up in it, a few pints in Lavery's on a Saturday night, then a pasty supper on the way home. Could there be a better life for a (semi-) professional athlete?

Coly, who spoke no English before he arrived, certainly seemed happy enough in an interview halfway through that season. "Are you happy in Belfast?" he was asked. "Yes, very happy. I'm enjoying myself. It's Linfield. Linfield is very good. Glentoran? Glentoran is ok."

Either way, he was gone at the end of the season, back to somewhere in Europe, probably (I cannot remember and can find no record of his whereabouts anywhere). There was never really much chance that a player like Coly would spend the rest of his career in the Irish League. But for a while there, when Tony was playing, even standing with wet feet in the cold at one of Northern Ireland's grimmer footballing outposts (Newry or Ballymena spring to mind), it felt like there was no better place to be watching football.

Bulgaria 1994
Adam Bate

The event is the World Cup. The arena is the Giants Stadium in New Jersey. It's the 78th minute of the quarter final between holders Germany and the unfancied Bulgaria. Ilian Kiriakov has the ball on the far touchline. He passes the ball inside to Zlatko Yankov who lofts a hopeful ball into the German 18-yard-box. The balding figure of Yordan Letchkov hurls himself at it with the conviction of a man determined to seize the moment. Bodo Illgner has no answer. Germany have no answer. And Bulgaria, improbably, are on their way to a World Cup semi final.

For many, this was *the* highlight of the 1994 World Cup. It was Bulgaria's brief day in the New Jersey sun. An unexpected but joyous moment that had come out of the blue and would be consigned to viewers' memory banks once the tournament was over. But for the country of Bulgaria - and for me personally - the story of that remarkable triumph had begun four summers earlier in the June of 1990.

That year my mother and father had a brainwave. As working-class parents in the 1980s they had played their own small part in turning Benidorm into the cliché-riddled dystopia that it is today. But this was the 1990s and that meant a brand new start – we were going to Bulgaria. I'd love to think it was out of an intrepid sense of adventure or an emotional desire to visit the Eastern bloc after the falling of the Berlin Wall. The truth is that they'd heard it was cheap.

What we discovered was a fascinating country at an extraordinary time in its history. The month we arrived saw the first free-elections Bulgaria had experienced since before the Second World War. This was a nation shrugging off the shackles of communism and taking the first tentative steps down a different road. Bulgaria's Communist leader Todor Zhivkov had been in charge since 1954 and few knew what to expect next.

As a result, the practicalities of a communist society were deeply entrenched. Western companies had yet to make inroads there. As exemplified by attempts to purchase a soft drink – any soft drink – in a bar or restaurant. Wonderfully, the reply would simply come back: "Juice?" At which point a nondescript, but enjoyable, seasonal fruit juice would be produced.

With the concept of tourism in its infancy and the local currency virtually worthless, the price of goods was also difficult to comprehend. A loaf of bread cost the equivalent of one seventh of a penny and a bottle of wine around 8p. It didn't take my parents long to realise this was the place for us.

Of course, the summer of 1990 is – to football fans at least – more commonly known as Italia '90. For me, actually watching the thing was something of a challenge. If there was a television set in the vicinity it would invariably be showing the tournament. But these mysterious televisions were far from readily available. In fact, we were reminded more than once how fortunate we were to have such a contraption in our room.

And so it was that – between power cuts – my experience of Mark Wright's headed goal against Egypt, Roger Milla's hip-swivelling antics and David Platt's extra-time winner against Belgium, came via a black-and-white 1970s television in a Bulgarian apartment.

It would be stretching the truth to claim that, back in 1990, the Bulgarians themselves had embraced what is now glibly referred to as World Cup fever. Their team had failed to even reach the tournament after finishing a dismal last place in a qualifying group containing Romania, Denmark and Greece. It was surely a disappointment but hardly a shock – up to this point they had yet to win a game at the World Cup finals. Even at the time this felt like a wasted opportunity. If ever there was a country in need of self-esteem it was Bulgaria. But change, in more ways than one, was just around the corner.

Some of the developments were immediately apparent when we returned to the country the following summer and again for a third visit in 1993. By now the confident requests for "juice" were greeted instead with surprise – "do you not want Coca-Cola?" As it happened, my sister relished this development so she at least was happy.

My parents were more worried about the increasing prices, and while they could be accused of not seeing the bigger picture regarding the upheavals of a post-communist society, they were not alone in their doubts about this brave new world.

Once engaged in conversation, many older Bulgarians were quick to voice their concerns. They spoke of rising prices and uncertain futures. Whereas communism provided jobs this new world offered no such guarantees. There was a sense that this was Russia and her oligarchs in microcosm – there would be winners and losers in the shake-up and for those on the wrong side of the line it wasn't going to be pretty. Fortunately, Bulgaria's footballers would be among the greatest benefactors of the change in circumstance.

Under communist rule, there were restrictions in place on Bulgarian players moving to foreign clubs until they were 28 years old. For example, the 1986 World Cup squad that failed to win a game contained only two who had experience playing abroad. When the rules were changed, the exodus was swift. Sixteen of the 22-man squad in 1994 had played their club football outside of Bulgaria in the preceding years. And what a squad it was.

When you look back at that side it really was quite the collection of characters. As the journalist John Nicholson put it, they "looked like the meanest bunch of desperados you ever saw in your life". In goal there was Boris Mikhailov – bald in 1992, but sporting a particularly dodgy wig come '94. At the heart of the defence there was the unmistakeable figure of Trifon Ivanov, aka 'The Bulgarian Wolf'. He was the sort of man people euphemistically refer to as having "seen things". He was also the owner of a rather fetching mullet and had a penchant for wild 45-yard shots *apropos* of very little.

They didn't really look like world beaters, but here was the thing: they were actually quite the team. Mikhailov may have been a figure of fun for the British media but on the field he did the business. Ivanov's Panini sticker had guaranteed that he'd become a cult figure before the tournament had even begun, but he was also an uncompromising and efficient defender.

There was the little 5'5" right-back Kiriakov who, curiously, was also ginger. I'm not sure how that one came about but he scurried up and down the right flank to good effect. Then there was Krasimir Balakov and his wand of a left foot. I particularly remember being transfixed by Letchkov. He had this loping stride and just never seemed to give the ball away. He'd also clearly not been talking to his goalkeeper because here was a man most definitely embracing his baldness. And all this without even discussing the mighty Hristo Stoichkov.

Ah, Stoichkov. The man who was to become the 1994 European Player of the Year had already won La Liga with Barcelona that preceding season before being denied the Champions League by the brilliantly ruthless Milan of Fabio Capello. Not only was he a genius, but he pretty much knew it. Not in the way Dimitar Berbatov knew it – the man who was to inherit his mantle as the talisman of the national team. Hristo knew it, but he ran, he harried and he carried the team through in the key moments. In short, he was the shit.

Of course, none of this would have mattered were it not for France's collapse at the Parc des Princes in the final qualifying game for the '94 tournament. David Ginola was famously made the scapegoat after looping a cross into the box rather than hold onto the ball in the corner. Bulgaria went down the other end, Emil Kostadinov fired the ball into the net and it was to be the Eastern Europeans who would be heading across the Atlantic instead.

A less well-known tale from that game is the story of how Kostadinov didn't actually have a visa to be in France at the time. It was only thanks to the 'local knowledge' of Mikhailov and fellow Mulhouse player Georgi Georgiev that the forward was able to elude French border security, slip into the country and ultimately score the goal that knocked France out the World Cup. A crueller man than I would suggest that this Bulgarian team not only looked like a bunch of amateur criminals but, well, you know the rest.

Anyway, this made my mind up. Bulgaria would be my team for USA '94. It was a decision made easier given England's failure to even reach the tournament thanks to the scandal of Ronald Koeman staying on the pitch and, perhaps more worryingly, Carlton Palmer finding his way onto it in the first place. So Bulgaria had my support. And like most teams cursed by that extraordinary gift they proceeded to lose. Emphatically so, as they crumbled 3-0 to Nigeria to be precise.

It was then that a very strange thing happened in the history of Bulgarian football. They won a World Cup match. The 4-0 thrashing of Greece was their first ever win. Given that their triumph over Germany 14 days later represents their last World Cup victory to date you might get some idea just how momentous this fortnight was.

The Greece victory meant Bulgaria needed just a point against Argentina to qualify from the group. These were the delightful days when third place finishes in a group of four could gain qualification to the next round and so most of the tournament was spent whittling the teams down from 24 to 16. Bulgaria weren't complaining and they stunned an Argentina side already rocked by Diego Maradona's mid-tournament drug ban. Stoichkov, again, and a last minute Nasko Sirakov goal secured a 2-0 win.

Sirakov's goal was significant in that it relegated Argentina to third in the group. The Argentinians were handed a tough tie against Romania and duly lost, while Nigeria, the group winners, faced Italy and were also beaten. Bulgaria got the best draw, against Mexico, and after an early Stoichkov goal, were pegged back to 1-1. With no goals in extra-time it went down to penalties. Despite Balakov's early miss, Stoichkov was not even required to take the fifth penalty as Mexico missed their first three – Mikhailov was the hero and Letchkov left the Hispanic community at Giants Stadium heartbroken with the winning strike.

When they returned to the same ground just five days later they were to make history. Germany were the defending world champions in 1994 and had reached the final game in five of the previous seven World Cups, including the last three. Two weeks earlier, Bulgaria had not even won a match at a World Cup. It was all heading for a tediously predictable outcome when Jurgen Klinsmann showcased his trademark simulation skills to win a second-half penalty that Lothar Matthaus, equally predictably, converted.

Enter Stoichkov, who curled in a wonderful free-kick. Then things got a little silly. Letchkov swooped to steer home the aforementioned header and the Germans were going home at the hands of the baldy man and Giants Stadium was going about as crazy as it ever could for a soccer match.

A couple of early Roberto Baggio goals for Italy killed off their hopes in the semi-final just three days later, but nothing could undo the events at the Meadowlands. The Bulgarian team returned to Sofia as national heroes. A country had been transformed. I've not been back to Bulgaria since, but I had seen a country come of age. They've knocked down that stadium in Jersey now, but the memories remain.

Manchester United 1992-93

Ryan Keaney

As clear as though it occurred yesterday, I can still remember the moment I discovered myself to be a fully-fledged Manchester United supporter. I went from being a shy, timid seven year old who loved nothing more than playing football to being a shy, timid seven year old Manchester United fan who loved nothing more than playing football.

Growing up in Northern Ireland, much of my football education comprised either playing with my friends or learning by way of television coverage. I couldn't draw any connection with a local team as none existed nearby other than the youth side I trained with and we didn't have a league to play in. I was left alone to be influenced by the games broadcast by Irish broadcaster RTE.

Each and every Saturday afternoon was spent in my grandparents' living room in front of the television digesting the English top-flight game that was beamed in at 3:00pm, as well as devouring a healthy dose of *Airwolf* and *Knight Rider* (things took their time before finding their way to Ireland). The huge numbers of Manchester United and Liverpool fans on the Emerald Isle meant that the broadcaster rightfully tried to appease the masses and ensured the games usually featured one of those two teams in action.

Steadily I grew an affiliation with Manchester United, although I refused to believe it. I told myself that I simply enjoyed watching football, any football. When pressed on the matter of affiliation in the playground and at school, I always declared my allegiance to the Red Devils to the delight of 50% of my friends and the horror of the other 50%. Afterwards, I told myself I didn't mean it. I simply didn't want to be the weird kid without a team to follow.

It wasn't until January 1993 and a discussion about a certain Frenchman that I felt myself make a commitment to the cause that I knew I was standing by. It was then that the previous years caught up with me and forced to me realise that I wasn't kidding anyone; least of all myself.

Less than two months earlier, Eric Cantona had made the £1.2m switch from First Division Champions Leeds United to my beloved Manchester United. To say I knew little about Cantona before the move would have been an understatement. I didn't like Leeds and didn't care for their players when watching them. I allowed their collection of eleven men to barely register. I watched the games when they were on, but only because I could root for the other team to win; no matter who that was. My opinion on Cantona as he signed his contract at Old Trafford may have been best summed up by a signature of the man himself – a barely emotive shrug. I didn't know enough to have an opinion, although I remember noting that it was nice for Andrei Kanchelskis to have a foreign friend at the club.

That was until someone in my extended Irish Catholic family dared to question the signing of Eric. Following one of my sixty-odd cousin's first holy communion, I was placed in a chair next to my brother, advised to behave myself and told to eat whatever I was given. Opposite me and my older brother sat a distant cousin of my father's. I think. Casting my mind back, I can only assume he got unlucky when he plumped for a pair of seats that were empty.

I had never seen the man or his wife before and I have not seen them since. Struggling for conversation with a seven- and nine-year-old, he quickly turned to football. Even quicker, he (a Liverpool fan) was soon berating the club for signing a buffoon like Cantona and daring to spend more than one million pounds on a disaster waiting to happen.

That was when I uttered a line that lives with me until now and one I have enjoyed repeating for the last 20 years: "Ferguson knows what he is doing." I was not in a mood to listen to the well-thought out, balanced and perfectly sound opinions of the Liverpool fan sitting opposite me. I was not prepared to put up with whatever he had to say.

It was then that I knew I'd been slowly sucked in by Manchester United. Here I was refusing to budge on an opinion that I'd plucked from the sky and refused to back down from.

"Ferguson knows what he is doing."

Thankfully, I proved to be right, although I had no right to be.

I had little more than blind faith and a fuzzy television screen to tell me otherwise and even then, I'm not one for making accurate and sound predictions (I've lost more money than I care to admit betting on Nicklas Bendtner to finish as top scorer of competitions). Much like their manner of victory at times, Manchester United and Alex Ferguson dragged me in without giving me a chance to understand what was actually going on.

Without knowing it or without perhaps wanting to let myself know it, Manchester United had won my heart because, after all, this is a matter of love. Sure, I was a football fan, but football was quite simply much better when the Red Devils were on the TV. The colours were brighter. The goals were much, much better. *Match of the Day* felt like something of a drag and quite tiring once United had been featured.

It's likely that the slight Irish slant in the squad with Denis Irwin at left-back and Keith Gillespie touted as a starlet in the next wave was a factor. Or perhaps the gentle influence of my father who, despite never being big football fan, would always enquire about United's score first when he arrived from work on a Saturday evening.

It's hard to pinpoint when it happened, but as I sat in the car on the way home from that Holy Communion, I knew a decision had been made. That team of Peter Schmeichel, Paul Parker, Gary Pallister, Steve Bruce, Denis Irwin, Lee Sharpe, Paul Ince, Brian McClair, Ryan Giggs, Eric Cantona and Mark Hughes were my first and my greatest footballing love.

Much like every person grows up knowing a different actor as their "ultimate" James Bond (Pierce Brosnan, as if you need to ask), every fan of the Red Devils identifies themselves by the player that delighted them most in that very special shirt. While others have been around for a couple of Champions League victories, Eric Cantona remains my number seven.

His movement, his confidence, his swagger, his goals and the collar; Cantona was everything I knew about foreign footballers. Sure, we had Kanchelskis at the club, but other than the difficult to pronounce name, he seemed like just another member of the squad. Eric was different.

He played in a different manner. Time threatened to stop when he was in possession of the ball. The dodgy analogue signal dared to get just a little bit better when he was at the centre of the picture. He forced me to catch my breath just to make sure I wasn't caught out when he did something special.

The Frenchman was the catalyst for Manchester United winning the first Premiership title, although I didn't quite understand it at the time. I didn't compute he was the missing part of the puzzle. I just figured my boys had finally got into the habit of winning more than they lost in a big way.

Then we beat Sheffield Wednesday. Sorry, then Steve Bruce single-handedly pulled us back from the brink to beat Sheffield Wednesday. It was incredible. It was mind-blowing. It was a feeling that could only be only bettered by the 1999 Champions League final.

In 1993, I was in front of the television and knew I'd witnessed something special. I was celebrating along with Alex, Brian and the players as they danced on the pitch. It was football in its greatest single moment. How could I not fall in love with the game?

Oxford United 1995-96

Sam Macrory

This piece opens with a confession. I didn't grow up in a footballing household. Looking back, I cringe to think that my mum phoned the BBC to demand why the football was still being shown when the listings had promised a cartoon, the lack of which left my brother and I devastated. It was May 20 1989, and the Liverpool-Everton FA Cup Final – which I later learned to be one of the great finals – had gone into extra time. But if that came at the expense of ten minutes of *Tom and Jerry*, then the schedulers should know better.

My eyes were first opened to football by the 1990 World Cup, and over the next year the BBC video of the tournament was played so often in our house that the tape snapped. I still know the commentary to every game – come back, Barry Davies – by heart, and while names like Lineker, Baggio, Careca, and Benjamin Massing fascinated me, a rather less glamorous side began to catch my imagination. My postcode gave me little choice: Oxford United became my team.

The team has got steadily worse ever since, and frequently they have been utterly rubbish. Even when they are at their best, the style of football seems to focus heavily on endless header rallies, a kick-off tactic which involves a rugby-style possession-seeking punt into the far corner of the pitch, goalkeepers with a chronic fear of roll-outs, and midfielders who appeared to be auditioning for the Peter Reid role of jogging behind an attacking Maradona. And playing against Oxford United could make any lower league journeyman look like the Argentine great.

Oxford's spectacular fall – over twenty years – from the dizzying heights of the old first division and a Wembley cup final victory into the depths of despair that is the Blue Square Premier League is hard to outdo. But, each season, I return to watch the horror unfold.

It began with a school trip round the old Manor Ground – hosted by Malcolm Elias, the youth team coach who would later unearth Gareth Bale and Theo Walcott at Southampton. A game against Watford, who featured a young David James in goal, followed, and over the next few years my Dad manfully bowed to his sons' growing interest and escorted us to watch what was then, briefly, a mid-table first division team.

We'd sit in the family stand, with Dad quietly reading his Guardian – embarrassing for his teenage sons, but not as much as when my mother, on a rare foray to the ground, was spotted leafing through Good Housekeeping during Oxford's 5-3 win over Swindon – before repeatedly asking me to identify John Byrne, apparently his favourite player of the time, or Jim Magilton, an elegant Northern Irish midfielder.

Looking back, it's astonishing to think that players of the calibre of Byrne and Magilton ever played for Oxford, while even the lack of appreciation shown to so-called striker Nick Cusack (10 goals in 61 games) now seems badly judged.

By the start of the 1995 season, Oxford were in what was then Division Two and is now League One, but really is the third tier of English football. Magilton, Byrne and even Cusack had gone on to better things, as Oxford pinned their hopes on 34-year-old Wayne Biggins, a striker firmly in the winding down stages of a recently undistinguished career.

Crucially, the season marked the moment when I graduated from the wooden benches of the family sitting area to the concrete slopes of the London Road stand, which was situated about two centimetres from the pitch, housed a permanently grumpy bookkeeper, and smelled of cigarettes and sweating fans. This was where the big boys went – one from our school claimed to start all the chants, despite his cracking adolescent voice – and the limb-breaking bundles took place, a dangerous land where my Dad and his *Guardian* would not survive. I was 14 now though, and my time – marginally later than the London Road 10 year olds who seemed to have been born with tattoos and a rich vocabulary of foul language – had arrived. As a result, the 1995/6 season took its place in one teenage boy's list of rites of passage moments.

Luckily I chose a rare season of success. Even my tactically naïve brain was able to tell the team was built on two centre halves who were far, far too good for that division: Matt Elliott and Phil Gilchrist. The latter would return a decade later, a slower, heavier, and flawed version, but Elliott remains one of the all-time Oxford greats. A defender who did the ugly stuff – the endless header rallies were child's play for him – while being able to hit 60-yard passes for the wingers to miscontrol, and score goals that Cusack could only dream of.

The team also contained two fine homegrown midfielders. At the time I thought Chris Allen was incredibly quick but had a terrible end product, but a review of my highlights video suggests I was unfair. Allen moved to Nottingham Forest early that season before falling out of the league by his 30s, while Bobby Ford, a wonderfully gifted midfielder with a range of passing never since seen at the club, later secured a big move to Sheffield United before returning to Oxford, losing interest in the miserable non-football of League Two, and quitting football at 29.

Also in the squad were the sideways passing – and running – trio of David Smith, Martin Gray, and Mickey 'Mad Dog' Lewis, while Les Robinson, so old that as a young footballer he had a moustache, was at right back.

But for that team, in that season, it was all about one striker. Not Wayne Biggins, who was soon playing for Leek Town, but Paul Moody, who on first glance played with a lumbering style that made Emile Heskey look like Lionel Messi.

However, Moody – who merits just a seven-word entry on Wikipedia – had the season of his life, an extraordinary campaign that included three hat-tricks, one within just 15 minutes after coming on as a substitute, and 24 goals. The team's style was simple. Get the ball to Moody, and see how far he could run with it – the ball was never quite under control – before he hit it as hard as he could towards the goal.

But just as important as the football was the (admittedly rose-tinted) way we watched it.

Match day began with headers and volleys with my friend Frank – not a retired 1950s footballer, despite the name, but an OUFC fan since the age of six – who lived round the corner from the ground. At 2:45 we ran the gauntlet of the dreaded Cuckoo Lane away end to pick up the programme – Mike Ford's 'Captain's Column' was a must-read – and made our way to the ramshackle prefab of the Manor Ground.

Highlights included an astonishing sloping pitch (six foot from one end to other), the never-functioning scoreboard, trees behind the away stand which were filled with turnstile-avoiding locals, and the long delays as balls were sent flying into the gardens of local houses, requiring one ball boy to find a new ball while his mate rang doorbells and asked – on behalf of a professional football club – for his ball back. In hindsight, it seems to belong to a black and white era of high-speed rattles, white horses, and toothless fans in flat caps, rather than the 1990s.

Minutes after full time we'd be back in Frank's front room for tea and toast, tuning in to watch the match highlights. "Mirror, mirror on the wall, who is the best south central side of them all?" When Tim Russon, the Partridge-esque presenter, hooks you in with lines like that, it's little wonder that we'd sprinted home so fast.

"Denis Smith, the Oxford wizard, stirred the pot", he announced after the Swindon away game, the climax of an excruciating conjuring-themed analogy which included 'Harry Houdini' left back Mike Ford and "magician" midfielder Ford. "Were the United defenders dazzled by the illuminations?" at Blackpool? Only Russon knows, but despite his flamboyant wordplay, the team was stuttering around the mid-table mark at Christmas.

Then manager Denis Smith pulled off a memorable transfer coup. Homegrown hero Joey Beauchamp was signed from local rivals Swindon on loan, later permanently for a bargain £75,000. Eighteen months previously, the absurdly talented Beauchamp had left to join Premier League West Ham for more than 10 times that fee, famously failing to play a game for the Hammers after the 60-mile commute left him overcome with homesickness.

The move delighted both us fans and Joey, and that April he scored a goal against Blackpool which would be voted the greatest in the

Manor's history. The team won 14 of their last 19 league games, an extraordinary run which included a 3-0 home win over Swindon, in which Beauchamp scored against his old a team, 6-0 win over Shrewsbury, when all six goals came from headers, and a 3-0 win at Wycombe, a result which Moody famously celebrated by performing the most unlikely of handstands while journeyman winger Stuart Massey swung deliriously on the crossbar.

On the last game of the season, Oxford needed to beat Peterborough to take the second promotion slot, annoyingly behind champions Swindon. I braved the London Road, but stayed law-abidingly rooted to the spot as fans charged on to the pitch to celebrate a 4-0 win. Moody was among the scorers, celebrating in extraordinary hip-shuddering fashion.

It was 10 years since that glorious Milk Cup triumph turned Wembley yellow and blue, but the club at last seemed to be heading towards more glory days. Work on a new stadium was underway, Denis Smith was highly rated and Beauchamp, Moody, and Elliott looked set to take the club back to where, in all honesty, it didn't belong.

Instead Matt Elliott joined Leicester for a club record sale of £1.6m the following season, while Moody moved to Fulham and broke both his legs. (He returned to Oxford in 2001 – by then the team was playing at such a low standard that even a semi-crocked Moody bagged 13 goals.) Saddest of all, Beauchamp retired with a toe-injury and developed a drink problem.

A decade after their promotion triumph, Oxford fell out of the league – Smith had returned for a disastrous second spell – and ended up playing in a soulless three-sided ground on the outskirts of the city. Financially precarious since the Maxwell family – the minutes silence after Sir Bob's death in 1991 was aborted after about 20 seconds – ran the boardroom, the club spiralled into debt and was taken over by a chairman with a penchant for sacking managers, not renewing playing contracts and egotistically naming three-sided grounds after himself.

Perhaps the 1995/6 season was the final hurrah of a team which had spent much of its existence over-achieving, but there is hope.

After four long years playing in grounds that made the Manor seem like the Emirates, OUFC returned to Wembley for a victorious play-off final and left the Blue Square Premier League.

Reassuringly the current goalkeeper still hates short goal kicks and all kick-offs still begin with a punt into the furthest corner of the pitch, but at least Oxford United are back in the football league. If only it had a Paul Moody, a Nick Cusack, or even a Wayne Biggins to take them a little higher. We didn't know how lucky we were.

Real Madrid 1990

Elliott Turner

During the winter of 1990, I ate quite possibly the worst Mexican food of my life in Wichita, Kansas. Why? Real Madrid, that's why. And my dad.

This is a story about fandom, childhood, and the power of sport to transport us from dreadful circumstances, if only for a moment.

I did not want to be in Wichita. However, there I was. Again. Mercifully, the chunk of the I-35 highway between my mom's house in Kansas City and my father's apartment in Wichita ran north-to-south. Travelling east-west in a state as horizontally long as Kansas barrages the psyche like Chinese water torture. The road and roaming prairie never end. Travelling north-to-south, though, gives the impression of false progress. Highway signs show the proximity of Oklahoma, a different state. No flint hills mar the horizon.

My dad had made the eight-hour round trip for the purpose of father-son bonding during a long weekend. My parents were separated, but not yet divorced. However, even my grade school mind and heart did not fathom nor harbour any hopes of reconciliation. Even now, my memories of my parents together revolve around shouting, slammed doors, and somebody staying the night at a friend or relative's. The separation had brought peace to the homestead, so I couldn't complain. Also, I wilfully permitted my dad to materially indulge me, both of us knowing that a wicked cool game system would make the weekend pass faster, but not change my mind about my choice of residence.

Yet there was still a major problem. My dad, like most folks at the time, could not find a cable TV option that showed La Liga soccer games. Cable TV had exploded in popularity and availability, yet European soccer had not yet penetrated the North American landscape.

The internet existed, but only for scientists with closets big enough to store enormous computers. This posed a serious problem because, as Mexican-Americans, my dad and I had a moral obligation to watch each and every Real Madrid game featuring *el tri* legend Hugo "Hugol" Sanchez. To do otherwise would betray the homeland before the homeland. The consequences would be divine spite, wave after wave of plagues and locusts.

Cable at the apartment was not an option and in those days, no Irish pubs or ex-pat hangouts existed in Kansas. Your best bet to catch a Real Madrid game was a semi-authentic Mexican restaurant and an answered prayer that the Real Madrid match did not conflict with a Mexican league fixture. Also, if the restaurant was too Tex-Mex and catered to gringos, then soccer would definitely not be on the TV. My first weekend in Wichita, my dad scoured the yellow pages for Mexican restaurants and we drove circles around town. Luckily, Wichita's roads were a collection of orderly straight lines that would make a gulag city-planner smile. This was a town where the streets formed straight lines, the trains ran on time, and folks comfortably sat down to eat dinner by 5:30pm. Our Mexican options were severely limited, but at least easy to find on a map.

We settled on a place just outside the Town West Square Mall that showed the games. We became regulars, even though the restaurant committed the cardinal sin of Mexican cuisine: serving nacho chips before the entree. If you ever want to eat authentic Mexican cuisine, a server brining you an endless supply of nacho chips is a tell-tale sign you are in Tex-Mex territory. Be prepared.to ingest unholy quantities of cheese.

Still, we formed fajitas with the store-bought tortillas (lamenting the lack of a *maiz* option) and downed *frijoles charros* ("cowboy beans") that still tasted of tin can. My dad may or may not have indulged in a margarita or two, depending on game time. If the margarita was as watered down as the food, he probably would have been better off with Sprite.

Still, the games played and we watched in our knock-off white Real Madrid kits. A few of the waiters paid attention too, and Hugo's goals always elicited a cheer. In the 1990-91 season, Real Madrid's *Quinta del Buitre* ("Vulture's Cohort"), spearheaded by the striking tandem of Hugol and Emilio "the Vulture" Butragueno, walloped the opposition into submission. Hugol won that season's *pichichi* ("top goal scorer award") and knocked in 38 goals. The team won La Liga, but cracks surfaced.

Hugo never felt accepted by his Spanish counterparts, and began to blow off steam in press conferences. More worryingly, Johan Cruyff had started to attract world-class talent to eon-old rival FC Barcelona. Ronald Koeman had led a 3-1 Barcelona rout of Madrid earlier that season. Any fan could see the window of success slowly closing at Madrid, but we had no idea how abruptly it would be slammed shut.

With that background, on February 15 my dad and I quietly sipped on bland tortilla soup and focused on the big screen TV above the bar. Real Madrid and Barcelona were tied 1-1. After years of coasting, the *cules* were finally putting up a fight. However, just before the half, Butragueno scored and then Hugo slammed home a penalty. Madrid reached half time with a nice two-goal lead and our entrees finally arrived. I can't recall the exact plate, but I know it was saturated in the classic "Mexican Cheese" blend of Monterrey Jack, cheddar, *asadero*, and *queso quesadilla*. The allegedly spicy sauce tasted like marinara with cilantro flakes and chunks of tomato.

We downed our meal as the teams trotted back out onto the field. The second half started off ragged, with Real Madrid bored and complacent. Then, in the 70th minute, Julio Salinas bagged his second goal for Barcelona. My stomach churned. A comfortable win had turned into a dogfight. Would this be Barca's time to slay Goliath? I looked into my dad's eyes for assurance, but could only see quiet intensity and a hint of desperation. Real Madrid rode their luck, fended off Barcelona, and held on for a 3-2 win. For 20 minutes, our stomachs writhed in agony and *pico de gallo* was not to blame.

And then it ended. We exchanged high-fives, pumped a fist or two, and some waiters hugged. Outside, the clouds formed a dark grey mass outside and snowflakes began to fall. Yet my dad and I could not be bothered by such concerns. Real Madrid had won, and beaten Barcelona no less. Another La Liga title was a foregone conclusion. Hugol's march to the *pichichi* knew no obstacle.

Our family life was torn to shreds, but the loose ends of sporting fiction were coming together nicely. Only two questions remained. How should we celebrate? And did we dare try the *arroz con leche* ("rice pudding")?

Tooting & Mitcham 2008-09

Chris Nee

October 28 2008 and 191 hardy supporters sit and stand in clusters around Imperial Fields, trying in vain to keep themselves warm on a bitterly cold evening in Morden. A spiky game does the job far better and Billy Smith's Tooting & Mitcham United take a deserved and most welcome point against Harrow Borough thanks to a goal from defender and captain Joe Vines, whose finish did more for the assembled Bog Enders than any polystyrene cup of overly gloopy Bovril ever could.

This was my first Tooting & Mitcham match, a night that forever changed the way I looked at football. Football has been a big part of my life for longer than I can remember; I have no recollection of my first games as a supporter or as a five-year-old no doubt teetering uneasily on my first set of studs. My birthright was Aston Villa and little has wavered in that respect, but it wasn't until adulthood that I came to consider my affections. Villa are in my blood and I am a football obsessive, but I loved a team, not a sport, until a freezing, floodlit introduction to the Terrors after moving to Tooting in London in my twenties.

I had always understood the depth of the English game and the importance of supporting one's local team. Despite this, I'd never really put my money where my mouth was – and, indeed, where it still is. As a youngster I'd been to see Poole Town while they played at AFC Bournemouth for a spell, and while I enjoyed their win over Fareham I felt no affection for either team or for the experience as a whole. Little did I know that this wasn't really Non-League, not in its purest form.

My next excursion into the depths was a mere scratching of the surface and a deeply unsatisfactory one at that. Having moved from the south coast to Guildford, I swaggered into Woking's wintry home fixture against Forest Green Rovers expecting to be entertained. It's fair to say that you get out of this life what you put in, and my half-arsed attempt that day was met with swift retribution from the heavens, for this was quite the worst football match I have ever seen.

Tooting & Mitcham was different from the moment I squeezed my bloated Premier League ego through the turnstile, and very much love at first sight. More than that, though, my experiences at the club taught me more about what football is really all about than I would ever have learned even higher up the Non-League pyramid. But by god, I wished I'd taken a pair of gloves.

I fancy much more of this, I thought, but there was no escaping that I was a Villa Park season ticket holder. Villa games meant quality time with my dad, too, so extricating myself from this situation was neither viable nor desirable, but on the odd weekend I would roll gleefully out of my rented flat on Garratt Lane and onto the 280 bus to Bishopsford Road. Intermittently accompanied by my friend Gary, each game made me feel more at home regardless of whether or not I attended alone. This was football. This was how we should be approaching this most bizarre of social creations.

In later years I'd interview Smith's replacement, Mark Beard, and become a much more frequent attendee. I eventually joined the Members Club, a collaborative minority owner of Tooting & Mitcham Sports & Leisure, the company that exists to own Imperial Fields and Tooting & Mitcham United. Although it turned out that being part of this organisation was akin to throwing a kernel of popcorn at The Thing, it was reaffirming to see how a dedicated bunch of supporters could help keep an ailing football club ticking over against the odds.

Before long I counted myself as one of them, one of the people making a contribution. Take it from me, being a programme editor at a club at Isthmian Premier level isn't exactly a bed of roses, but it offers an insight into how clubs are run that one just doesn't get as a regular supporter. Given that they're the ones who paid their way while I offered only my labour suggests that's a problem with transparency, but I gained a lot from the experience nonetheless.

But it was Smith's Tooting, the team I wished I could have supported more often, that I look back upon with most fondness, that truly drew me in to the club that changed my perceptions.

The highlight of their – sod it, our – many achievements under Billy and his right-hand man, George Wakeling, was a glittering FA Cup run in 2009. The team battled their way out of some remarkable lost causes to reach the first round proper. Both the club and Smith himself have an affinity with the Cup, and the Terrors' most famous game was a 2-2 draw against eventual winners Nottingham Forest in the third round in 1959. Tooting & Mitcham had been 2-0 up. They went a round further in the 1970s as part of a series of impressive runs achieved by a team that featured Smith the player.

The 2009 team might not have quite the historical reverence afforded to the team of '59 but they earned their first round game at Stockport County by expending everything they had to achieve some victories.

They entered at the first qualifying round and faced league rivals Horsham at home, a fixture in which Tooting & Mitcham had a poor record. With the game poised at 2-2 at the beginning of injury time, Horsham goalkeeper Rob Tolfrey, now a tower of strength for Kingstonian, got himself sent off in ridiculous circumstances. The home team converted the penalty and scored a fourth for good measure.

A win over Canvey Island and an upset against Slough Town followed, putting Smith's side into the fourth qualifying round against Conference outfit Eastbourne Borough. On this occasion injury time was less enjoyable and the Terrors squandered a 3-1 lead in front of a large home crowd and had to head to the south coast for a replay. They had to fight tooth and nail for a 4-3 extra time win, and, despite losing 5-0 at Stockport, it was worth every bead of sweat.

But what really brings Non-League to life is not the matches, it's the people involved in them. Smith's Tooting team had countless players who are still held in high regard in SM4. I quickly had a favourite, a young man who became the player I wished I'd be when I was a kid. Paul Vines was, and is, too good a striker for the Isthmian League and plays with a swagger and a confidence that endears him to many in the region.

Vines scored great goals and was key to that FA Cup run, and he was generally able to tie defenders in knots. His cause was aided by a new partner, Simon Parker, who made his debut in the cup win over Horsham and was a perfect foil for Vines until a new job took him back off to the north of England. Parker was a scruffy looking player, bearded of face and awkward of gait, but his quality on the ball and his instinctive ability to play with Vines was something to behold.

Sharp-eyed readers will have spotted mention of two Vines', and they are indeed brothers. Joe, who scored the first goal I ever saw Tooting & Mitcham score, is a fantastic Non-League defender. He has a reputation for backing down from nobody, which is fair and accurate, but he's a smart cookie on and off the pitch. He sweats blood for his team – whichever it might be – and now dedicates some of his time to helping one-time opponent Francis Duku improve the lot of the Non-League player.

Despite getting plenty of verbal from opposition supporters, Joe is a hugely popular and well-respected character in the London game and a superb representation of exactly why Tooting & Mitcham took my existing love for the game to another level.

So too is Jamie Byatt, in many ways the heart and soul of Smith's wonderful Terrors team. "Busy" was another who would leave no stone unturned or opponent unkicked in his desire to win, but a bad knee injury took him out of action a few years ago. The extent to which supporters rallied around Byatt, who lost his job as a labourer as a result of his injury, spoke volumes for a club that looks after its own. Byatt himself embodied that more than most before he eventually left the club under subsequent management.

The sights, sounds and smells of Non-League football are different. It's not about being "better", or more "real", it's just different. Some people suit it and some people don't, but I found a new home at Imperial Fields in 2008 and I miss it enormously since I moved away in 2012. Freedom for Tooting & Mitcham!

Yugoslavia 1990

Dominic Bliss

He didn't know it as he warmly announced himself down the phone, but Dragan Stojković once made me cry.

You see, my earliest memories of football are as a five-year-old, experiencing the 1990 World Cup, a tournament that Stojković and his Yugoslavia team-mates graced with some breathtaking attacking football and a vulnerable side that appealed to fans of the underdog.

Of course, those few weeks in Italy have a safe place in the nostalgia section of the English collective memory because of the heroics performed by Bobby Robson's team on their way to semi-final heartache at the hands of eventual winners West Germany. And, aside from some wayward penalty-taking, nothing has come to symbolise the nation's grief that night in Turin more powerfully than Gazza's tears.

But I remember that tournament for a salty-cheeked moment of my own, one I suppressed for years to come due to its sheer ludicrousness. That is because my first footballing tears weren't shed for the flawed genius of Paul Gascoigne, or for any of England's nearly men. No, I had already poured my heart out at the quarter-final stage, when Yugoslavia were defeated by Argentina after another penalty shoot-out.

I couldn't help it. I saw the Argentinian players celebrating afterwards and I just could not control myself – I cried my eyes out like five-year-olds do when they sense an injustice. And for years afterwards, my older brother, Oli, would sneeringly use my strange outburst of emotion to put me in my place, especially if I embarrassed him in front of his mates.

"Yeah, but Dom," began the taunt that made my heart sink. "You cried when Yugoslavia lost in the World Cup."

"I was *five*!"

Yet there was a reason I was reduced to tears when a country I had previously never heard of lost at football. Just hear me out...

Prior to that tournament, I recall my mum handing me and Oli a sampler packet of *Panini* stickers, which must have come free with a breakfast cereal or something similar, and soon afterwards the wardrobe in our bedroom was adorned with images of international footballers in Belgium and Yugoslavia shirts. Oli's door was now decorated with Eric Gerets' beard and I had two new heroes of my own – Darko Pančev and Dragan Stojković (both clean-shaven, since you ask).

So, aside from trying to work out why Yugoslavia was pronounced the way it was when it was spelled with a 'J' on the stickers, we also gained an allegiance to the teams whose players we had each been introduced to at random by a box-stuffer at Kellogg's. I therefore became a Yugoslavia supporter for the duration of the 1990 World Cup, which explains how I came to be in tears as a result of a missed penalty by the man who, more than two decades on, ended up on the other end of the phone waiting to be interviewed by me.

Suppressing a smile at the memory, I realised that, in my new life as a football writer, there was no way I could seriously suggest to Stojković that we had shared that moment of grief 22 years earlier – him on his knees in the centre circle of Florence's Stadio Artemio Franchi, head in hands; me turning mournfully away from the telly in Banstead, stickle bricks falling from my trembling, snotty fingers.

I settled instead for an opportunity to speak to my first footballing idol about his incredible career. We spoke for almost an hour about his playing days, his move into management and the state of the game in general and, with his openness and his charm, Stojković put to bed the myth that you should never meet your heroes.

The part he played in the magical experience that was my first World Cup stood out above all the rest for me and, let's face it, there was no shortage of material to capture a child's imagination at Italia '90.

This was the World Cup of Rene Higuita, Colombia's crazy sweeper keeper and Roger Milla, the snake-hipped veteran striker from

Cameroon; the World Cup of Carlos Valderrama – his through balls, his one-twos and his hair.

It was the World Cup of Luciano Pavarotti, New Order and John Barnes rapping; of Eastern European mullets; American mullets; Middle Eastern moustaches; German moustaches; shell-suited coaches and suspect shorts. It was the summer of Frank Rijkaard's phlegm, Toto Schillacci's wide-eyed joy and David Platt's happy little goal face.

As Brazil played Argentina in a breathless last-16 encounter, my dad turned to me hopefully and said: "Why don't you sit down and watch this, it's a lovely game." And when Oli and I went out into the road to play football that evening, we were Maradona and Caniggia!

The next evening, I shouted "Packie Bonner!" in a high-pitched voice, in honour of the Irish goalkeeper's heroics in their shootout win over Romania, as I saved a penalty in the garden.

Yet, among all the iconic men and moments that made it such a rich tournament for a young boy, it was Yugoslavia who drew me in as a supporter. I was gripped by England's journey to the semi-final, but the Balkan side appealed to me for some intangible reason – perhaps it is the intangibleness of it all that has made it stick in my memory.

In their first group stage game, Yugoslavia faced the mighty West Germans and, with UAE and Colombia as their other opponents in the first phase, they were touted as the only side who could give Franz Beckenbauer's men a run for their money.

They were duly stuffed 4-1, with Lothar Matthäus scoring one of the goals of the tournament for good measure.

I thought I'd picked a dud, but Yugoslavia came good in the next two matches, playing some good stuff in a 1-0 win over the Colombians before taking out the embarrassment of their opening defeat on the poor old UAE, registering a 4-1 win of their own this time. Pancev, one of the men whose face graced my wardrobe door, scored two –and could he strike the ball!

This was a good side, after all. The technical football they played; the scud missiles sent flying towards goal by Pancev; the back three with a roaming sweeper, and the number 10, Stojković, who popped up all over the pitch with the ball at his feet and all the time in the world to use it.

They certainly had a style. I could never have appreciated that at the time, yet I feel as though somehow I did when I consider things retrospectively. Something must have rubbed off because I still admire that style of football above all others. Even my favourite memories of England's Italia '90 (I did support my home nation too, after all) are of the games when they switched to a back three and seemed to find time and patience from somewhere.

A five-year-old cannot fully grasp those things, but he can get a feel for the intensity in the room, and people just seemed to be calmer when the sweepers and the playmakers were in control. The commentators, the pundits, my dad – everyone seemed to understand that this was the way the game *should* be played.

As is the case for so many football supporters, the lineup for the last 16 of my first World Cup remained settled in my mind as the elite of international football as I grew up. It took some getting used to when France emerged as a power in the decade to come – they hadn't been there when my brother and I were pencilling Costa Rica and Czechoslovakia into our table football World Cup draw in 1990!

That was a round of classic games, by the standards of any tournament: Brazil v Argentina; Ireland v Romania; England v Belgium; Italy v Uruguay; West Germany v Holland; Czechoslovakia v Costa Rica. And, on the final day of last 16 fixtures, came the big one – the game in which my arbitrarily chosen side overcame one of the big boys.

Yugoslavia v Spain.

Watching the match again recently, I realised that it wasn't really much to write home about, particularly in light of the excitement thrown up in the other games that week. However, when a cross from the left wing fell to Stojković at the back post, with 12 minutes remaining, I was treated to a moment of technical perfection.

He could have swung a boot at it and snatched at the shot, but he didn't. Instead, he calmly brought the ball down on the far corner of the six-yard box, killing it with the inside of his right foot and simultaneously committing the defender, before nonchalantly rolling the ball inside the far post, beyond the reach of Andoni Zubizarreta.

The arrogance of it. The sheer front of doing that in a World Cup knockout tie against Spain. It was beautiful. Just beautiful.

Spain equalised on 83 minutes, through a tap-in from Julio Salinas, but two minutes into extra time, it was a case of *Enter the Dragan.*

Stojković confidently strolled up to take a free kick on edge of the 'D', just to the right of centre. Faced by a five-man wall, he simply stroked the ball between the faces of the two men on the end and watched it dip at speed into the far corner of Zubizarreta's net. Stojković swept away to celebrate his winning strike with a jump, a punch of the air and a sign of the cross, his pious emotions showing he could be humble too.

Then it was Argentina in the quarter-finals, and what I now understand was a nothing game really – except for the intensity of the situation, and that is what you notice as a small boy.

0-0 at full-time; goalless after extra time – the game had to be decided by a penalty shootout.

I'd seen Ireland win this way in the previous round and knew it could be fun, but when my new hero rattled the crossbar with a casually lifted effort, it started to feel like things might not go to plan this time around.

By the time it came around to the fifth round of penalty kicks, I was fully aware of the importance of this game. In fact, if you had asked that five-year-old boy from Surrey what he wanted more than anything else at that moment, he would have told you it was for Yugoslavia to go through to the semi-finals of the World Cup.

Then Faruk Hadžibegić placed the ball on the spot.

"If he misses, Yugoslavia are out…

...Oh, what a great save!"

I don't know if it was the way Stojković covered his face with his shirt to hide his anguish, or Maradona – who also missed with a tame effort – feverishly celebrating after Hadzibegic's crucial miss. Maybe it was my dad, seemingly unabashed by his youngest son's attachment to a completely alien nation, sympathising with me.

Whatever the catalyst, I burst into uncontrollable tears and, although I hid that truth for many years afterwards, I now look back on that as a seminal moment in my relationship with football.

Watching Dragan Stojković kneeling, inconsolable, in the middle of that pitch in Florence, I was distraught. But at that moment I was introduced to the emotionally charged and largely irrational nature of the game that has been central to my life ever since.